# Understanding
## GERHART HAUPTMANN

# UNDERSTANDING MODERN EUROPEAN and LATIN AMERICAN LITERATURE

**James Hardin,** *Series Editor*

### ADVISORY BOARD

Understanding Günter Grass
*by Alan Frank Keele*

Understanding Graciliano Ramos
*by Celso Lemos de Oliveira*

Understanding Gabriel García Márquez
*by Kathleen McNerney*

Understanding Claude Simon
*by Ralph Sarkonak*

Understanding Mario Vargas Llosa
*by Sara Castro-Klarén*

Understanding Samuel Beckett
*by Alan Astro*

Understanding Jean-Paul Sartre
*by Philip R. Wood*

Understanding Albert Camus
*by David R. Ellison*

Understanding Max Frisch
*by Wulf Koepke*

Understanding Erich Maria Remarque
*by Hans Wagener*

Understanding Elias Canetti
*by Richard H. Lawson*

Understanding Thomas Bernhard
*by Stephen D. Dowden*

Understanding Heinrich Böll
*by Robert C. Conard*

Understanding Céline
*by Philip H. Solomon*

Understanding Gerhart Hauptmann
*by Warren R. Maurer*

# Understanding

# Gerhart Hauptmann

by
Warren R. Maurer

University of South Carolina Press

Library of Congress Cataloging-in-Publication Data

Maurer, Warren R.
    Understanding Gerhart Hauptmann / by Warren R. Maurer.
        p.   cm. — (Understanding modern European and Latin American
    literature)
    Includes bibliographical references and index.
    ISBN 0–87249–823–9
    1. Hauptmann, Gerhart, 1862–1946.
    2. Authors, German—20th century—Biography.   I. Title.
    II. Series.
    PT2616.Z9M365   1992
    832′.8—dc20                                                    92–14308
    [B]

For Jadzia

# Contents

# CONTENTS

# EDITOR'S PREFACE

*U*nderstanding Modern European and Latin American Literature has been planned as a series of guides for undergraduate and graduate students and nonacademic readers. Like its companion series, *Understanding Contemporary American Literature,* the aim of the books is to provide an introduction to the lives and writings of prominent modern authors and to explicate their most important works.

Modern literature makes special demands, and this is particularly true of foreign literature, in which the reader must contend not only with unfamiliar, often arcane artistic conventions and philosophical concepts, but also with the handicap of reading the literature in translation. It is a truism that the nuances of one language can be rendered in another only imperfectly (and this problem is especially acute in fiction), but the fact that the works of European and Latin American writers are situated in a historical and cultural setting quite different from our own can be as great a hindrance to the understanding of these works as the linguistic barrier. For this reason, the UMELL series emphasizes the sociological and historical background of the writers treated. The peculiar philosophical and cultural traditions of a given culture may be particularly important for an understanding of certain authors, and these are taken up in the introductory chapter and also in the discussion of those works to which this information is relevant. Beyond this, the books treat the specifically literary aspects of the author under discussion and attempt to explain the complexities of contemporary literature lucidly. The volumes are conceived as introductions to the authors covered, not as comprehensive analyses. Nor do they provide detailed summaries of plot since they are meant to be used in conjunction with the books they treat, not as a substitute for the study of the original works. The purpose of each volume is to provide information and judicious literary assessment of major works in the most compact, readable form. It is our hope that the UMELL series will help to increase our knowledge and understanding of the European and Latin American cultures and will serve to make the literature of those cultures more accessible.

Professor Maurer's *Understanding Gerhart Hauptmann* recounts the life and career of a writer whose longevity and literary creativity call to mind

Goethe and Thomas Mann. And in fact Hauptmann was a celebrity in Germany, and even—for a short time—in America. But in spite of the fact that he lived until 1946, when he died a physically and psychically broken man, having witnessed the fall of Germany and quite specifically the fire-bombing of Dresden, his most enduring works were those of his naturalist period, his epoch-making plays *Vor Sonnenaufgang, Die Weber,* and *Die Ratten* and his tragic novella, *Bahnwärter Thiel.* It is in the discussion of these early works—which mirror so uniquely the peculiar oppressive atmosphere of both the provinces and Berlin in the late nineteenth century—that Maurer's book is most fascinating. Hauptmann's portrayal of families (every family has a secret, good or bad, he said, and the writer must seek it out) of all social strata is gripping to the present-day reader. His probing of the sexuality, the drives (conscious and otherwise) and illusions of these people, who in the last analysis are to be pitied, not blamed, has the power to shock and embarrass vicariously. And that is the power of Hauptmann's literature, which in some respects (setting, deterministic theory of character, and so on) is dated and yet is shaped by timeless archetypal patterns of behavior that verge on the myth. Hauptmann's best works are great, and Maurer's authoritative and lively book helps to show why this is so.

J. H.

# PREFACE

Although more has been written about Gerhart Hauptmann than about any other modern German author (a recent bibliography of secondary material lists almost 8,000 titles),[1] and, although his dramas continue to be frequently performed on the German stage, he has faded from the Anglo-Saxon consciousness. Whatever the reasons for this—they likely have more to do with translation and political problems than with intrinsic literary merit—no study of modern European or American theater is complete without consideration of this prolific and influential author. Admired and imitated by such disparate writers as James Joyce, Maksim Gorky, Anton Chekhov, Eugene O'Neill, and Arthur Miller, Hauptmann has left an indelible impression on the literary landscape of the twentieth century.

The present study is intended primarily as an introduction to Hauptmann, the man and the writer, for students and teachers of German and comparative literature, or for the general reader whose literary interests transcend the narrowly parochial yet whose knowledge of German is limited or nonexistent. As the author of an earlier study published in 1982,[2] I now can treat Hauptmann's works from new perspectives, incorporating recent research in my discussions and analyzing eight dramas and two prose narratives excluded from the earlier book. Because of the prodigious number of Hauptmann's works, I have been obliged to make choices as to which can best represent his achievement. Works selected fall into the following categories: (1) some ten or twelve dramas and three narratives whose titles are easily recognized by sophisticated German readers; works that have been the subject of a great deal of critical attention and that constitute the essential Hauptmann canon; (2) a group of lesser, albeit significant and/or especially popular works; (3) works selected because of a possible specific interest to Anglo-Saxon readers (for example, a chapter on Hauptmann and *Hamlet*); and (4) works that are available in English translation.

It would be remiss not to express here my gratitude to The University of Kansas for granting me a sabbatical leave for the academic year 1990–91, which greatly facilitated the completion of this book, and to the editor of this series, Professor James Hardin, for his encouragement, patience, and much helpful advice.

## NOTES

1. See Sigfrid Hoefert, *Internationale Bibliographie zum Werk Gerhart Hauptmanns*, 2 vols. (Berlin: Erich Schmidt Verlag, 1986–89), 2:23–520.
2. See Warren R. Maurer, *Gerhart Hauptmann* (Boston: Twayne, 1982).

# AUTHOR'S NOTE

Unless otherwise indicated, dates referring to Hauptmann's works indicate premieres (of dramas) and first printings. Translations of titles for works that have not been translated into English are my own. They appear in parentheses following the German title and are not italicized. All translations into English from both German primary and secondary sources in this book are my own.

Quotations from Hauptmann's works are translated from *Sämtliche Werke. Centenar-Ausgabe zum 100. Geburtstag des Dichters, 15. November 1962*, 11 vols, edited by Hans-Egon Hass and continued by Martin Machatzke. Frankfurt/M.: Propyläen, 1966–74. Citations in parentheses throughout are to this edition and are given in Arabic numerals, with the numerals preceding the colon indicating volume number and those following the colon indicating page numbers.

# CHRONOLOGY

1862    November 15: Hauptmann born in Ober-Salzbrunn, Silesia, the fourth child of Robert (1824–98) and Marie Hauptmann, née Strähler (1827–1906).

1868    Begins attending village elementary school.

1874    Attends school in Realschule am Zwinger in Breslau with brother Carl (1858–1921).

1875    Writes first preserved poems.

1877    Robert Hauptmann loses hotel Preußische Krone to creditors.

1878    Agricultural trainee on estate of uncle in Lohnig and then Lederose; exposed to Herrnhut Pietism.

1879    Participation in Pangermanic brotherhood.

1880    Admitted to sculpture class of the Königliche Kunst- und Gewerbeschule in Breslau; writes alliterative Hermann epic.

1881    Writes *Liebesfrühling* (Spring of Love) for wedding of brother Georg (1853–1899); is engaged to Marie Thienemann (1860–1914); begins work on *Germanen und Römer* (Germanic Tribes and Romans); participates in utopian Pacific Society (Gesellschaft Pacific).

1882    Leaves art school and, in the fall, begins one semester of study at the University of Jena.

1883    Mediterranean trip; October 1883 to March 1884 works as sculptor in Rome, where he contracts typhoid fever; recovers and returns home.

1884    Attends drawing class in Königliche Akademie in Dresden; studies at University of Berlin, works on *Promethidenlos* (The Fate of the Prometheans) and *Das bunte Buch* (The Varicolored Book); takes acting lessons.

1885    May 5: Marriage to Marie Thienemann; couple lives briefly in Berlin before moving to Erkner; first visit to island of Hiddensee; begins Jesus studies.

1886    Son Ivo born; extended visit to Putbus on island of Rügen.

1887    June 17: Speech on Georg Büchner before Berlin literary society Durch; witness at "socialist trial" in Breslau; son Eckart born; writes *Fasching* (Carnival).

1888    Spring-fall: Stay in Zurich with Carl Hauptmann and his family; psychiatric studies with Professor Auguste Forel; friendship with Frank Wedekind; chance meeting with "nature apostle" Johannes Guttzeit; work on autobiographical novel; *Bahnwärter Thiel (Flagman Thiel)*.

1889    Son Klaus born in Erkner; Hauptmann meets fourteen-year-old Margarete Marschalk (1875–1957). October 20: Turbulent premier of *Vor Sonnenaufgang (Before Sunrise)*.

1890    *Das Friedensfest (The Coming of Peace)*; *Der Apostel (The Apostle)*.

1891    *Einsame Menschen* (Lonely Lives); meets Johannes Brahms, Henrik Ibsen, and Richard Strauss; moves to Schreiberhau in Silesia; research trip to locale of *Die Weber (The Weavers)*.

1892    *Kollege Crampton (Colleague Crampton)*; public performance of *The Weavers* prevented by authorities; study trip to Franconia for *Florian Geyer*.

1893    February 26: premier of *The Weavers* under auspices of Freie Bühne; *Der Biberpelz (The Beaver Coat)*; *Hanneles Himmelfahrt (Hannele)*; close ties with Margarete Marschalk and beginning of Hauptmann's decade-long marriage crisis.

1894    Pursues wife and children to United States; *Hannele* premiers in New York; renewed separation from wife and family upon return to Germany.

1896    *Florian Geyer;* awarded Grillparzer Prize for *Hannele;* Kaiser Wilhelm II prevents award of Schiller Prize; *Die versunkene Glocke (The Sunken Bell)*.

1897    Trip to Italy with Margarete; intense dispute with brother Carl during Christmas season.

1898    *Furhmann Henschel (Drayman Henschel)*; lives in Berlin-Grunewald; death of father.

1899    Second Grillparzer Prize (for *Drayman Henschel)*; Kaiser Wilhelm II again prevents award of Schiller Prize; deaths of brother Georg and friend Hugo Ernst Schmidt.

1900    *Schluck und Jau (Schluck and Jau)*; son Benvenuto born to Hauptmann and Margarete Marschalk; *Michael Kramer*.

1901    Moves with Margarete into magnificent Haus Wiesenstein near Agnetendorf in Riesengebirge of Silesia; *Der rote Hahn (The Conflagration)*.

1902    *Der arme Heinrich (Henry of Aue)*.

1903    *Rose Bernd;* illness; work on novel fragment *Der Venezianer* (The Venetian).

1904  Divorce from Marie and marriage to Margarete; fragmentary *Das Hirtenlied* (Pastoral) published; signs exclusive contract with theater director Otto Brahm.

1905  Awarded third Grillparzer Prize; *Elga;* honorary doctorate from Oxford University; visit to Stratford upon Avon; meets George Bernard Shaw; infatuation with Ida Orloff.

1906  *Und Pippa tanzt!* (*And Pippa Dances*); meets Konstantin Stanislavsky.

1907  *Die Jungfern vom Bischofsberg* (*The Maidens of the Mount*); long–awaited trip to Greece.

1908  *Griechischer Frühling* (Greek Spring); *Kaiser Karls Geisel* (*Charlemagne's Hostage*).

1909  *Griselda;* honorary doctorate from University of Leipzig; lecture tour to Berlin, Hamburg, Leipzig, Munich, Prague, Vienna, and Zurich.

1910  *Der Narr in Christo Emanuel Quint* (*The Fool in Christ Emanuel Quint*).

1911  *Die Ratten* (*The Rats*); birth of son, Gerhart Erasmus, who dies after two days.

1912  *Gabriel Schillings Flucht* (*Gabriel Schilling's Flight*); *Atlantis;* Nobel Prize for Literature; death of Otto Brahm.

1913  *Festspiel in deutschen Reimen* (*Commemoration Masque*) provokes nationalist opposition and is suppressed by order of the Crown Prince after eleven performances.

1914  *Der Bogen des Odysseus* (*The Bow of Odysseus*); outbreak of First World War inspires Hauptmann to write nationalistic poetry and newspaper articles.

1915  *Magnus Garbe* completed; death of first wife, Marie.

1917  *Winterballade* (*Winter Ballad*).

1918  *Der Ketzer von Soana* (*The Heretic of Soana*).

1920  *Der weiße Heiland* (*The White Savior*); Rainer Maria Rilke participates in drama rehearsals.

1921  *Peter Brauer;* honorary doctorate from University of Prague; Hauptmann denies that he is a candidate for Reichspräsident.

1922  *Indipohdi;* Hauptmann festival in Breslau, where fourteen of his dramas are performed; tumultuous sixtieth birthday celebration throughout Germany.

1923  Hauptmann and Thomas Mann spend fall vacation in same Italian hotel; Hauptmann provides model for Peeperkorn character in Mann's *The Magic Mountain.*

1924   *Die Insel der Großen Mutter* (*The Island of the Great Mother*); awarded Pour le mérite.

1925   *Veland.*

1926   Hauptmann reads from *Till Eulenspiegel* before German Reichstag; *Dorothea Angermann;* parts of *Mary* published.

1927   Hauptmann directs own version of *Hamlet* in Dresden; *Die blaue Blume* (The Blue Flower).

1928   *Wanda; Till Eulenspiegel;* member of the literary section of the Prussian Academy of Arts.

1929   *Die schwarze Maske* (The Black Mask); *Witches' Ride* (*Hexenritt*).

1930   *Das Buch der Leidenschaft* (The Book of Passion).

1931   *Die Spitzhacke* (*The Pickax*).

1932   *Vor Sonnenuntergang* (*Before Sunset*); second (this time triumphal) trip to the United States, where he meets numerous celebrities; seventieth birthday celebration throughout Germany.

1933   *Die goldene Harfe* (The Golden Harp); advent of Hitler regime, to which Hauptmann expresses loyalty; gradual withdrawal from public life.

1934   *Das Meerwunder* (The Sea Miracle); attends funeral of Jewish friends Max Pinkus and Samuel Fischer, his publisher.

1935   *Hamlet in Wittenberg.*

1936   *Im Wirbel der Berufung* (In the Maelstrom of Vocation); excerpts from *Der große Traum* (The Great Dream) published.

1937   *Das Abenteuer meiner Jugend* (The Adventure of my Youth); radio speech to Germans abroad.

1938   *Tochter der Kathedrale* (Daughter of the Cathedral); *Ulrich von Lichtenstein; Der Schuß im Park* (The Shot in the Park).

1941   *Iphigenie in Delphi.*

1942   *Das Märchen* (*The Fairy Tale*); on the occasion of Hauptmann's eightieth birthday S. Fischer publishes the seventeen-volume *Gesammelte Werke,* including some previously unpublished items such as *Magnus Garbe.* Correspondence between Alfred Rosenberg and Josef Goebbels concerning an appropriate Nazi political stance regarding Hauptmann.

1943   *Iphigenie in Aulis;* fragments of *Der neue Christophorous* (The New Christophorous).

1945   Hauptmann witnesses the destruction of Dresden by allied bombers on the night of February 13–14.

1946  June 6: Hauptmann dies; buried on the island of Hiddensee.
1947  *Die Finsternisse* (The Eclipse) published in New York; *Agamemnons Tod* (Agamemnon's Death); *Elektra; Mignon.*
1952  *Herbert Engelmann.*

# Understanding
## GERHART HAUPTMANN

# INTRODUCTION

It appears now that only two twentieth-century German playwrights—Gerhart Hauptmann (1862–1946) and Bertolt Brecht (1898–1956)—have achieved world literary stature. And although Brecht is better known today, it would not be unreasonable to argue that Hauptmann had a wider range, was more productive, and created a greater number of unforgettable characters who, free of his compatriot's Marxist ideological ballast, appeal to a more universal range of human instincts and emotions. Although no one familiar with Hauptmann's oeuvre would argue its uniformly superior literary quality (occasionally he seems to have succumbed to the temptation of trading on his celebrity for quick profit), its sheer volume is astonishing. The standard edition of the works contains within its almost 14,000 pages some fifty plays, twenty-five novels and shorter prose pieces, half a dozen verse epics, and hundreds of poems, in addition to an abundance of fragments, essays, speeches, epigrams, and the like. To this must be added a massive quantity of largely unpublished manuscript material, of interest mainly to specialists, now in the possession of the Staatsbibliothek Preußischer Kulturbesitz in Berlin. In addition to Hauptmann's private library of more than 10,000 volumes—valuable for the author's often revealing underlinings and marginal notations—and roughly 60,000 letters, the collection also includes 774 volumes and folders of differing format, containing variants and rough drafts of works, diaries, newspaper clippings, handwritten aperçus, and so forth. Even to catalogue this material will require years; a historical-critical edition remains a perhaps utopian desideratum.

Due in part to the highly developed, highly subsidized theater system of Germany, Hauptmann's plays achieved a popularity undreamed of by an American dramatist. Thus *Die Weber* (*The Weavers*) was published in no fewer than 253 editions between 1892 and 1942; *Die versunkene Glocke* (*The Sunken Bell*) in 160 editions between 1896 and 1930, and *Der Biberpelz* (*The Beaver Coat*) in 108 editions between 1893 and 1942. Not only were Hauptmann's plays performed when they first appeared, but a consistent nucleus of ten or twelve of them continues to be performed, competing only with such classics as plays by Shakespeare, Goethe, and Lessing, while even surpassing in popularity such traditional favorites as Molière and Schiller. A random

1

theater season—1958–59—shows forty-two productions of fifteen different dramas for a total of 823 performances; *The Beaver Coat,* the most popular of the comedies, was accorded 329 productions and some 700 performances between 1948 and 1962 and carried its popularity into the 1980s. That such popularity should extend to other media is also hardly surprising. There have been at least twenty-one film and television adaptations of Hauptmann's works to date—another record not equaled by any other German author.[1] His accomplishments were recognized and honored throughout his life, both at home and abroad. He received the prestigious Grillparzer Prize on three occasions, collected a number of honorary doctorates (the first from Oxford in 1905), and was awarded the Nobel Prize for Literature in 1912 and the Goethe Prize in 1932.

In spite of the difficulties inherent in the process of translation (about which more later), Hauptmann's work has been made available worldwide through some 670 renderings into thirty-nine languages, including Chinese, Japanese, Hindi, and Esperanto. In eastern Europe he has sometimes competed favorably with domestic authors. The first edition of his collected works in a foreign language appeared from 1902 to 1905 in Russia, where for a time he was that country's best-loved dramatist. *The Weavers,* translated by Lenin's sister, was exploited in the Russian Revolution, and its author—himself indebted to Tolstoy and Dostoyevski—exerted his influence on Gorky, Chekhov, and the influential director and theoretician Stanislavsky.[2] A recent Hauptmann festival in Poland confirms his continued importance for the cultural life of that country as well.

In the Anglo-Saxon world, James Joyce, Eugene O'Neill, and Arthur Miller (among others) have expressed indebtedness to Hauptmann. Joyce learned German to read him in the original, translated *Vor Sonnenaufgang* (*Before Sunrise*) and *Michael Kramer* into English but failed in his efforts to get the plays performed by the Irish Literary Theatre. Admiring the playwright almost to the point of idolatry, Joyce liked to think of himself as the third in an illustrious line from Ibsen through Hauptmann; he expressed his homage in notes and a letter and more allusively in *The Dead* and *A Painful Case* (from *Dubliners*), in *A Portrait of the Artist as a Young Man,* and in *Ulysses.* Especially the German's psychological skills, his depiction of marital and family problems, and his "epiphanies" (for example, the last scene of the artist-drama *Michael Kramer*) impressed him deeply. Overall, as one critic has observed, "it is difficult to imagine a modern author more helpful for the study of Joyce than Hauptmann."[3]

2

In the United States Hauptmann's reception has been decidedly mixed.[4] The amount and quality of scholarly preoccupation with him here compares favorably with that found in Germany, and, until approximately the outbreak of the Second World War, he was a relatively familiar figure to educated Americans not indifferent to the arts. Some of his plays, notably *The Sunken Bell* and *The Weavers*, had successful runs on Broadway and in some of the larger cities east of the Mississippi. Popular actors such as Basil Rathbone and Ethel Barrymore performed in his works; Barrymore, in fact, considered her title role in *Rose Bernd* a high point of her career. Hauptmann's visit to the United States in 1932—by which time he was a world-renowned celebrity—perhaps occasioned the most tumultuous celebration ever accorded a German visitor to this country. Here he was awarded yet another honorary doctorate (by Columbia University); delivered a lecture on Goethe on that occasion, and then at Harvard, in Baltimore, and in Washington, D.C.; was presented to President Hoover in the White House; and met such contemporary luminaries as Theodore Dreiser, Sinclair Lewis, Eugene O'Neill, Helen Keller, and Lillian Gish. Although the precise extent of his influence is not easily quantifiable, he also had some impact on the course of American literature. Perhaps O'Neill expressed this elusive relationship best during their meeting when he pointed out that contemporary American drama was inconceivable without Ibsen, Strindberg, and Hauptmann and, in a more personal note, added that ever since he had begun to write plays he had taken Hauptmann as his model.[5]

That Hauptmann was not better appreciated in America derived from a variety of factors that have little to do with literary quality. When his first plays, *Before Sunrise* and then *Hannele* (originally *Hanneles Himmelfahrt*), were performed in New York in 1892 and 1894 respectively, they were burdened by a number of handicaps. As a dramatist Hauptmann was at the mercy of a theater tradition which could not compare with that of his homeland; as an author identified with Naturalism he was conjoined with a movement that would remain largely alien to Americans for some twenty more years; and as a Silesian German he drew his characters, situations, language, and inspiration from a milieu that was almost incomprehensible to American audiences. To be sure, German drama had been steadily performed in New York (and also in Philadelphia, Boston, Chicago, Milwaukee, and St. Louis) since William Dunlap's 1798 adaptation of August von Kotzebue's long-forgotten *Menschenhaß und Reue* as *The Stranger*. Unfortunately this choice remained typical of the sentimental, farcical, superficial fare that was to dominate the

American stage for years to come. Even the German immigrants of 1848, many of whom arrived with relatively sophisticated cultural interests, were soon absorbed into the New World mainstream and began patronizing the vapid, Americanized, happy-ending versions of French plays by the likes of Rostand and Sardou and later preferred the melodramatic Hermann Sudermann over his compatriot Hauptmann by a wide margin. By the mid-1890s the profit motive and star system were already so dominant in New York that even Heinrich Conried had to prostitute his fine Irving Place Theatre with performances of ephemera in order to finance an occasional culturally significant German play.[6]

Compounding Hauptmann's problem, his most congenial mode, Naturalism, was antithetical to the optimistic, didactic, and puritanical contemporary American spirit. When Ibsen's *A Doll House* was staged in 1883 it had been given a "happy" ending in the form of a sermon about woman's place in the home, and in 1937 the theater historian Norman Hapgood was still claiming that "it must be recognized that great as the power of Ibsen and Strindberg may be, they present those facts of life which men must forget if life is to be noble or even endurable."[7] It was, of course, precisely "those facts of life" that the Naturalists had vowed to stress.

An equally daunting problem (as even Joyce found out) was that of translation. As Lilian R. Furst has summarized, "a translation is no guide to a Naturalist play. . . . Precisely because of the German achievement in the field of dramatic language, characteristic speech-patterns, dialectical coloring, verbal gestures, silences, etc., the problems of translation apply to German Naturalism more than to any other movement and largely account for its unwarranted neglect outside Germany."[8]

## Formative Years

Before elaborating on the specifically German component of European Naturalism, it may be well to take a closer look at the formative years of the man generally regarded as its most important practitioner. This approach suggests itself not only because it will provide at least some sense of time and place for what is to follow, but, more important, because Hauptmann's work is firmly rooted in personal experience. As his publisher Samuel Fischer put it, "Hauptmann, the man and his work, form a unity of rare legitimacy; they are completely identical." Even Daiber is not far off the mark when he claims, "[Hauptmann] didn't publish books; he published himself."[9] Especially the first quarter century, the period described in great detail in the autobiography *Das Abenteuer meiner Jugend* (The Adventure of my Youth) supplied the "humus" (the author's term) from which grew a luxurious harvest of works spanning more than fifty years.[10]

Gerhard Johann Robert Hauptmann (at birth his first name was spelled with a final *d*) was born around noon on Saturday, November 15, 1862, the fourth child of Robert (1824–98) and Marie (Straehler) Hauptmann (1827–1906). The youngest of his siblings, Carl (1858–1921), was four and a half years older, while Johanna (1856–1943) and Georg (1853–99) were too old to figure prominently in his childhood as companions. Of great significance for Hauptmann's future development was his birthplace, the spa hotel Zur Preußischen Krone (Prussian Crown) in Ober-Salzbrunn, Silesia—taken over by Robert Hauptmann from his father and located in present-day Poland. For a growing child such quasi-public surroundings were a mixed blessing. The constant, hectic activity needed to satisfy the needs and whims of hotel guests left the parents with little time (especially during the summer season) to devote to their children. As a result the boy was often left to his own devices or in the care of a brutal, superstitious nursemaid. His earliest memory, he claimed later, was of being whipped by this peasant woman, whose choleric rantings came to represent for him his "first contact with the Prussian non-com" (7:457) mentality. Little wonder, perhaps, that his earliest years were pervaded by an "almost cosmic sadness" (7:460) and that he fell into the habit of oppressive dreaming, of which he complained most of his life.

Unintentional as it may have been, the neglect had a positive side also. It allowed the child to roam about the hotel and its environs, bringing him in direct contact with an undomesticated nature and with certain strata of society which a more cautious upbringing might have excluded. Hotels are microcosms, and the hotel Prussian Crown was no exception. Here the boy was exposed to German, Polish, and Russian nobility whose pampered children aroused his envy, but also to the unceasing drudgery of those who served them. Part of the ground floor was leased for a time to an actor who ran a tavern which catered to a less select clientele, but it was also the crowded home of drayman Krause and his poor family. Here Hauptmann moved easily from the standard German spoken by his father and the guests to the local dialect; ate with gusto from the communal bowl in which the meals were served; and, treated as one of the family, entertained the younger children for hours at a time with invented fairy tales. Wanderings into the surrounding countryside exposed him to the even more dire poverty of weavers' huts and the miserable quarters of exploited coal miners.

The Hauptmann household offered minimal cultural enrichment for a future author. A full-length, life-size oil painting of King Wilhelm and consort expressed the father's monarchical predilection and was prominently displayed in the "blue room" of the hotel. (Robert also managed to pass on much of his boundless enthusiasm for Bismarck to his son.) Another room displayed copies of a Raphael and a Rembrandt, but aside from a piano on which Hauptmann "improvised" without benefit of formal instruction, there was little to attract a child to the arts. Nor was the relationship of the parents conducive to a cooperative, harmonious effort to help their offspring realize their highest potential. The father was an aloof, cerebral type with a penchant for fine clothes, fine manners, and fine horses, while the mother, although the daughter of an intimidating local official, was from a deeply pietistic background, tended to wallow in self-pity, complained to her children about the father's allegedly spendthrift ways, and dressed so as to be hardly distinguishable from a scullery maid—whose work she performed anyway in the hotel kitchen. Very early the family began to assume that any intellectual distinction would accrue to Carl, while his mother encouraged Gerhart—even in his late teens—to pursue a career in gardening. Robert Hauptmann did not neglect his son's practical education completely. While Hauptmann was still a child, his father began plying him with liquor in the belief that this would inoculate him against future alcoholic excess!

Like many other creative individuals of his day Hauptmann loathed school and continued to have nightmares about it long after he had become an adult. His first village schoolmaster, the perpetually irritable, sadistic Brendel, personified the worst aspects of a system in which "simple words, a kindly manner, friendly support of the student were despised. They were considered soft, they were considered unmanly. The invisible, authoritative figure behind the pedagogue was not Lessing, Herder, Goethe or Socrates, but the Prussian noncom" (7:623). While Brendel was unable to break him, Hauptmann also resisted learning from him and learned to read by himself from translations of Defoe's *Robinson Crusoe* and Cooper's *Leatherstocking Tales*. So intoxicated was he by the latter that for years he identified with Leatherstocking's noble friend Chingachgook and was pleased when his older brother Georg took to calling him by that name.

Having survived the terrors of Brendel, Hauptmann may have thought the worst of school behind him. He was wrong. When he was eleven years old his parents sent him to nearby Breslau (now Wrocław) to join Carl in a nonclassical secondary school. Here, in addition to the humiliation heaped on him by teachers, schoolmates, and even his own brother, the living conditions were horrendous. The school was located in a disreputable part of the city amidst taverns and prostitute hangouts, and the brothers lived with some thirty other adolescents on the fourth floor of a crowded, noisy, vermin-invested tenement house that was hot in the summer and freezing in the winter. The only bearable periods of this "exile" were Hauptmann's vacations at home, opportunities for telling stories to the children of his landlord and visits to the nearby Breslau theater. Although he had been intrigued by the spa theater in his home town and had enjoyed playing with a cardboard Hamlet and stage as a small child, this was his first exposure to theater of high quality. When the renowned Meininger troupe arrived for an engagement, he attended its productions of *Macbeth, Julius Caesar,* Schiller's *Wallenstein* trilogy and *Wilhelm Tell,* and Kleist's *Die Hermannsschlacht (Battle of Arminius).*

As he recalled later, however, the dubious high point of his stay in Breslau was the death and burial of a cousin, Georg Schubert, who died suddenly of meningitis. The pride and joy of his parents and the Straehler family (the boy's mother was a sister of Marie Hauptmann), Georg was considered a child prodigy and had been tirelessly promoted as a model for Hauptmann. While the confrontation with the majesty of death and the abrupt realization of its inevitability had a profound effect on Hauptmann, he also had an inappropriate but honest feeling of joy and release because of the lavish affection Georg had received and he had been denied. But Georg was not to be gotten rid of that easily. After dropping out of school in 1878 in order to accept an offer from the Schuberts (Julie and Gustav) to live with them as an agricultural trainee, first in Lohnig and then in nearby Lederose, Hauptmann gradually realized that he was meant to serve as a kind of surrogate for the dead cousin—another role he despaired of being able to fulfill to anyone's satisfaction.

Adding to his misery, he suddenly found himself subjected to hard physical labor from 4:30 A.M. until he could retreat to bed at night. It was at this time that he developed lung problems which concerned him greatly for a number of years and which his aunt and uncle refused to acknowledge. Soon his mental health also began to deteriorate. Ignorant of sex (his father had told him that abstinence was probably harmful) and surrounded by the fecundity of the barnyard and of the robust peasant women who worked the fields, he succumbed to masturbatory fantasies and practices. As an isolated problem this might have been harmless enough. In his case, however, it was conjoined with a level of self-esteem already at its nadir and with an oppressive, guilt-inducing religious atmosphere. The suffocating pietism of the Schuberts (and the veritable death cult practiced by the mother on behalf of Georg), the ravings of lay preachers who roamed the countryside, and his sudden obsessive preoccupation with the New Testament and his own "sins" led Hauptmann to the threshold of religious mania. Indeed only when he was convinced that the end of the world was at hand and rushed home to warn and prepare his parents for the coming apocalypse—but was met instead by the cold bath of Carl's skeptical rationalism—was he finally saved.

Immediate suffering notwithstanding, the Lederose experience was to prove invaluable for Hauptmann's later development. Without his exposure to rural life and immersion in the Bible and religious sects, such masterpieces as *Rose Bernd* and *Der Narr in Christo Emanuel Quint* (*The Fool in Christ Emanuel Quint*) would have been stillborn. In addition, thanks to aunt Julie's talent in that area, a love of music (Bach, Handel, Protestant chorales) was stimulated, and the rural sojourn even broadened the author's political horizon. Comments by farm laborers with whom he worked, ignorant of the fact that he understood their dialect, disabused him of the notion that everyone accepted the glorious Prussian status quo. Praise of Bismarck elicited only sullen silence from them; Field Marshall von Moltke was dismissed as a coward, and even local Protestant pastors were accused of aligning themselves with the rich and powerful while ignoring the example and teachings of Christ.

In 1880 Hauptmann returned to Lederose for a short vacation. There he met and fell passionately in love with his successor, the trainee Anna Grundmann, but was thwarted by a jealous uncle in his attempt to win her in marriage. The beautiful verse epic *Anna* (1921), reminiscent of Goethe's *Hermann und Dorothea*, goes a long way toward capturing the ineffable atmosphere of Lederose as the author experienced it.

Continuing his string of failures—at least he now had the legitimate excuse of ill health for giving up agriculture—Hauptmann returned briefly to Breslau, where he joined his brother Carl, Alfred Ploetz, and another friend, Ferdinand Simon, in an idealistic blood brotherhood with the wildly extravagant goal of uniting all Germanic nations and peoples. Inspired by the spiritual preceptors of the small group, the popular historical authors Felix Dahn and Wilhelm Jordan, he wrote a dramatic fragment, *Fritihofs Brautwerbung* (Fritihof's Courtship) and an alliterative "Hermannslied" (Lay of Arminius) in emulation of their patriotic works. A chance meeting with an artist acquaintance of his father, however, soon diverted his attention to the plastic arts, and in spite of patently deficient preparation for such a move, he managed to enroll in a sculpture class of the Breslau Royal Art and Vocational School (Königliche Kunst- und Gewerbeschule) in the fall of 1880. Whether seduced by his changed circumstances and new companions or simply feeling the need to assume a role commensurate with his image of an artist, Hauptmann suddenly underwent a radical transformation. From a shy, introverted adolescent he became a proponent of nudism (for which he continued a vocal predilection the rest of his life); squandered what little money his parents sent him in cheap bars (often in the company of James Marshall, one of his professors); wore shoulder-length hair and worn-out clothing; pawned even his mattress; and was reduced to begging. As was the case with his previous literary efforts, the sculpture he produced was conventional and derivative. However, his expulsion from art school was not due to such shortcomings but to "bad behavior and insufficient industry and attendance" (7:807). Fortunately a reading from his "Lay of Arminius," arranged by faculty who supported him, not only brought him his first taste of (local) fame but achieved his reinstatement. He remained in school, working under the supervision of one of his defenders, the sculptor Robert Haertel, until the spring of 1882

During this time a virtual miracle occurred, one which solved Hauptmann's financial problems, gave him the freedom to pursue his personal inclinations, and, for this reason, deserves substantial credit for his future success. It began when his brother Georg met Adele Thienemann, the daughter of a wealthy widower who lived near Dresden with four other daughters and a son. When Robert Hauptmann learned of his son's engagement and of the Thienemann family's circumstances, he could hardly suppress his glee and is said to have exclaimed, "I tell you, a nest of birds of paradise!" (7:843). The Hauptmann brothers were quick to act, and within a few years all three were married to Thienemann sisters: Georg to Adele, Carl to Martha, and Gerhart to Marie (or Mary, as he preferred to call her). Although Gerhart Hauptmann's marriage did not take place until 1885, he soon began to enjoy the benefits of his fiancée's largesse, starting on a day early in 1882 when she visited him in Breslau, discovered the extent of his poverty, and silently pressed a pile of gold coins into his hand.

Still unable to choose between sculpture and literature, he dictated a drama, *Germanen und Römer* (Germanic Tribes and Romans), with which he intended to outshine Heinrich von Kleist, to an "old unemployed gymnastics instructor" (7:883). (The habit of dictating his works—while pacing to and fro, often holding a volume of Goethe in his hand—was to stay with him throughout his life.)

Again with the intercession of Robert Haertel (Hauptmann still lacked credentials), he enrolled in 1882 for one semester at the University of Jena, where he busied himself with two very different areas of study: the materialist views of science and heredity as expounded by the Darwinist Ernst Haeckel, and the study of Plato and ancient Greece. With his newly acquired interest in Greek antiquity providing the incentive (and Mary's money the means), Hauptmann set out alone by steamer from Hamburg in April of 1883 on a Mediterranean trip. Unfortunately Carl decided to join him in Genoa, and his constant bickering so poisoned the atmosphere that the trip was broken off before they reached Greece. Nevertheless it exposed Hauptmann to a number of new experiences: the power and grandeur of the sea; unimaginable degradation in the opium dens and prostitution cribs of Málaga, and the glory of Michelangelo's sculpture in Rome.

Indeed, so inspired was he by Michelangelo that he returned to Rome in October, set up an atelier in the Via degli Incurabili, and had cards printed grandly announcing himself as "Gherardo Hauptmann, Scultore." Ambitious to a fault but lacking practical know-how, he spent some ten weeks modeling a colossal Germanic warrior in clay, only to see it begin to shift and sag one night—defying his frantic efforts to prop it up—and collapse in a heap on the floor. His remaining work was destroyed in a fit of madness by a German neighbor, and, to complete the disaster, he contracted a virulent typhoid fever which plunged him into a "splendid, holy" coma in which he felt "unspeakably well" (7:986) while actually hovering on the brink of death. Returning home, he spent a final six weeks attending a drawing class in Dresden before deciding, once and for all, to concentrate his creative energies on literature.

The first products of this renewed interest were an epic in verse, *Promethidenlos* (The Fate of the Children of Prometheus), written in a Byronic vein and incorporating some of Hauptmann's Mediterranean experiences, and a book of poetry, *Das bunte Buch* (The Varicolored Book). In spite of their Romantic overtones, both these works express strong compassion for the downtrodden and condemnation of the city as an instrument of corruption.

We get a further glimpse of the nature of Hauptmann's sociopolitical leanings at this time through an episode involving a planned utopian colony in the United States. Together with Carl and some student friends, he had learned about the attempt by Étienne Cabet and his followers to establish model communal settlements in Illinois and Texas some thirty-five years earlier. Attempting a similar experiment, the group founded a Pacific society (Gesellschaft Pazifik) and appointed Carl and Gerhart ministers of science and culture respectively for the enterprise. Alfred Ploetz, the president–designate, actually undertook a reconnaissance trip to the United States in 1884. He soon discovered, however, that Cabet's settlements had fallen into a sad state of decline and that American conditions were not conducive to a realization of utopian plans. Abortive and unrealistic as it was, this episode contributed to Hauptmann's reputation as a socialist agitator and complicated the later reception of some of his works.

Hauptmann and Mary Thienemann were finally married in Dresden on May 5, 1885, under inauspicious circumstances. Their areas of incompatibility were formidable. Raised without a mother and educated in the gloomy atmosphere of a Pietist school, Mary inclined toward melancholy, held conventional views of sexual morality, and worried about money matters to the point of distraction. Hauptmann, on the other hand, had shaken off the grip of sectarianism, was more cheerful and positive in his outlook, was beguiled by ideas of free love and the "natural" polygamous nature of the male much in vogue at the time, and spent Mary's money freely—on his friends as well as himself. Both had health concerns. Mary suffered from a debilitating anemia; Gerhart still had his lung problems. The fact that he was coughing up blood relieved him from compulsory military service but didn't augur well for his future. A dashing young cavalry officer, observing the bridegroom with disdain through his monocle just after the wedding, was heard to remark to his female companions, "That fellow is going to kick the bucket before the end of the first week!"[11]

The couple's first household was established in Berlin, where, since the fall of 1884, Gerhart was again enrolled at the university. While the intensive theater and concert activity of the metropolis was ideal for a future playwright—here he was first exposed to Ibsen and took acting lessons from a former theater director, Alexander Heßler—the noise and hyperstimulation of urban life were especially irritating to his bride, and by September they moved to Erkner, a nearby village popular as a summer resort. Although he could not know it at the time of the move, the four years spent in Erkner were also to prove highly fortuitous for his future work. Located near enough to Berlin for village residents to see the city's red nighttime glow and for Hauptmann to feel the need for protection from the unsavory characters who wandered out from the city (he bought himself two dogs for this purpose), yet providing also the advantages of country life (walks in the deep forest, iceskating on a moonlit lake), Erkner was an ideal place for an aspiring author to establish himself. Here he met a variety of people who would serve as models for characters in later works, fathered three sons in rapid succession, wrote his first important works, and cultivated ties to publishers and to a group of young literary activists including Arno Holz (1863–1929) (with whom, next to himself, the German Naturalist movement is most strongly identified). An example of the way in which his literary taste was changing is provided by a lecture and reading before the Berlin literary society Durch in which he introduced the then almost forgotten Georg Büchner (1813–37) to his listeners. This prescient early-nineteenth-century dramatist who despised hypocrisy, flirted with atheism, and—especially in his masterpiece *Woyzeck*—championed the weak and disenfranchised made a profound and lasting impression on young Hauptmann.

A final stage in young Hauptmann's personal development, and one that also left a lasting impression on his work, resulted from a stay in Switzerland during the summer of 1888. In Zurich he joined Carl and Martha and a growing colony of idealistic young artists and scientists disillusioned with the censorship and repression synonymous with Bismarck's Germany. Sharing with his friends a strong faith in science as the ultimate solution to human problems, he was especially attracted to the teachings of Professor Auguste Forel, the director of Burghölzli, the local insane asylum. From Forel, whose lectures he attended and whose patients he was allowed to observe, he not only gained valuable insights into the human psyche but was also swayed, at least for a time, by his mentor's passionately held views on such subjects as female emancipation and the evils of alcohol. Notebook in hand, he recorded for later use the behavior not only of individuals but of the Salvation Army and various religious sects as well. During conversations with another aspiring author, Frank Wedekind (1864–1918), he spoke frankly about his own sexual problems—confessions, he claimed later, which led to Wedekind's first big success, the sensational *Frühlings Erwachen* (1891) (*Spring's Awakening*). By this time he was also making plans for a drama about the plight of Silesian weavers and had decided on a definite program for the future: he would write about people, problems, and locales with which he was intimately familiar and would do so in scrupulously realistic language finely attuned to the nuances of each character's speech habits.

## German Naturalism

It was another stroke of luck (the first was Mary) that Hauptmann's literary intentions and talents were so perfectly attuned to the increasingly naturalistic tendencies of his epoch. His absorption in the life around him, his preoccupation with psychology, his intuitive gift for observation, even his naive idealism coincided with the general tenor of a movement which was on the brink of fruition, especially in nearby Berlin.

It is an oversimplification to think that Germany merely attached itself uncritically to the movement of European Naturalism; the ground had been prepared in the social, religious, political, and economic life of the country and to a lesser extent in domestic literature and the universities as well. How far back we wish to trace these developments would seem to be a matter of arbitrary choice, but the deaths of Hegel (1831) and Goethe (1832) are acceptable markers with which to date a distinctively new outlook. Within a short time the German nation experienced rapid advances in natural science and sociology; a new antimetaphysical outlook based primarily on the theories of Charles Darwin but also on the positivism of Auguste Comte and Hippolyte Taine; the atheistic materialism of Ludwig Feuerbach; the attacks on Jesus as an "affable madman" by David Friedrich Strauß; and the scientific socialism of Marx and Engels—not to forget the impact that such inventions as photography had on life and the arts.

To a much greater extent than before, literature began to limit itself to corporeal man, subject to the laws of organic life and free of transcendental delusion. While this state of affairs would seem to represent an impoverishment of the traditional image of man—as a being endowed with a soul and spirituality—it was accepted with surprising equanimity. "The distinctive feature of our life at that time," Hauptmann was to recall later,

> was confidence. Thus we believed in the irresistible progress of mankind. We believed in the victory of natural science and in the ultimate unveiling of nature. The victory of truth, we believed, would also negate the deceptions and delusions of religious blindness. Within a short time, we believed, the self-laceration of humanity through war would be no more than a superceded chapter of history. . . . One day the last crime would have died out with the last criminal, like certain epidemics, as the result of hygiene and other prophylactics of medical science. (7:1071)

The immediate future, to be sure, was more problematical. The unification of Germany, after its victory over France in 1871 and its sudden ascendancy under Bismarck to the rank of a world power, was accompanied by waves of nationalism; the rise of labor-saving technology widened the gap between proletariat and bourgeoisie; the sudden shift from an agrarian, handicraft society to industry and trade put a severe strain on the economic system; and the rapid growth of cities like Berlin—the result of a phenomenal flight from the land—intensified the social misery of the masses.

Finding a commensurate literary form for expressing these changed conditions required trial and error but was eventually accomplished by an extension of certain trends from domestic literature and by adapting techniques of contemporary foreign authors to German circumstances. For drama, the most successful naturalist genre in Germany, the direct line of descent is via the eighteenth–century Storm and Stress period, followed by Heinrich von Kleist and later nineteenth–century dramatists such as Büchner, Friedrich Hebbel, and the Austrian Ludwig Anzengruber. Storm and Stress authors such as Heinrich Leopold Wagner (*Die Kindesmörderin* [*The Infanticide*]), but especially Jakob Michael Reinhold Lenz, had dealt with biting, realistic social criticism and drastic action such as infanticide and self-castration, Kleist, perhaps naively, had dared to suggest in *Der Prinz von Homburg* (*Prince of Homburg*) that even a member of the Prussian nobility could disintegrate abjectly in the face of death, and in *Penthesilea* that extreme mental anguish can lead to extreme perversity. Apparently instinctively, and almost alone, Hauptmann had discovered the most direct precursor not only of the Naturalist movement but, more specifically, of his own early work: Georg Büchner. A pioneer of the social movement of the nineteenth century, Büchner like Hauptmann opposed political decadence and stagnation and a conservative government whose only allegiance was to the rich and powerful. He too subscribed to a doctrine of radical realism, including such naturalistic techniques as the minute observation and reproduction of seemingly trifling detail; and long before Taine and Zola, he recognized the fateful consequences of heredity and environment for character. For Büchner, too, the exploration of character superseded plot in importance and, like Hauptmann, he dismissed the concept of the villain as unscientific, believing rather that we are all victims of circumstances beyond our control.[12]

In Germany the theater itself was also beginning to move in a direction that would make a naturalistic style viable. Since its founding in 1866 by Duke Georg II of Saxony-Meiningen, the Meiningen Court Theater emphasized an almost excessive realism in costumes, stage-setting, lighting, and other details. Attention was lavished on historically accurate heavy oaken furniture; special weaving methods were researched to provide authenticity in costuming; and live animals such as horses appeared on stage. Limited financial resources precluded the hiring of performance stars, but that situation was turned to advantage in the development of ensemble acting, which also tended to inhibit the bathos of traditional German theater. It was the Meiningen troupe which first introduced Ibsen to Berlin in 1876 with a production of his early drama *The Pretenders* (1863), and it was the same troupe which influenced the style of Otto Brahm—Hauptmann's influential, long-time director.[13]

Naturalism, of course, was not an indigenous movement, nor was it limited to literary art. The term itself was imported into literary criticism from the fine arts, probably by Zola in the preface to the second edition of the novel *Thérèse Raquin* of 1867,[14] and there is much truth to Ziolkowski's remark that in Germany "the 'movement' . . . received its name largely in its obituaries; not until Hermann Bahr wrote in 1891 about *Die Überwindung des Naturalismus (Overcoming Naturalism)* could the term be used confidently with any assurance of common understanding."[15] The movement first flourished in France in the 1870s and early 1880s, reached Germany and Italy a decade later and England at the turn of the century, while in the United States it became dominant only between the two World Wars, in such authors as Theodore Dreiser, Sinclair Lewis, Jack London, Upton Sinclair, and John Steinbeck.

The main foreign influences on German Naturalism came from France, Scandinavia, and Russia. Zola, Ibsen, and Tolstoy were the key figures abroad for Hauptmann. Through Zola the Germans were exposed to the literary exploration of heredity and environment on character and the concomitant need for precise, detailed information (he too was rarely without his notebook). Tolstoy showed how drama could serve as a shock to complacency, and his first strong impact came with the *Power of Darkness,* which Hauptmann saw performed in January of 1890.[16] This play, with its stark depiction of peasant lust, adultery, and gruesome infanticide (an infant is crushed "flat as a pancake" under some planks) and the protagonist's overwrought confession in the last act, helped dislodge tabus previously imposed on such crassly naturalistic portrayal. But Ibsen was more important for Hauptmann than either Zola or Tolstoy. Berlin suffered a virtual "Ibsen fever;" performances of *Ghosts, An Enemy of the People, The Wild Duck,* and *Pillars of Society* were staged there in 1887; *The Lady from the Sea* in 1889; and *A Doll's House* in 1890. Most important was Ibsen's exposure of the "lies of society," and the critic Hermann J. Weigand claims that Hauptmann "took over from Ibsen the medium of prose; the strict abandonment of the time-honored stage devices of the monologue and the aside; the imperceptible introduction and filling in of the exposition, the analytic technique, presupposing a long latent crisis which bursts into the open, reducing the play itself to the unfolding of a catastrophe that runs its course swiftly, in the space of a few days, or even a few hours."[17]

What made Hauptmann really distinctive, however, was his linguistic virtuosity, and here he owed a debt to a man who, out of professional jealousy, was later to become his ardent enemy: Arno Holz, the most significant theoretician of German Naturalism, whose experiments helped revolutionize literature well into the twentieth century. Holz's starting point was Zola's treatise in *Le roman expérimental* (The Experimental Novel) of 1880, in which he claimed that—given sufficiently detailed information about fictional characters—one could predict their interaction with one another with the inevitability of a chemical experiment in which all the ingredients are known; and that, furthermore, such experimentation could provide a valuable probe for human behavior. Holz welcomed this causal-mechanistic adaptation of scientific method to literature but differed with Zola over the mimetic equation "art = nature $-x$," in which "$x$" represents the temperament (we might substitute "individuality") of the artist. Holz, who abhorred the traditional idea of artistic genius, at first tried to eliminate the "$x$" completely, and when he realized that this was impossible, insisted that its influence be reduced to an absolute minimum. Literature, he held, should be a manufactured product, influenced, to be sure, by the skill of its producer but devoid of such concepts as inspiration. (Perhaps this explains the ease with which he was able to work with a collaborator, Johannes Schlaf, in writing their two best known Naturalist works, *Papa Hamlet* and *Die Familie Selicke* (*The Selicke Family*). To achieve his ends, Holz subscribed to a "second-by-second style" (*Sekundenstil*) which aimed for a running, photographically-phonographically accurate reproduction of reality in narrative or drama. Here Holz's linguistic experiments proved especially productive. What one first notices on looking at *Papa Hamlet* is the extensive use of dialogue (so extensive that it is sometimes confused with drama) and the nature of the dialogue—much of it is in dialect. But although the use of dialect is a laudable innovation for serious work directed at a sophisticated audience, and it certainly encouraged Hauptmann and others to follow the lead, there is another aspect to such speech mimicry which is more important. By focusing our attention on the exact way in which characters speak, stutter, cough, remain silent (the possibilities are extensive), we learn something of the inner life and motivation, conscious or unconscious, of the characters themselves. And so, paradoxically, Holz's attention to *external* minutiae (a similar case can be made for his stage settings) provides a better insight into the *internal* dynamics of what is being presented.

It is in this approach to language—and in this approach only—that Hauptmann acknowledged a debt to Arno Holz. In depicting his own breakthrough in the play *Before Sunrise* he attributes a great deal of influence to Ibsen's *Ghosts* and continues:

Then came Tolstoy with *Power of Darkness*. This drama opened even further my access to life: under its impression I felt my own property [*Besitz*] completely and began to coin my gold.—*Papa Hamlet* was no drama, but

*Before Sunrise* was the first drama [in the new style] and the *Selicke Family* only arose under my direct and energetic encouragement: these are the facts. From *Papa Hamlet* I took the creation of the language—nothing, nothing at all for my drama: which is also proven by the fact that Holz rejected it as not in accord with that which he called his theory and which is humbug.[18]

It is a central irony of Hauptmann's work that, although he is generally recognized as the greatest Naturalist dramatist, he consistently rejected the Naturalist label for himself. And though the scientific and naturalist tendencies of his age served as a catalyst to his own productivity and are reflected by it, he remained too strongly offended by their ultimately dehumanizing implications ever to accept them completely. For Hauptmann, Holz's "laws" were little more than banalities, fit only for training shoemakers. One of his rare theoretical essays, *Gedanken über das Bemalen der Statuen* ("Thoughts Concerning the Painting of Statues"), although written in 1887, expressed his lifelong credo. "The purpose of all art," he wrote, "is not the absolute imitation of nature, because that is an impossibility. If it were possible it would coincide with nature, and art would be excluded. . . . The purpose of art is . . . the expression of the innermost essence of the object represented, elevated to type" (6:896). Like generations of Classical and Romanticist writers before him, Hauptmann strove to employ art in the search for (and revelation of) eternal, human verities.

Holz's rejection of the concept of genius was particularly repugnant to Hauptmann because it diminishes both artist and man.[19] By the same token, and in spite of personal sympathy for many of the goals of socialism, he himself rejected the concept of agitprop in preference to the belief that the artistic quality of a drama stands in direct proportion to its freedom from party politics of any kind.[20]

## NOTES

1. See Bernhard Zeller, ed., *Gerhart Hauptmann. Leben und Werk: Eine Gedächtnisausstellung des Deutschen Literaturarchivs,* (Stuttgart: Turmhaus-Druckerei, 1962), pp. 283–85. See also Roy C. Cowen, *Hauptmann Kommentar zum dramatischen Werk* (Munich: Winkler, 1980), pp. 68, 78; and Gert Oberembt, *Gerhart Hauptmann: Der Biberpelz* (Paderborn, Munich, Vienna, Zurich: Schöningh, 1987), pp. 166, 169.

2. See Sigfrid Hoefert, " 'Gerhart Hauptmann und andere'—zu den deutsch-russischen Literaturbeziehungen in der Epoche des Naturalismus," in *Naturalismus. Bürgerliche Dichtung und soziales Engagement,* ed. Helmut Scheuer (Stuttgart, Berlin, Cologne, Mainz; W. Kohlhammer), pp. 244–52; Hans Daiber, *Gerhart Hauptmann. Oder der letzte Klassiker* (Vienna, Munich, Zurich: Molden, 1971), pp. 88; and Eberhard Hilscher, *Gerhart Hauptmann. Leben und Werk* (Frankfurt/M: Athenäum, 1988), p. 344.

3. Dougald McMillan, "Influences of Gerhart Hauptmann in Joyce's Ulysses," *James Joyce Quarterly* 4 (1967): 118. See also H. D. Tschörtner, *Ungeheures erhofft. Gerhart Hauptmann—Werk und Wirkung* (Berlin: Der Morgen, 1986), pp. 207–08, 214–15.

4. See Edith Cappel, "The Reception of Gerhart Hauptmann in the United States" (Ph.D. dissertation, Columbia University, 1953). This dissertation provides the most detailed record of Hauptmann's reception in the United States available to date. See also my article "Gerhart Hauptmann in the United States," in *The Fortunes of German Writers in America: Studies in Literary Reception*, ed. Wolfgang D. Elfe, James Hardin, and Gunther Holst (Columbia: University of South Carolina Press, 1992), 99–120.

5. See Frederick W. J. Heuser, *Gerhart Hauptmann: Zu seinem Leben und Schaffen* (Tübingen: Niemeyer, 1961), p. 87.

6. For the status of the American theater in 1894 see Peter Bauland, *The Hooded Eagle: Modern German Drama on the New York Stage* (Syracuse: Syracuse University Press, 1968), esp. pp. vii, 1, 4, 23–24, 43; see also Cappel, 10–21.

7. Quoted by Bauland, 4.

8. Lilian R. Furst and Peter N. Skrine, *Naturalism* (London: Methuen, 1971), 64.

9. Daiber, 9. See also Zeller, 286.

10. See Philip Mellen, "A Source of Hauptmann's Michael Kramer," *Germanic Notes* 17 (1986): 35.

11. See Zeller, 39.

12. See also Cowen, *Kommentar*, 38–41, and Warren R. Maurer, *The Naturalist Image of German Literature* (Munich: Fink, 1972), pp. 226–28.

13. See John Osborne, *The Naturalist Drama in Germany* (Manchester: Manchester University Press; Totowa N.J.: Rowan & Littlefield, 1971), pp. 10–11.

14. See Furst and Skrine, 4.

15. Theodore Ziolkowski, review of *Literarische Manifeste des Naturalistmus: 1880–1892*, by Erich Ruprecht. *Germanic Review* 38 (1963): 308.

16. See Oberembt, 29.

17. Hermann J. Weigand, "Gerhart Hauptmann's Range as Dramatist," *Monatshefte* 44 (1952): 319.

18. Gerhart Hauptmann, *Die Kunst des Dramas: Über Schauspiel und Theater*, ed. Martin Machatzke (Frankfurt/M.: Propyläen, 1963), pp. 196–97.

19. Cf. Peter Sprengel, *Die Wirklichkeit der Mythen: Untersuchungen zum Werk Gerhart Hauptmanns* (Berlin: E. Schmidt, 1982), p. 57.

20. Cf. William H. Rey, "Der offene Schluß der *Weber:* Zur Actualität Gerhart Hauptmanns in unserer Zeit," *German Quarterly* 55 (1982): 150.

# CHAPTER ONE

# Family Tragedy

*Before Sunrise*

When *Before Sunrise* was performed three evenings in succession, beginning on January 11, 1892, in New York's German–language Thalia Theater, it was the first play by Hauptmann to reach an audience in the United States. Only one critic, an anonymous reviewer for the *New York Times,* deigned to comment with these meager remarks:

A study in socialism, by Gerhart Hauptmann, one of the German followers of Ibsen, was brought forward at the Thalia Theatre last night under the title of "Vor Sonnenaufgang." Briefly recapitulated, the story of the play has to deal with the inevitably irrepressible conflict between capital and labor. A young journalist is sent into the mining regions to investigate the relations between employers and employed. While thus concerned he is thrown into contact with the charming daughter of one of the hated monopolists. He is an ardent lover and he captivates the girl. But he is likewise a young man with a theory. His investigations show that the father of his bride-expectant is a drunkard and her mother is an infidel. This determines him, and he relentlessly breaks off the match, and the young woman kills herself with a convenient household utensil—a carving knife. And capital continues triumphant, while labor languishes.[1]

The flippant tone of these remarks fails to camouflage the writer's superficial understanding of what he has just seen. The "mother" referred to quite inaccurately as an "infidel" ("adulteress" or "hypocrite" are better descriptors) is actually the heroine's stepmother; the term "monopolists" has connotations which hardly apply to a nouveau riche, degenerate peasant; the suicide is apparently with a hunting knife, not the ludicrous "household utensil"; and the entire play is much more than the implied simplistic socialist tract. As the renowned Berlin novelist and man of letters Theodor Fontane pointed out the day after its tumultuous German premiere during the afternoon of October 20, 1889, "the tone with works such as this, which have much of the ballad about them, is almost everything."[2] Given the obvious inattentiveness of the *Times* reporter, it would have been too much to expect him to be susceptible to anything as elusive as the "tone" of Hauptmann's landmark drama. Nor, considering the conservative and provincial state of American theater at the time, could he be expected to appreciate the fact that even naturalistic art can benefit from virtuosity and that the play would remain a memorable compendium of the ideas and moods of the people, places, and events it reflects.

Written almost effortlessly in Erkner during the "summer-bright hours before daylight" of 1889, *Before Sunrise* was the first German Naturalist drama to appear on a stage. It represented Hauptmann's own most extreme concession to the tenets of theoretical Naturalism and, in the author's proud words, "introduced a unique, powerful German literary epoch" (7:1082).

Originally called *Der Säemann* (The Sower)—the changed title was suggested by Arno Holz—it was rejected for publication by the Munich Naturalist periodical *Die Gesellschaft* (Society) before being published in book form in Berlin in mid-August. With its dedication "to Bjarne P. Holmsen, the most consequential realist, author of 'Papa Hamlet' . . . in enthusiastic recognition of the decisive inspiration of his book" (1:10), it appears that Hauptmann was angling for Holz's support. (Holmsen was a pseudonym chosen by Holz and Schlaf in the belief that a Scandinavian author would find easier acceptance in the Germany of the day than a pair of Germans.) Holz was impressed, soon calling *Before Sunrise* "the best drama that has ever been written in the German language" and adding with more enthusiasm than concern for accurate detail, *"Tolstoy included!"*[3] The second edition of the book, which appeared after the premiere, substituted a new dedication, this one to the theater director Otto Brahm and his colleague Paul Schlenther, who had made the staging of the play possible and would henceforth hold Hauptmann's future as a dramatist largely in their hands.

Even before its premiere—probably the most outrageous of German theater history—the play was widely read and discussed. Its drastic depiction of drunkenness, adultery, and attempted incest was seen as a shocking innovation, and its perceived flirtation with socialism—at a time when the Socialist party was outlawed in Germany—made it a prime topic of gossip among conservatives and liberals alike. Again Fontane must be mentioned as one who could see beyond the immediate sensationalism and who used his considerable influence to promote the young author. Praising him as a new Storm and Stress Schiller and as an Ibsen without the clichés, he went on to claim that "[Hauptmann] presents life as it is, in its full horror; he doesn't add or subtract anything and thereby achieves his colossal effect. At the same time (and that is the funny part and the main reason for my admiration) he displays, in that which appears to the layman to be simply a transcription of life, a measure of art which cannot be imagined any greater."[4] Urging Otto Brahm to produce the new drama, while impishly suggesting that it might not be to the liking of all the ladies in the front row, he was pleased to learn that such a production was already planned.[5] By staging it under the auspices of a private theater, the newly founded Freie Bühne (Free Stage), Brahm tried to militate against adverse reaction but, as it turned out, to little avail. The performance was frequently interrupted by whistles and foot-stamping, largely orchestrated by Dr. Isidor Kastan, a well-known Berlin physician and journalist who, during the protracted off-stage birth scene of the last act, brandished gynecological forceps at the stage and shouted, "Are we here in a bordello or in a theater?"[6] The scandal was kept alive in the newspapers and periodicals during the following days. Most of the reviews were negative (Fontane again providing the notable exception), and Hauptmann found himself vilified as "the most immoral playwright of the century."[7]

*Before Sunrise* represents an excellent example of Hauptmann's creative modus operandi: the skillful blending of personal, political, religious, and literary influences. Among the latter, *Papa Hamlet* has been mentioned for its impact on the author's use of language; Tolstoy's *Power of Darkness* encouraged the exploitation of daring subject matter; Zola had prepared the way for the depiction of low-life types and stressed the importance of heredity for character development and depiction. Ibsen contributed strongly with his ensemble treatment of family drama into which an outsider is introduced as a catalyst to the action, with his analytic technique, and with his frequently encountered theme of a progressive individual in conflict with a conservative society. *Ghosts* and *The Wild Duck* especially appear to have left their mark on certain of Hauptmann's characters, as did also perhaps Büchner's play *Dantons Tod* (*Danton's Death*).[8]

Somewhat misleadingly subtitled a "Social Tragedy," *Before Sunrise* is more accurately a character drama in which the hero, Alfred Loth, is exposed to a series of episodes that cast an appalling light on certain economic and social conditions of the day. Recently released from prison for his part in a utopian socialist adventure in America (as a member of the Vancouver Island Society—almost identical in its aims and description to Hauptmann's Pacific Society), he has come to the small community of Witzdorf to investigate the rumored exploitation of local miners. Before beginning his research he visits a former friend, Hoffmann, who has, in the meantime, married into the mine-owning Krause family and become one of the worst exploiters. (Again the situation derives from autobiographical experience. The Krauses are nouveau riche peasants such as Hauptmann had known in Weißstein near

21

Salzbrunn—people who suddenly found themselves enormously wealthy because the coal needed to fuel the Industrial Revolution happened to be found under their land and who, abruptly relieved of the need to work or structure their lives, succumbed to various extravagances and sins of the flesh.)

Loth, it turns out, has two obsessions, social welfare and eugenics—both of which are certain to bring him into conflict with the Krause's mores. His intention to investigate and expose the miserable working condition of the miners naturally estranges him from Hoffmann but is never followed through because he finds it expedient to leave before the task is even begun. It is the second obsession—eugenics—that actually determines the outcome of the play. Like some of Hauptmann's acquaintances (including Forel and Ploetz), Loth firmly believes that alcoholism (as opposed to a *predisposition* to alcoholism) is a hereditary disease, from which there is no escape. Only gradually does he learn that the Krause family is sorely afflicted by this scourge, which is strongest on the father's side. Krause himself and his daughter Martha, Hoffmann's wife, provide especially frightening examples. The former spends his days and nights in an alcoholic stupor while Martha, who is awaiting the birth of a second child in an upstairs room, is described as completely ravaged by her addiction. While all this might have remained academic for Loth—another horrific example to confirm him in the correctness of his views—the fact that he and Helene, Martha's sister, have fallen in love in the meantime puts an entirely different complexion on the matter. Although Helene herself displays no obvious symptoms of the disease and has clearly come to see marriage to Loth as a way out of the Krause morass, he allows his principles to outweigh his professed affection and flees. The result, as the *Times* reviewer noted, is Helene's suicide.

But it is neither the plot nor its themes that have kept the play memorable. Much of its success can be attributed to the detailed attention lavished on even minor characters. An example is already found in the *dramatis personae,* where we notice that the characters fall into two groups: locals and people who came to Witzdorf from elsewhere. The former have typical Silesian names (Krause, ''Willem'' Kahl, Beibst, Baer, Gosch, Guste, Liese, and Miele) while the latter do not (Hoffmann, Loth, Schimmelpfennig, Spiller, and Eduard).[9] Each of these characters has his or her own distinctive speech patterns and idiosyncrasies. A man delivering a package of children's toys (intended for the newborn) speaks his two lines in sing-song tones suggesting the forced cheerfulness of those dependent on gratuities. Eduard, a politically aware servant from Berlin, speaks in the dialectal inflections of that city.

Beibst, a long-suffering laborer who has lost two sons in the mines and has been shot and crippled by his employer, Kahl senior, is understandably taciturn and irritable but speaks in Silesian dialect when he needs to express himself. Mrs. Spiller, a sycophant whose livelihood depends on playing the subservient lady-in-waiting to the crude Mrs. Krause, has developed a tic, the repeated expression of an *m* sound in her speech. Mrs. Krause herself, a would-be grand lady not up to the role by virtue of background, education, or native intelligence, sprinkles her speech liberally with mispronounced foreign words and malapropisms. Baer, the retarded village pariah who sells sand (for strewing on floors) from a child's wagon and who is nicknamed Hopslabaer for his compulsion to leap into the air on command, speaks his one-word line "saaa-a-and" (1:71) in an odd, bleating voice. And—a final example—Kahl, the malicious, hunting-obsessed fiancé of Helene, who spends his nights in bed with her stepmother, is a severely afflicted stutterer. In addition to the psychological insights such distinctive speech patterns suggest, they also—especially in combination—provide a pervasive aura of cruel humor. When called to task by Loth for shooting at anything alive, Kahl defends his practice of hunting field mice with the remark "T. . . t. . . m. . . m. . mouse, isn'. . . in. . . in. . infamous. . . am. . am. .amph. . . phii. . . blan" (1:31). When two such individuals (for example, Kahl and Mrs. Spiller) converse, the effect is both painful and funny.

Hauptmann's success in vivifying even minor characters results not only from reproducing such externals but from an enviable ability for empathizing with all manner of humanity. In describing poor Hopslabaer he could draw on personal experience as a pariah (such as his treatment vis-à-vis Georg Schubert or his inferior position to Carl within his own family), and when he has Loth become enraged over Kahl's hunting of larks, he must surely have recalled his own shameful shooting of songbirds as a youthful "good-for-nothing" (7:1006).

If Freud was correct in his observation regarding "the inclination of the modern writer to split up his ego, by self-observation, into part-egos and in consequence to personify the conflicting currents of his own mental life in several heroes,"[10] it may not be too farfetched to approach at least the three central male characters from this perspective. By coincidence, Hoffmann, Schimmelpfennig, and Loth, who knew each other as idealistic, socially conscious, and mildly revolutionary students, find themselves involved with the same family. Like Hauptmann, Hoffmann has married into money and has paid a price: life with a sickly wife inadequate to his emotional and physical needs. (This helps explain—without excusing—his sexual designs on his sister-in-law.) Not a simple villain—he seems very much to want a child and shares his wife's suffering—he has learned to compromise his ideals and to substitute expediency for principle, while proclaiming his all-purpose exculpatory slogan: "Whatever will be, will be!" (1:20).

Dr. Schimmelpfennig, who comes to the Krause household to assist in the birth of Martha's child, is the embodiment of that absolute faith in the future of natural science experienced by Hauptmann in Zurich. His outward cynicism and bluster are a physician's carapace to protect him from the cumulative effects of the suffering to which he is exposed daily through his patients. He does care; he works hard at the practical task of alleviating as much pain as possible but, in spite of himself, cannot hide his own flawed humanity. His final revelation to Loth about the depth of Krause depravity, and the suggestion that if Hoffmann has not yet actually ruined Helene, he has certainly already ruined her reputation, are cruelly gratuitous and suggest the possibility of ulterior motive.

Of all the characters Alfred Loth has caused the most consternation and disagreement among critics.[11] Bauland sums up his positive and negative attributes when he writes:

> Hauptmann always demonstrated an inherent fairness in characterization, and Loth surely has his positive side. It is impossible not to be moved by his awareness and articulation of outrageous social injustices, and we can consider his long-range goals nothing short of admirable. An audience must share Hauptmann's own ambivalence toward his reformer, and it cannot discount what Loth says just because it may not like him personally. At the same time that we agree with and approve of Loth, we find it hard to forget that he is a narcissistic, pompous, self-righteous, humorless ass who is insensitive to the needs of others and incapable of listening to them. . . . Even when his thoughts and feelings are sound, he is an infuriatingly rigid fanatic. . . . A salient part of his personality is Hauptmann's portrait of that peculiarly German mentality that so often has perpetrated incalculable horrors in the name of lofty (and sometimes not so lofty) principles.[12]

Alfred Loth is a composite figure based on at least three real-life models: Alfred Ploetz, Henrich Lux, and Hauptmann himself. As an outgrowth of the Pacific Society adventure, all three were drawn into the Breslau Socialist Trial of 1887 (Hauptmann only as a witness), which ended in a one-year prison sentence for Lux (not Loth's two–year sentence for his Vancouver Island Society activities). The most radical in his scientific opinions was Ploetz, the later "race hygienist" and author of such articles as "Alcohol and Progeny."[13] His extreme views are reflected in Loth and Schimmelpfennig.

In a reply to his critics, written in 1889 but not published until 1963, Hauptmann tried to distance himself from his fictional character. Pointing out (revealingly?) that he has "almost as little in common with Alfred Loth as with Hoffmann" (11:754), he cites the former's taste in literature as contrasting with his own. In a conversation with Helene, Loth dismisses Goethe's *Werther* as "a stupid book," praises Felix Dahn's potboiler *Kampf um Rom* (*Battle for Rome*) for depicting humanity not as it is but as it should become, and rejects Ibsen and Zola as "not authors at all but necessary evils" (1:46). We recall, of course, that there had been a time when Hauptmann's own impression of Dahn had been much more favorable, and contemporary acquaintances report that, around the time of his stay in Zurich, he too tried to live by a rigid set of principles, including the adherence to a strict vegetarian diet and the complete rejection of alcohol (something he could never again be accused of during the remainder of his long life).[14] In an interview from 1894 he also admitted that he had perhaps "been possessed by the zeal of a reformer"[15] in his early works and especially in *Before Sunrise*.

The most attractive character of the play is Helene Krause. Although Hauptmann uses her relationship with Loth to reflect certain elements of the zeitgeist—notably the preoccupation with female emancipation—she is largely spared the programmatic naturalist ballast which burdens the other characters. She was, to be sure, educated in a pietist school for girls (and thereby escaped some of the detrimental impact of life in Witzdorf), but even so her nature is such that she can be expected to follow her own best instincts. The fact that she does so and is crushed by the force of circumstances makes her an early precursor of such memorable Hauptmannian heroines as Rose Bernd. Her suicide is more than a rash act over an unrequited love affair. It is an autonomous act, superseding the determinism of naturalist theory. Her nature rebels at the thought of being drawn ever deeper into the moral morass around her.

Had Arno Holz examined *Before Sunrise* more closely, he must surely have noticed that it was more than a naturalistic "slice of life" in which the author maintains a scientifically objective distance from his material. Far from trying to estrange his viewers emotionally from what was happening onstage, Hauptmann was interested in getting them involved—emotionally as well as intellectually. To this end he "wrote *Before Sunrise* in such a manner as though the stage did not have three, but four walls"[16] and strove to entertain as well as to edify his audiences—realizing that in the theater the one is hardly possible without the other.

One way to assure audience participation is through suspense, and *Before Sunrise* is, from this perspective, exemplary. Partly because of Loth's obtuseness the audience realizes long before he does the conflict between his principles and the Krause reality. As a result the spectator is constantly occupied with questions that have a bearing on the outcome. What, for example, was the "frightful end" (1:54) of Hoffmann's deceased three-year-old son mentioned in the third act? (In the last act we learn that he cut his throat on a bottle he thought contained alcohol.) Will Loth meet Martha and recognize her condition? Will the malicious Kahl, or Loth's planned meeting with Schimmelpfennig, reveal the true state of affairs? And, finally, when the inevitable has happened, what will be the effect on the lovers?

But the drama is more than suspenseful melodrama. Through a carefully structured combination of humor, irony, foreshadowing, effective opening and closing of acts, meaningful repetition, snatches of folksongs, and pantomime, it displays a "stupendous measure of art"—to borrow one more phrase from Fontane.[17] The delicate love scene between Loth and Helene in act 4 demonstrates once and for all that Naturalism is not restricted to the depiction of the ugly and revolting. And the entire last act is a small masterpiece of pantomime and stagecraft, especially the handling of the stillborn birth of Martha's child and the suicide of Helene—with their unknowing drunken father's voice reverberating from offstage, "Ain't I got a coupla pretty daughters?!" (1:98).

With time it has become ever more apparent that even in this, his most naturalistic work, Hauptmann was not willing to dispense completely with a mythic dimension. Taking their cue from the original title (*Der Säemann* [The Sower]), the name of the hero (Loth = Lot), and the fact that Hauptmann was deeply involved with "Jesus-Studies" during 1885–90, several critics have linked the Biblical story of Lot, his daughters, and Sodom and Gomorrah to *Before Sunrise*.[18] If such a connection was intentional, and it appears reasonably certain that it was, it represents an early example of the atavistic wellsprings of the author's art.

## The Coming of Peace

On January 4, 1907, Hauptmann attended a rehearsal of Max Reinhardt's production of a play Hauptmann had written seventeen years earlier, which bore the ironic title *Das Friedensfest. Eine Familienkatastrophe* (*The Coming of Peace: A Family Catastrophe*). He was much impressed by Reinhardt's staging but even more by his own play. Having achieved some distance from it, he now pronounced it "a masterful work replete with a dark Romanticism."[19] In a lengthy panegyric he sought to put its essence into words with the help of atmospheric imagery: "Biting, chilling blasts of wind come forth from the invisible, and warm aroma-saturated currents, which appear to come laden with sweet premonitions, from blessed meadows. Simultaneously come powerful blasts and explosions as if from nocturnal thunderstorms struggling with stagnant vapors, blasts related to those expressed powerfully and violently in Beethoven symphonies, frightful and purifying."[20]

This is hardly imagery easily associated with works like *Before Sunrise,* or with Naturalist "poor folk art" in general, and it seems to point toward a discrepancy between the author's intention and the way in which *The Coming of Peace* was, for a long time, understood. Written in 1889, the same year as *Before Sunrise,* and dedicated to his faithful benefactor Theodor Fontane, the new play was not at all what might have been expected from a sensational new author who had just succeeded in scandalizing the theater world. Forsaking politics and the lurid subject matter of Zola and Tolstoy for a more Ibsenian dissection of bourgeois family life, Hauptmann has been credited with initiating "the interiorization or psychologizing of drama"[21] with this work. Such judgments, to be sure, have begun to appear with any frequency only since the 1960s. Earlier critics tended to see just another treatment of the effects of heredity and environment on family life; their response generally ranged from lukewarm to hostile. Even Fontane registered doubts about the author's abrupt shift from the depiction of external to internal action.[22] That Hauptmann expected some such resistance to his new approach is clear from a lengthy quotation from Lessing with which he prefaced the drama and in which his eighteenth-century predecessor had argued that "action" doesn't literally require "the lover to fall to his knees" and that "every inner struggle of passions, every series of diverse thoughts, where one cancels out the other, is also action" (1:101). Because of Hauptmann's insistence on his premise that "what one gives to the action, one takes from the characters" (6:1043) and his firm belief that progress consists of "understanding more and more of that which is 'undramatic' in dramatic terms" (6:1040), the plot of his new play must have seemed rather threadbare to the young author's ill-prepared contemporaries.

Reduced to essentials, the play describes an involuntary Christmas reunion of estranged family members. After a six-year absence, Wilhelm Scholz has yielded to the pleading of his betrothed, Ida Buchner, and her mother to return home to visit his own mother, where he also meets his sister Auguste and his brother Robert. His father, the medical doctor Fritz Scholz (who has likewise been away for six years) returns quite unexpectantly, whereupon it becomes necessary for the Buchners to plead with Wilhelm again not to run away immediately. Contrary to all expectations a miracle occurs. Father and son are reconciled and Christmas Eve becomes a "festival of peace" (*Friedensfest*) for everyone. The harmony is short–lived, however. A gradual accumulation of seeming trifles evokes the old acrimonies and recriminations, and it soon becomes clear that the past weighs too heavily upon the Scholz family to be suppressed for any length of time. Even the death of his father in the last act fails to alleviate Wilhelm's apprehension. Although the last stage direction has him going hand in hand, "upright and composed" (1:165), with Ida into the room where his father lies dead, Wilhelm (and the audience) can by no means be sure that the Scholz family past will not continue to poison the future. The open ending leaves the audience pondering the fate of the young couple.

Hauptmann once remarked, "Every family bears a secret curse or blessing. Find it! Make it your basis!" (6:1042). During the course of three acts he seeks out and attempts to illuminate the "secret curse" of the Scholz family. As is typical in analytic drama, the decisive events have taken place in the past, and the audience (along with the unknowing Buchners) is left with the task of reconstructing that past from present evidence and then examining what has been learned for its possible ramifications for the future— especially as it relates to Wilhelm Scholz and Ida Buchner. Gradually the audience learns that six years ago, in a fit of oedipal rage, Wilhelm had physically attacked the feared and hated paterfamilias, Dr. Scholz. (The Buchner women learn this later.) Though the attack led to a final breakup of the family with the departure of both Wilhelm and his father, it was only the expression of deeper, more complex forces—hereditary, environmental, social, psychological, and even, perhaps, archetypal—that were active before the children were born and are beyond the control of any of the protagonists.

Again, as in *Before Sunrise*, Hauptmann subscribes to the modern, naturalistic credo of describing conditions and results rather than apportioning blame. As he succinctly expressed it: "Thou shalt love thy characters—hate none among them!" (6:1036). And again the action of the drama derives largely from the nature and behavior of the characters, individually and in combination with each other.

Through a variety of techniques Hauptmann insures that, by the end of the play, we are thoroughly familiar with his characters. In part they are exposed by their own actions, language, and gestures and by what others have to say about them, sometimes before they appear on stage; but he also carefully guides his actors and directors with extensive, detailed stage directions in which practically nothing is left to chance or directorial whim. Accompanying the dramatis personae, for example, is the instruction (one surely difficult to fulfill!) that "as far as possible [for the Scholz family] a family similarity must be expressed in the makeup" (1:103). This is followed by almost a page of description in which not only a very specific setting but also a particular atmosphere is established and evoked. It reads in part:

> The action of this work takes place on a Christmas Eve of the eighties in a lonely country house on the Schützenhügel near Erkner (Mark Brandenburg). The scene of all three acts is a high, spacious hall, painted white and hung with old-fashioned pictures as well as antlers and animal heads of all kinds. A chandelier of stag antlers attached in the middle of the timbered ceiling is garnished with fresh candles. In the center of the rear wall is a projecting vestibule with a glass door through which one can catch sight of the heavy, carved, oaken portal of the house. On top of the vestibule is a stuffed, male, wood grouse in mating posture. To the side and above the vestibule, a window each to the left and right, frosted and partially drifted with snow.

Additional objects include "an old grandfather clock on the top of which perches a stuffed screech-owl" and furniture consisting of "old, heavy oak tables and chairs." The doors are all "varicolored, the door frames provided with primitive paintings representing parrots etc." (1:103).

Especially when printed as part of the program, such descriptions not only plunge the theatergoer into a richly evocative atmosphere, they also provide clues regarding the inhabitants (here the Scholz family) of the premises described. It is Christmas Eve, a festive time of year and a plausible one for reunions but also one of excitement and tension during which family relationships have a tendency to become strained. The time is contemporaneous with that of the first audiences, and the action takes place in one room of a house near Erkner and Berlin in Prussia (an area so real and familiar to the author that he must have felt perfectly at home in it). The cold outdoor climate insinuates itself into the interior of the house and is exacerbated by the rather severe decorating scheme. The general ambience suggests owners who belong at least to an upper middle class with no immediate financial concerns. The emphasis on such details as antlers, preening grouse, and a screech owl may seem puzzling if not gratuitous at first, but it makes sense when we recall that the Naturalists had a preference for "fang and claw" imagery and metaphor with which to suggest the dangerous, atavistic predisposition of the human species. (Even the name *Schützenhügel,* with its overtones of rifle–shooting matches, may have been used with something like this in mind.) Finally there are the primitive and exotic door-frame paintings that serve a similar purpose but also point to Dr. Scholz's exotic past.

Before the play opens, and then as each character is introduced, Hauptmann supplies additional detailed information for his actors and directors (or readers). From these stage directions it soon becomes evident that he is interested in developing strongly contrasting personalities who will find it difficult or impossible to understand each other. The first such pair of opposites to be introduced is that of the two mothers. Mrs. Buchner is described in almost exclusively positive terms. At the age of forty-two she is a natural, healthy looking, friendly woman, genuine in manner, well-spoken, and nicely dressed; she exudes an air of satisfaction and well-being. Mrs. Scholz, on the other hand, though only forty-six, has aged beyond her years and is already beginning to show the frailties of old age. She is overweight, with whitish gray hair; she is indifferent to her appearance; she wears glasses. Her movements are abrupt and restless. She usually speaks in a whining voice, with frequent lapses into dialect, and makes the impression of constant excitation. "Whereas Mrs. Buchner seems to exist only for others, Mrs. Scholz has enough to do to take care of herself" (1:105).

Not surprisingly the outlook of the two women is also totally different. Aware of the estrangement of Wilhelm and his father but not of the details, Mrs. Buchner tries to convince Mrs. Scholz of the possibility of reconciliation. The latter responds typically with a mixture of religious and superstitious clichés: "Honor father and mother: the hand that is raised against one's own father . . . such hands grow out of the grave" (1:111). When Mrs. Buchner persists in her belief that human beings can influence their own destiny and tries to extol the virtues of willpower, she is rudely interrupted by Mrs. Scholz: "Willpower, willpower! Just forget it! I know better. A person can will something, and will it, and will it a hundred times, and everything will stay the same. Naw, naw!" (1:112). For a time, during the remarkable love feast of the second act, it appears that the optimism of the attractive Mrs. Buchner will carry the day. For Hauptmann, however, things are not that simple. Musing on the optimist/pessimist opposition he once wrote: "Optimism

30

as such has something suspicious about it, more: something vulgar, more: something banal, more: something vile!— But pessimism too gives the impression of something shopworn and is in every sense an appropriate contrast to the above: for concepts are totally inadequate when it is a matter of even so much as touching upon the mystery of existence'' (6:998).

After the newly found family harmony has begun to unravel, it is Mrs. Buchner who is assailed by doubt and shaken in her confidence. Speaking to Wilhelm, she has lost much of her self-assurance (expressed also by her hesitant, groping speech) as she confesses, ''I know, you will try with all your strength to make my daughter happy. It won't be a matter of willpower, but now . . . no I have, so many things . . . now I've seen so much here— experienced. . . . I came here with a firm, cheerful belief. I'm downright ashamed. What did I think myself capable of! I wanted to control such personalities, I a weak, foolish person! Now everything is wavering. I suddenly feel my frightful responsibility . . . '' (1:155). Of all the characters, only Mrs. Buchner undergoes a noticeable change. The fact that she is shaken from her optimistic confidence to doubt and uncertainty—at best—needs to be taken into account as the audience contemplates the future of the young couple.

Central to the appreciation of the Scholz family dynamic is a recognition of the parents' mésalliance. The difference in ages—she is forty-six, he sixty-eight—suggests a marriage contracted from motives other than love, and the characterization of the principals soon increases our suspicion. While Dr. Scholz is an educated, widely-traveled, and sophisticated man of science, his wife betrays minimal evidence of formal schooling, takes refuge in simplistic, fundamentalist religious slogans, and displays no intellectual or cultural proclivities whatsoever. Coming from a nouveau riche family—the most obvious explanation for Dr. Scholz's initial interest in marrying her—she believes a wife's obligations are duties such as keeping her husband supplied with warm socks; she lacks any understanding of a deeper, more spiritual companionship. Trying to explain the ramifications of such a marriage to Mrs. Buchner, the cynical brother Robert launches into a typical diatribe:

A man forty marries a girl of sixteen and drags her into this godforsaken corner. A man who served as a physician in Turkey and travelled in Japan. A cultivated, enterprising spirit. A man who is still preoccupied with the most far-reaching plans gets together with a woman who, until a few years ago, was completely convinced that one could see America as a star in the heavens. Really! I'm not joking. Well, and it turned out accordingly: a stagnant, rotten, fermenting swamp from which we have the dubious

pleasure of originating. Hair-raising! Love—not a trace. Mutual understanding—don't ask; and this is the [flower] bed upon which we children
grew. (1:120)

(Here Hauptmann has Robert reflect a prevalent viewpoint of the times: that
loveless marriages inevitably produce defective progeny.) As Robert summa-
rizes, the children "are all thoroughly botched. Botched in origin; completely botched in upbringing" (1:121).

The audience hears from Wilhelm what this upbringing was like. While he
admits that his father's intentions may have been good, he insists that the
results were disastrous. Vacillating between periods of brutal authoritarian-
ism and callous neglect, Dr. Scholz seems to have been more concerned with
triumphing over his wife's influence than with his sons' welfare. Both brothers largely blame this environment for their inability to cope with life.

Although the discord between parents and children may rest in part on generational differences, this does not account for the enmity between Robert
and Wilhelm. Both are artists manqué: Wilhelm a pianist hoping for his inner
turmoil to subside so that his talent can freely express itself, Robert a writer
who has gotten into the habit of hiding his sensibility behind a veneer of cynicism and has settled for a job writing commercial advertisements. Both also
reflect the prevalent turn-of-the-century idea that artistic talent and mental
(or physical) health are not compatible,[23] and both seem to have inherited
some of their father's paranoia. For Hauptmann the mere fact of brotherhood
itself conceals elemental dangers. He sees "fraternal strife in history" as "in
every way the most horrible phenomenon of the human psyche. . . . The
problem of brotherhood encroaches on the doppelgänger problem. Complete
doppelgänger would have to attack each other blindly, without hesitation,
with daggers. They would have to provoke a boundless mutual hatred, that
primal hatred [Urhaß] which is a compulsion, a command to destruction"
(6:1014). Seen from this perspective the hatred between brothers is itself basic and archetypal, and only the way it is expressed varies with the circumstances. For Robert, Wilhelm's attack on the father and his relationship with
Ida are sufficient motivation. Though Robert might just as plausibly have attacked his father himself, given his impetuous nature and abhorrence, he
chooses to blame Wilhelm for having done so, since this provides a convenient weapon to use against his brother. By the same token, and although the
motive has been introduced with utmost subtlety, Wilhelm's accusation that
Robert is envious of him because of Ida's affection is quite plausible. In act
1, for example, Robert is left alone on the stage when he notices a purse Ida

had crocheted for her deceased father and brought as a Christmas present for Wilhelm. The stage direction reads, "Looking about nervously like a thief, he bends down again, hastily seizes the yellow silk purse, brings it closer to his eyes and, with a sudden passionate movement, to his lips. This movement shows the flash of an uncanny, pathological ardor" (1:123). Later, when Ida presents her gift to Wilhelm, Robert ridicules it and, by his uncouth behavior, turns the festive occasion into one of acrimony and thereby destroys the possibility of a lasting reconciliation.

The remaining characters, Friebe the house servant, Auguste Scholz, and even Ida Buchner, can be discussed more briefly. Friebe, although not a consistently humorous figure, provides a touch of comic relief in an otherwise somber work. He is fifty years old, recalcitrant, and bowlegged; he has a "little unshaven monkey face" and wears hand-me-down clothes from Dr. Scholz that are meant "for a man twice his size" (1:106). His absolute loyalty is to Dr. Scholz, who in turn trusts him more implicitly than any member of his own family. Auguste serves as both a foil to Ida and as further confirmation of the force of heredity. As Mrs. Scholz remarks, "Auguste is . . . so nervous! . . . Just like her father . . . " (1:110). She also shares her mother's "pathological, offensive manner" and exudes "an atmosphere of dissatisfaction, uneasiness, and hopelessness" (1:107). Ida, by contrast, is a virtual compendium of admirable traits. Only twenty years old, she is blond, attractive, tastefully dressed, intelligent, and irrepressibly positive in her outlook. Perhaps for these reasons she also comes across as less interesting than the other characters. Unlike her mother she maintains her optimism, and if Wilhelm is to escape the toils of his past, she represents his best opportunity for doing so. Unlike the elder Scholzes also, the young couple, if only by virtue of the fresh blood of the Buchner line, enjoys a better chance for a reasonably successful marriage.

In recent times critics (like Hauptmann before them) have begun to appreciate *The Coming of Peace* as more than a positivistic demonstration of the workings of heredity, or even psychology, and have stressed the metaphysical undertones of the work. Here the focus has been on the masterful pantomimic scene of the second act, the midpoint of the drama, in which faith, hope, and love briefly break through the pervasive hatred and animosity. Unlike his renowned predecessor Lessing, the modern Hauptmann has lost the absolute faith in language to describe and solve all human problems. Continuing a trend begun as early as Büchner, he realizes that words can confuse issues as well as clarify them. "It is not as contradictory as it sounds," he observed later, "if one declares as the purpose of all art: to express the great silence silently'' (6:1027). During the scene in question, Wilhelm has just confessed to Ida his transgression against his father when the old man appears on the staircase—descending from his upstairs apartment, where he had previously lived separated from his family and to which he had immediately retreated upon his return. Wilhelm's usual articulateness forsakes him when he sees his father, and, in a scene of great intensity, he stammers out his guilt, receives his father's forgiveness, and falls into a state of deathlike unconsciousness from which he is revived fresh and free of his furies. In a process familiar to readers of Goethe's *Iphigenie*, Kleist's *Prince of Homburg,* and other works by Hauptmann in addition to *The Coming of Peace*, catharsis follows emotional suffering too great for human endurance. There is a lapse into a substratum of authentic existence, a state of lucid unconsciousness, in which the antinomies of good and evil, innocence and guilt, even life and death are rescinded and from which the sufferer emerges with that ''peace which passeth all understanding.'' Unfortunately, it is also in the nature of such epiphanies that they remain ephemeral.

Much (perhaps too much) has been made of the role played by Frank Wedekind and his family in the genesis of *The Coming of Peace*. It is true that he had confided the unsavory details of his family history to Hauptmann in Zurich and was subsequently angered by what he considered his friend's betrayal of his trust in exploiting the information for his drama. Frank's father, a widely traveled medical doctor like Fritz Scholz, had withdrawn into an upper story of the family residence, Lenzburg castle, met members of his family only when it was unavoidable, and stamped his foot on the floor when he wanted his meals delivered. His strong patriarchal tendencies likewise led to familial estrangement, and when Wedekind returned from the University of Munich insisting that he wanted to become an author rather than the lawyer his father had decreed, they came to blows and he was thrown out of the house.[24] In Hauptmann's play Wedekind saw himself split into the two Scholz brothers: Wilhelm, the neurasthenic musician who had struck his father and was desperate for reconciliation; and Robert, the cynical would-be author who, like Wedekind himself for a time, was reduced to writing advertising slogans. Still it is a serious oversimplification to accuse Hauptmann of plagiarizing his *Coming of Peace* from Wedekind's family troubles. He was always keenly aware that ''he who takes something as an author that he does not already possess will end up, even as a master thief, with empty barns'' (1:1035). As has been demonstrated in some detail elsewhere,[25] the characters of Robert, Auguste, and Minna Scholz are much more reminiscent of Hauptmann's own brother Carl, his sister Johanna, and his mother Marie than they are of anyone from the Wedekind clan. The Buchners, introduced to enhance the drama's dialectic of light and darkness, optimism and pessimism, seem not to derive from any clearly identifiable models.

If we compare *The Coming of Peace* with *Before Sunrise* we note, first of all, a narrowing of broad, amorphous social problems (alcoholism, poverty) to more intimate, archetypal ones (enmity of brothers, father-son conflict, heterosexual love). To be sure, certain aspects of these themes (the oppressively patriarchal father; "marriage lie") were more topical in 1889 than they are today. As Fontane noted, "Things don't look much different in thousands of families. What is presented here is typical, and it is truthfully reproduced and without exaggeration."[26] Nevertheless, the basic dynamics of interpersonal relations remain constant and susceptible to universal empathy.

The greater progress is found in the increased subtlety, ambiguity, and sheer artistry of *The Coming of Peace*. To take just one example, alcohol also plays a role in this drama, but it requires a greater degree of audience sophistication to catch its significance. Instead of being subjected to the drunken revelry of old Krause, the viewer or reader is dependent on subtle stage directions and comments to provide clues as to what is happening. Thus shortly after the arrival of Dr. Scholz and his retreat to the upstairs apartment, Friebe is seen leaving the cellar "carrying, in his left hand, three bottles of red wine . . . in such a manner that the necks are clamped between his fingers—, under his left armpit a bottle of cognac" (1:118). Later Friebe, who is almost constantly alone with the old man, is depicted as quite patently inebriated, and Dr. Scholz himself appears with "drink-reddened face" (1:143). That Robert, too, has been imbibing freely is revealed by his mother's remark: "If only Robert didn't drink so much." Wilhelm naively assures her, "Oh, mother, today . . . today all that makes no difference!" (1:144). While the "difference" is probably not decisive in itself, it may well have exacerbated the vehemence of Robert's destructive outbursts; contributed to the intensity of the persecution mania that seizes Dr. Scholz the last time we see him alive, and made the short-lived reconciliation all the more difficult to maintain.

## Lonely Lives

Hauptmann began writing his next play, *Einsame Menschen* (*Lonely Lives*), in June of 1890 and attended its premiere on January 11, 1891. Seen as the final work of a Naturalist trilogy (after *Before Sunrise* and *The Coming of Peace*) in which an "angry young man" first attacks society and then the contemporary family, this drama portrays the tensions which arise during a transitional age—here especially the transition from a conservative, orthodox Protestant religious outlook to one increasingly dominated by the sciences. Reminiscent of Ibsen's *Rosmersholm* (1886), and also a play by Hermann Bahr, *Die neuen Menschen* (1888) (New Man),[27] *Lonely Lives* was the first of Hauptmann's dramas to find a clearly positive reception on the public stage. In 1941 the author still considered it decidedly superior to its predecessors, and when it first appeared Anton Chekhov found it an invaluable inspiration to his own artistry; as Stanislavsky reported, he preferred it to his own plays.[28] Unfortunately, time has been less kind to *Lonely Lives*. Not so much the themes, but the almost hysterical earnestness with which they are expounded tends to provoke unintended laughter among modern audiences, and directors and actors often collude in transforming a work intended as a tragedy into something close to farce.

Like *The Coming of Peace,* this play deals with generational conflict within an upper-middle-class family. Johannes and Käthe Vockerat live in a country house in Friedrichshagen near Berlin on the shore of the Müggelsee lake. Johannes, twenty-nine, is a self-employed scholar and adherent of the latest scientific and philosophical ideas, working on what he hopes will become his magnum opus. His wife, who has enjoyed no more than the average education for a woman of her generation and class, devotes her days to maintaining a comfortable household for her husband and infant son while trying to keep Johannes's spendthrift ways in check. The elder Vockerats, conservative in religion and politics, have come from their rural Silesian home to attend the baptism of their grandson, which Johannes has permitted only with extreme reluctance and as a concession to his parents; he considers such ceremonies inappropriate and beneath the dignity of a sophisticated, modern intellectual.

Tension mounts within the family with the arrival of Anna Mahr, one of the first female students admitted to the University of Zurich. Although she is actually an acquaintance of Braun, a rather cynical, shaven-headed friend of the younger Vockerats, she and Johannes soon discover themselves to be kindred spirits. Despite Johannes's insistence to his wife and parents that his new relationship is strictly platonic—he even tries to elevate it to a universal, high-minded blueprint for the future which will transcend sexual considerations entirely—a long, drawn-out kiss, reciprocated with equal ardor by Anna, would seem to indicate that his practice is outrunning his theory. Johannes's parents are understandably upset by what they consider adultery of the heart and what they fear may go further, and Anna is finally persuaded that she should return to Zurich. In the final scene Johannes exits toward the lake. Although the content of the note he leaves behind is never communicated to the audience, Käthe's reaction to it and the fact that he had threatened suicide several times suggest that he intends to drown himself. Whether he actually does so remains a matter of conjecture.

In addition to the symbolism inherent in its location—halfway between the bucolic countryside and the noisy metropolis of Berlin—Friedrichshagen was for Hauptmann and his contemporaries as much a state of mind as a place. A kind of artists' colony, it included in its inner circle writers like Wilhelm Bölsche, Bruno Wille, and the brothers Heinrich and Julius Hart, men who were dissatisfied with the narrow definition of Naturalism (and the extreme emphasis on natural science from which it derived) promulgated by the likes of Arno Holz and Conrad Alberti. Turning again to philosophical speculation, mysticism, or any approach that promised a more intimate communion with the cosmos, they soon attracted writers, bohemians, and socialists of every stripe, eventually including among their ranks the Naturalist authors Otto Erich Hartleben and Max Halbe; the Swedish playwright August Strindberg; the Polish satanist Stanislaw Przybyszewski; Frank Wedekind; the irreverent poet Richard Dehmel, and, as frequent visitors, Carl and Gerhart Hauptmann. Among the topics that interested them especially were those involving personal ethical problems concerning individual freedom versus societal constraints of the type depicted in *Lonely Lives*. Because these people represented a new spirit which was becoming more and more prevalent among the young, we can imagine that when Hauptmann dedicated his drama "to those who have lived it," (1:168) they too may well have felt themselves addressed.

The primary addressees, as we know, were Hauptmann's brother Carl, Carl's wife Martha, other members of Hauptmann's family, and a Polish student named Josefa Kodis-Kryzanowska. While living in Zurich with Martha in 1888 Carl had become involved in an affair with Kodis-Kryzanowska which would have destroyed his young marriage if his wife had not been able to cope with the situation better than Käthe Vockerat is able to do.[29] Like Johannes, he was possessed by an impatient idealism and an almost pathological irritability while struggling with a study dealing with a dynamic theory of life, the first volume of which actually appeared in 1893 under the title *Metaphysik der modernen Physiologie* (*Metaphysics of Modern Physiology*).[30] Similarly the elder Mrs. Vockerat owes some characteristics to Hauptmann's mother, as does Käthe to both Mary Hauptmann and Carl's wife. Typically, however, Hauptmann's characters transcend such real-life prototypes and reflect an amalgamation of ideas and personalities he himself had experienced. He too had known female students in Zurich (including one who smoked big black cigars) and had become dangerously infatuated with the brilliant, intellectual daughter of a professor during his trip to Italy while he was already engaged to Mary. Likewise, some of the incidents depicted in the play (for example, Johannes's resistance to the baptism, the fact that his mother comes to help care for the newborn baby, and the complaints over squandered money) derive from Hauptmann's direct experience.

A closer look, particularly at the male protagonists of the first three plays, reveals an evolving typology of Hauptmannian characters. Loth, Wilhelm Scholz, and Johannes Vockerat are all youthful, agitated, self-centered, professed idealists who treat the women who love them (Helene, Ida, and Käthe) in a callous manner which belies the sensitivity to which each would surely lay claim. Each cherishes an almost megalomanic ambition (as social activist, musician, or writer) but has, so far, nothing to show for it. In a very real sense they are all weaker than the more instinctive and natural women who try so hard to support them in their work.

Each of these central characters also has an alter ego, a brother or male friend, who is (or pretends to be) cynical and world-weary but who, upon closer inspection, is revealed to be in open or secret conflict with him. Schimmelpfennig seems more than a little anxious to help Loth separate himself from Helene; Robert Scholz is patently envious of his brother's relationship to Ida; and Braun goes out of his way to denigrate Anna Mahr while complaining, "I don't suit her" (1:215).

In the figure of Anna Mahr, Hauptmann did manage to create a distinctively new kind of female character for the German stage. Making her own way in a male world, she recognizes and opposes the ethical and social evils of her generation without sacrificing her femininity. Although subject to the same temptations as Johannes, she vacillates briefly and then follows her better moral instincts by withdrawing her disruptive influence from the young family. She too is a victim of historical transition. Whereas Johannes finds it difficult (or impossible) to adapt to a world that is rapidly changing its religious, scientific, and philosophical orientation, she bears the additional burden of being in the vanguard of a women's movement struggling for some minimal rights (work-related, social, political, and sexual) against a firmly entrenched male hierarchy. Aside from advances in the depiction of female characters, it is, perhaps, in the evocation of a uniquely lyrical atmosphere that *Lonely Lives* surpasses its predecessors. As one critic has described it, "an autumnal glow envelops the play in a romantic haze that belies its realistic label and gives it a strong flavor of fin-de-siècle morbidity."[31] Although music was used in *The Coming of Peace* to provide ironic counterpoint to the atavistic behavior of the Scholz brood, here music, literary allusion, and references to the Bible and folklore provide a subtext accessible to educated German audiences of the day. As has been convincingly demonstrated, "the many folkloristic allusions give accurate clues to personality and behavior. Thus Johannes' references are filled with pathos, showing no sense of irony, while Anna Mahr's are ironic and Braun's downright cynical. Käthe's show a child-like but foreboding imagination, while her parents-in-law are shown to be pious rustics. In each case Hauptmann quickly establishes the ambience of the characters by setting up associations in the spectator that deepen his response, in the manner of musical themes."[32] Only after having been alerted to this profusion of quotations, snatches of verse, and lyrical "inserts" can one appreciate the subtle skills with which the author plays upon the emotions of his listeners. A good example occurs in the last scene. While Johannes is presumably drowning, his mother tries to help Käthe fall asleep by reading to her from Grimms' *Fairy Tales,* and the effect is at once sad, funny, and disconcerting.

## NOTES

1. *New York Times,* 12 January 1892, p. 4.

2. Theodor Fontane, "Gerhart Hauptmann, 'Vor Sonnenaufgang,' " in *Gerhart Hauptmann,* ed. Hans Joachim Schrimpf (Darmstadt: Wissenschaftliche Buchgesellschaft, 1976), p. 13.

3. Quoted by Bernhard Zeller, ed., *Gerhart Hauptmann. Leben und Werk: Eine Gedächtnisausstellung des Deutschen Literaturarchivs* (Stuttgart: Turmhaus-Druckerei, 1962), p. 52.

4. Quoted by Hans Daiber, *Gerhart Hauptmann. Oder der letzte Klassiker* (Vienna, Munich, Zurich: Molden, 1971), p. 51.

5. Zeller, 60–61.

6. Quoted by Daiber, 53.

7. Quoted by Eberhard Hilscher, *Gerhart Hauptmann. Leben und Werk.* (Frankfurt/M.: Athenäum, 1988), p. 96.

8. Cf. John Osborne, *The Naturalist Drama in Germany* (Manchester: Manchester University Press; Towota, N.J.: Rowan & Littlefield, 1971), pp. 78, 84–85; and Roy C. Cowen, *Hauptmann Kommentar zum dramatischen Werk* (Munich: Winkler, 1980), pp. 162–63.

9. See Warren R. Maurer, "Gerhart Hauptmann's Character Names," *German Quarterly* 52 (1979): 459.

10. Sigmund Freud, "Creative Writers and Daydreaming," in *Literature and Psychoanalysis,* ed. Edith Kurzweil (New York: Columbia University Press, 1983), p. 27.

11. See Sigfrid Hoefert, *Gerhart Hauptmann* (Tübingen: Metzler, 1974), p. 15.

12. Peter Bauland, *Hauptmann's Before Daybreak,* (Chapel Hill: University of North Carolina Press, 1978), p. xvi.

13. "Alkohol und Nachkommenschaft," *Neue deutsche Rundschau* 6 (1895): 1108–12.

14. See Daiber, 43; and Osborne, 87.

15. Quoted by Frederick W. J. Heuser, *Gerhart Hauptmann: Zu seinem Leben und Schaffen* (Tübingen: Niemeyer, 1961), p. 43.

16. Carl F. W. Behl, *Zwiesprache mit Gerhart Hauptmann: Tagebuchblätter* (Munich: Desch, 1949), p. 121.

17. Quoted by Karl S. Guthke, *Gerhart Hauptmann: Weltbild im Werk* (Munich: Francke, 1980), p. 71.

18. See Philip Mellen, "Gerhart Hauptmann's *Vor Sonnenaufgang* and the Parable of the Sower," *Monatshefte* 74 (1982): 139–44, and W. A. Coupe, "An Ambiguous Hero: In Defence of Alfred Loth," *German Life and Letters* 31 (1977/78): 13–22.

19. Quoted by Peter Sprengel, *Die Wirklichkeit der Mythen: Untersuchungen zum Werk Gerhart Hauptmanns* (Berlin: E. Schmidt, 1982), p. 160.

20. Sprengel, 160.

21. Neville E. Alexander, *Studien zum Stilwandel im dramatischen Werk Gerhart Hauptmanns* (Stuttgart: Metzler, 1964), p. 39.

22. See Zeller, 62, 64.

23. Cf. Peter Sprengel, *Gerhart Hauptmann. Epoche-Werk-Wirkung* (Munich: Beck, 1984), p. 197.

24. See Heuser, 230.

25. See Warren R. Maurer, *Gerhart Hauptmann* (Boston: Twayne, 1982), pp. 38–39.

26. Quoted by Günther Mahal, *Naturalismus* (Munich: W. Fink, 1975), p. 233.

27. See Daiber, 64.

28. See Behl, 70; and Hoefert, 246–47.

29. See Heuser, 253–54.

30. See Daiber, 64.

31. Henry A. Lea, "The Specter of Romanticism: Hauptmann's Use of Quotations," *Germanic Review* 49 (1947): 278.

32. Lea, 275.

# CHAPTER TWO

# Everybody Has a Longing

### The Weavers

With the premiere of *Die Weber, Schauspiel aus den vierziger Jahren* (*The Weavers: A Drama from the Forties*) in February of 1893, Hauptmann achieved world literary stature. First written in the impenetrable dialect of the Eulengebirge and then translated into a more widely accessible version, tinged with the Silesian dialect, the play's political repercussions and its intrinsic power and emotional intensity carried its author's reputation far beyond the borders of his homeland, where he was already the leading dramatist. Together with *The Beaver Coat*, which followed almost immediately, *The Weavers* represents a high point not only of German Naturalism but of European Naturalism as well. Although ostensibly Hauptmann's first attempt to apply the principles of literary Naturalism to historical subject matter, the drama, while brilliantly achieving this goal, also went far beyond it—transcending both history and conventional, contemporary ideals of form. Because the historical conditions it depicts were almost indistinguishable from those prevailing during its creation, they remained as topical as ever, while the formal innovations (such as the use of masses of people as a collective hero, an epic structure which substitutes a series of stations or tableaus for traditional plot, and reliance on documented facts) foreshadowed Expressionism, Brecht, and even the documentary drama of the postwar years.

If it were not for the fact that choice of subject matter may also reflect the genius of an artist, one might say that Hauptmann was extremely lucky when he chose to write a drama about the plight of a group of poor, exploited Silesian weavers and their abortive revolt in 1844. A predisposition to the topic deriving from personal, political, and religious motivations; virtuosity in a literary style ideally suited to the material; and, especially, an audience prepared by contemporary events to appreciate every nuance of his message were all in place by 1891. According to its dedication to the author's father, Robert, the "germ" of the work was Robert's stories about *his* father, "who, as a young man, was a poor weaver who had sat behind the loom like those depicted" (1:321). In his own youth, Gerhart had become intimately familiar with the impoverished weavers around Salzbrunn, but only his contact with a group of textile workers in Zurich in 1888 finally inspired him to write his play, and by the spring of 1890 he had begun work on it. In the same year the dire need of the Silesian weavers, exacerbated by a failed potato harvest, had again attracted widespread public attention, and it was reported that "cries of hunger from the Silesian mountains were reverberating throughout Germany."[1] As in 1844 a government commission was dispatched to study conditions firsthand, but it was a Protestant pastor, Ernst Klein, who, through articles in the popular press, made the country aware of the severity of the weavers' misery and set about raising money to help them. Fearing that such publicity and support would play into the hands of the fledgling socialist workers' movement, the local Breslau government prohibited Klein's activities; but, by now, the topic was on everyone's lips and Hauptmann must have recognized the incendiary potential of his material.[2]

The identification of the revolt of 1844 with the contemporary situation (which Hauptmann tried to deny but which later brought him into conflict with the authorities) had also been well established by 1891—largely through the efforts of militant social democrats. All that remained was to concentrate and focus the intense public interest that had been generated by current events in a veristic literary work. Assuring the credibility of the characters depicted and of their desperate situation required considerable research. In a process familiar to students of modern documentary drama (but also of Büchner's *Danton*), Hauptmann exploited historical works by Alexander Schneer and Wilhelm Wolff that had documented the situation around 1844, as well as Alfred Zimmerman's *Blüthe und Verfall des Leinengewerbes in Schlesien* (Flourishing and Decline of the Linnen Trade in Silesia) of 1885, which demonstrated that the horrendous conditions of the earlier period persisted.[3] From these materials he took not only an account of the course of events but actual names, incidents, and anything else that would contribute to the verisimilitude of his drama. Not content, however, with secondhand information, he took a research trip to the scenes of the revolt, Peterswaldau and Langenbielau, in 1891, after having written a first draft. How deeply disturbed and moved he must have been is reflected not only in the finished drama but also in the remark of an acquaintance who saw him upon his return: "[Hauptmann] reported on the impressions, which he had had, with trembling lips, nervous and tormented, he looked miserable and exhausted. . . . "[4]

The first act of the play provides an overview of the weavers' economic plight, introduces one of the eventual leaders of the revolt, and reveals the first faint glimmerings of rebellion. Masses of weavers—wretched, emaciated creatures dressed in rags—have assembled in the shipping room of the

42

wealthy factory owner Dreissiger to deliver the fustian cloth they have woven in their hovels, to bargain for a few extra pennies, or to beg an emergency advance on their paltry salaries. The shipping clerk, Pfeiffer, himself a former weaver who owes his position as Dreissiger's right–hand man to his talent for sycophancy, criticizes their workmanship and takes every opportunity to depress their wages even further. Only Bäcker, a young, atypically robust newcomer from another village, stands up to their exploiters and dares to complain loudly about their abominable treatment of their workers. When Dreissiger himself is called to deal with the disturbance, he recognizes Bäcker as one of a group of young men who had been singing the weavers' forbidden song of protest—the "Lied vom Blutgericht," (Song of the Court of Blood)—in front of his mansion the previous evening. The tense situation is defused when a small boy, sent by his family to deliver its completed piecework, collapses from hunger. Visibly embarrassed before his employees, Dreissiger has him taken to his private office, where he complains about the irresponsibility of parents who would send a child to deliver such a heavy load of goods, complains in self-pity about the risks and responsibility to which he is subject as an entrepreneur, and promises to hire two hundred more weavers—although that will only lower the wages of those already in his employ.

Whereas the first act serves as a general introduction to the problems of the Silesian weaving industry, the second provides an intimate look at a typical weaver's family in which everyone, from small children to the sick and infirm aged, must work long hours just to keep from starving. Old Baumert, who has eaten no meat for two years, has had his little dog butchered (he could not bear to do it himself) and is happily stewing the meat in a pot. He has just returned from picking up new yarn for the loom and, on the way, has met the reservist soldier Moritz Jäger, who has come home with him bearing a precious bottle of schnapps. Jäger amazes his listeners with stories about the luxury of a soldier's life in the city and then begins to rail against the local capitalists. When it turns out that, unaccustomed to the rich fare, old Baumert's stomach rejects the dog meat, and he breaks down weeping, Jäger begins reading the weaver's song aloud and with increasing passion. Those who hear him are carried along by the emotion and vow that conditions must and will be changed.

Act 3 is set in Welzel's tavern in Peterswaldau, a scene that Hauptmann uses to elaborate on the weavers' problem from yet a different perspective. A traveler new to the area is struck by what he considers the peculiar funeral customs of the locals. Chewing vigorously on his chopped steak he muses, "I just don't understand . . . wherever one looks, in any newspaper, one reads the most horrible stories about the weavers' suffering, as if the people here were already three-quarters starved. I just came into the village. Brass band, school teachers, school kids, the pastor and a parade of people, my God, as though the emperor of China were being buried. Well, if the people can still pay for that . . . !'' (1:383). After an embarrassed silence Wiegand, the local cabinetmaker (who also does a brisk business in coffins) explains that, precisely because of their miserable earthly lives, the relatives feel obligated at least to provide the dead with a spectacular send-off, even if it means going deep in debt to do so. Besides, the local clergy derive a good portion of their income from the practice and actively resist modest burials. The traveler's arrogant ignorance and his crude attempts at flirtation with the serving girl gradually increase the animosity of a group of young weavers present. Spurred on by the blacksmith Witting, they again start singing their protest song. The attempt of the village gendarme (a man known as much for his corruption as for his propensity for drink) to stop them leads only to his inglorious retreat. The young weavers now take their song to the street.

The fourth act focuses more strongly on the Wilhelminian collusion of church, capital, and state. In strong contrast to the previous locales, we now find ourselves in the cold elegance of Dreissiger's home. During an intimate social gathering Weinhold, a young theology candidate and tutor to Dreissiger's sons, dares, however timidly, to question the social conditions under which the weavers are forced to eke out their existence. Kittelhaus, an older pastor comfortable with Dreissiger's hospitality, encourages the young man to change his attitude. With frequent Bible references, he argues the cliché that the poor will always be with us and that a few starving weavers are not reason enough for disturbing the sociopolitical and economic status quo. Weinhold persists, however, and so enrages his employer that he is dismissed from his tutoring position. Meanwhile the rebellious weavers have advanced on the residence. Dreissiger's workers have captured Jäger, their leader, and brought him to the mansion for interrogation by police commissioner Heide—another friend of the household. When Jäger is placed under arrest and led out into the street the riot breaks out in earnest; he is freed by his comrades, the police are beaten, and Dreissiger and his family just barely escape before the mob demolishes the house and everything in it.

The last act shifts to a new locale: the impoverished quarters of Hilse, an old weaver who lives with his extended family in the neighboring village of Langenbielau. Informed by his peddler friend Hornig that the raging mob is moving to drive out the profiteers here too and that troops have already been raised to beat down the revolt, he is greatly concerned. A pious man who has lost an arm in the service of his country, he sees revolt as futile, subscribing instead to the stubborn belief that the just will find their reward in heaven. His daughter-in-law Luise interprets his attitude as cowardice and welcomes the revolt with fanatical enthusiasm. The revolutionaries, led in part by Hilse's friend old Baumert, who has fortified his flagging courage with alcohol, call for their comrades to join them in the street, but the old man refuses. The soldiers fire their weapons at the mob but are driven back temporarily by a hail of rocks. Hilse remains sitting at his loom, where he is killed by a stray bullet.

A comparison of Hauptmann's sources with his *Weavers* reveals how accurate the play was. Hilse's death, the only episode to reflect obvious artistic manipulation, is nevertheless eminently believable given the conditions prevailing during the 1844 uprising. If anything, the author's depictions of poverty are understated, perhaps to minimize their inherent pathos. Thus, for example, Hauptmann uses one episode from Schneer in which an old weaver relates how fortunate he had been to find a dead horse to nourish his family; but he rejects another incident, equally heart-rending: a family in which the husband and wife had hidden a piece of bread six years earlier at their marriage, in accord with the prevailing superstition that it would protect them forever from hunger, suddenly remembers it during a time of dire need, retrieves it, and shares the moldy remains.[5] Hauptmann had seen the effects of similar suffering with his own eyes during his research trip: old people dying of starvation; small children forced to work long hours almost from the time they learned to walk; a mother and her newborn infant covered with peat litter because there were neither blankets nor rags to keep them warm; children six and seven years old with nothing to cover their nakedness—in short, conditions even worse than those presented in the play.[6]

It is, of course, not the materials but their treatment (not the "what" but the "how") that accounts for the worldwide success of the drama. Had Hauptmann chosen to write an essay or a monograph deploring the plight of Silesian weavers, he could have reasonably expected no greater response than that accorded Schneer, Wolff, or Zimmermann. Only by exposing the scandal in that most public of media arenas, the stage—especially in a country as theater-obsessed as Germany—did he guarantee himself a large and varied audience. Recalling later his artistic ambition for the drama, he wrote, "But the social drama, even if at first an empty schema, was in the air as a postulate. To call it to life was, at that time, a prize challenge which, if solved, was the equivalent of making one the initiator of a new epoch. . . . I could write *The Weavers* . . . because . . . I knew the folk dialect. I would, I decided, introduce it into [serious] literature. . . . I wanted to return to dialect its dignity'' (7:1078–79).

Although, as we recall, Hauptmann had also used dialect rather extensively in *Before Sunrise, The Weavers* would be inconceivable without it. Whereas earlier German authors had largely reserved it for provincial literature and exploited it for its sentimental and/or humorous overtones (a tendency still evident in Holz and Schlaf), *The Weavers* elevated it to a form of artistic expression as appropriate for its purpose as the classical language of Goethe and Schiller had been for theirs.

A comparison of *The Weavers* with Hauptmann's previous dramas shows a continuation of trends found earlier but also some daring innovations which increasingly distance it from its more traditional predecessors and from the more theoretical tenets of Naturalism itself. The already extensive stage directions become even longer and more detailed. The concept of the outsider who serves as a catalyst to the action (for example, Mrs. Buchner, or Anna Mahr) is less obvious but still present in the agitators Bäcker and Jäger. More significant is the changed hero. Whereas the earlier works also focused less on an individual than on the clash of a number of personalities than had been customary in traditional drama, the individual is now almost completely subordinated to the collective. No specific weaver—not even Hilse—carries the action in any traditional sense. What we find instead is a great number of characters, each individualized by language, gesture and appearance, but each also subsumed within a composite figure defined by similar physical and psychological characteristics, and especially by a shared suffering. Again the stage directions seem intended as much for a reader as for a viewer. As the curtain rises we are introduced to this collective hero (in part) as follows: "Something depressed clings to [these people], something characteristic of the receiver of alms who, going from humiliation to humiliation, conscious of being only tolerated, is accustomed to making himself as small as possible. In addition there is a rigid expression of ineffectual, tormented brooding on all the faces. The men, who resemble each other, half dwarfish half school-masterly, are by and large flat-chested, coughing, wretched people with dirty, pale, complexions: creatures of the loom whose knees are bent from so much sitting" (1:325). Here are the debilitating effects of environment at work. Hauptmann, again in accord with his sources, also implies hereditary damage, which becomes especially acute in small, closed groups with a great deal of intermarriage. One of Mrs. Baumert's children, for example, a twenty-year-old son capable of doing only the simplest tasks, is described as "imbecilic, with a small torso and head, and long, spider-like extremities" (1:351).

Such detailed and extensive stage directions imply a strong epic tendency in the drama that is reinforced by the very nature of the events requiring dramatization. Because of the physical limitations of the stage, especially in the final act, Hauptmann can only present a *pars pro toto* impression of the effects of mob violence. He does so by bringing the action indoors, into Hilse's cottage and before the audience, through a series of reports supplied by such eyewitnesses as Hilse's old friends Horning and a now inebriated Baumert; and also through the naive comments of his small granddaughter, who exclaims at one point, "Dear grandfather, grandfather, they've shot with rifles. A few fell down. . . . One wriggled like a sparrow when you pull off his head. Oh, Oh, and so much blood squirted out!" (1:477). These reports are intensified by the constant, loud noise produced by the berserk rioters and soldiers: snatches of drunken song; shooting; and wild cries of "hurrah" which are ironic because the shooting of Hilse also signals the death of the revolution to Hauptmann's knowledgeable audience.

Almost from the beginning and continuing at least until 1970, there were complaints that *The Weavers* deviated markedly from the traditional idea of a well-made drama of five acts, each developing logically from its predecessor, with a climax in the middle of the third; a minimal number of characters; and a complete, satisfying resolution of the action at the end of the play.[7] Naturalism, with its aim of presenting "a slice of life," should never have been forced into such a rigid, formalized structure. Nonetheless, and although Hauptmann went further in his formal experimentation than most of his German Naturalist contemporaries (such as Max Halbe, Hermann Sudermann, and Otto Erich Hartleben), his dramas before *The Beaver Coat* still pay homage to the traditional "closed" ending (although the suicides, or implied suicides, of Helene Krause and Johannes Vockerat, and even the death of Hilse, have something artistically arbitrary about them). Hauptmann was, as he never tired of asserting, above all a literary artist, and only then a reluctant Naturalist; and a closer look at *The Weavers* reveals a number of techniques he used to impose a strong sense of unity on what appears, at first reading, to be only a series of loosely connected tableaux. This sense of unity is achieved in various subtle ways: Old Baumert appears in all five acts (as does one or the other of the fanatical revolutionaries Bäcker and Jäger); act 5 represents a recapitulation of the rising tide of revolt begun in the previous acts; and the protest song from its first hesitant introduction in act 1 to its use as the noisy public voice and battle cry of act 5, traces the crescendo of violence. As has been shown, the acts themselves are also orchestrated for maximum effect. Reduced to schematic form they represent a fever chart of the revolt. Thus the second, third, and fourth acts each begin at a higher emotional pitch than their predecessor and end higher still. Act 5, on the other hand, in keeping with its function as a recapitulation, begins somewhat lower on the scale but then rises higher than all the others.[8] In the final analysis, the most profound unity of the play is centered in the suffering of the weavers themselves.

It would be naive to ascribe the international success of *The Weavers* exclusively to its artistic qualities. Regardless of what Hauptmann's intentions may have been, he managed, almost immediately, to affront both the political Right and Left. Although censorship no longer officially existed in Germany, contemporary Prussian laws regarding the maintenance of order were broadly interpreted and marshaled against the new play so that Hauptmann soon found himself embroiled in "the most spectacular censorship trial in the history of German literature."[9] When the director of the Deutsches Theater applied for permission to present the play in the spring of 1892, the police chief of Berlin rejected the request with the argument that, given recent increases in unemployment, such a performance would be detrimental to class harmony and represented a veiled incitement to revolution. Hauptmann's lawyer, responding that the work was purely historical, made little headway since it was clear to everyone that current conditions among the weavers were just as bad as in 1844 and that contemporary workers were just as susceptible to its alleged message.[10]

In order to avoid further delay, the Freie Bühne (as a private theater not subject to the laws regarding public performances) scheduled a staging for February 26, 1893. This performance was hailed enthusiastically by the Marxist critic Franz Mehring as socialist agitprop and as being both "revolutionary and highly topical."[11] Meanwhile, Hauptmann's lawyer took the case to an appeals court, where he finally won release of the play for performances in the Deutsches Theater. The judges, while under no illusions as to its incendiary nature, were persuaded by the cynical reasoning that the class of society most susceptible to its message was too poor to afford tickets! When the first public performance in Germany took place on September 25, 1894, the uproar it provoked among various factions of the audience rivaled that of the premiere of *Before Sunrise*. The next day the Rightwing press castigated it for alleged socialist tendencies, and Kaiser Wilhelm II canceled his subscription box seat in protest.[12]

It took somewhat longer for the socialists to make up their mind about the work. Like Mehring most were initially carried along on its revolutionary fervor and were anxious to claim the author as one of their own. Unfortunately for them, the quietism of the Hilse episode, and Hauptmann's own views, made it increasingly difficult for them to do so. As he expressed the crux of the matter: "Although I stood close to socialism, I never felt myself to be a socialist" (7:1047).

Paradigmatic for the situation of Hauptmann and socialism is his relationship to Bertolt Brecht. Like Mehring, Brecht was initially a great admirer of his famous older compatriot but then, around 1920, abruptly changed his attitude. Disregarding the historical outcome of the revolt of 1844, he criticized the author of *The Weavers* for not having tried hard enough to change society directly along more militant ideological lines and for being satisfied with trying to arouse some compassion in his bourgeois audiences. Such appeals to emotion Brecht equated with mere "culinary art"; a refusal to accept the responsibility of a modern author, as he saw it, specifically to support the coming proletarian revolution and more generally to change the world instead of merely describing it. For Hauptmann, on the other hand, art and political propaganda were antitheses. Although hardly an aesthete, he despised agitprop and all forms of fanaticism (religious as well as political) as simplistic and dangerous. In an 1894 note he complained, "The Social Democratic Party is a party which aspires to be a champion of specific interests. Don't its leaders see what a literary work would look like that devotes itself only to specific interests? Are you nothing but socialists? Are you not also human beings—that so much humanity is foreign to you?"[13] It is ironic that Brecht, who placed his work at the disposal of a specific, dogmatic political agenda, never wrote a drama that achieved as much international political resonance as *The Weavers*.

When it was performed on May 29, 1893, in the Théâtre Libre of Paris—the first performance of a German play in France since the Franco-German War of 1871—its revolutionary aspect was emphasized and it enjoyed enormous success. Translated into Russian by Lenin's sister, it had an impact not only on Russian literature but on the Russian Revolution itself.[14] American readers may be interested in learning that it was also capable of arousing strong passions in the United States. Here, as was frequently the case in Europe, it was exploited as an overt attack on capitalism. First presented in German on the evening of October 9, 1894, by amateurs in the Thalia Theatre under the sponsorship of a labor group calling itself Freie Bühne von New York (Free Stage of New York), it featured the well-known anarchist-terrorist

John Most in the role of Old Baumert. Not only was the cast woefully inadequate to the task of bringing Hauptmann's subtle masterpiece to life, but the producer tried to sharpen the political attack. "Not that he omitted passages," as Blankenagel has described his meddling, "but rather that he arbitrarily made additions which Hauptmann never would have written. There were more vulgarisms, tirades, and a long bombastic speech by Jäger in which he attacked the manufacturer Dreissiger. As a result the fourth act became a botched farce."[15] When, a few weeks later, Most tried to produce the play in Newark, New Jersey, the *New Yorker Volkszeitung* of October 29 declared on its front page: "*The Weavers* Dangerous to the State. Performance of Hauptmann's Play Prohibited by the Newark Police, Due to the Presence of Strikers." A meeting of the politically powerful—including the mayor, his police commissioner, and the district attorney—had been called, and in it the mayor declared that, except for the fact that the play was "crass, tasteless, and therefore not ennobling," he had nothing against it; but the district attorney reminded his honor that "we are the guardians of morality."[16] Finally, the arguments of the police commissioner prevailed. Pointing out that there were a thousand local workers who had been unemployed for nine weeks and whose families were starving, he thought it dangerous to allow an agitator like Most to stir them up further. Should he dare to speak he would be arrested. Permission to perform the play was denied.[17]

Before leaving *The Weavers* it is necessary to comment briefly on what might be called the Hilse controversy. From the earliest to the most recent discussions of the drama the character and death of Hilse have elicited intense critical attention, and the interpretations have tended to reflect the political, metaphysical, and literary orientation of the critics themselves. The various approaches, which have been discussed at greater length elsewhere,[18] can be summarized as follows: (1) Hauptmann wanted things both ways; disturbed by the political direction the work seemed to be taking, he added a fifth act as a diplomatic compromise which would somewhat mollify the authorities while permitting him to speak out on a subject of wide concern. (2) Old Hilse's attitude and his death confirm a Marxist orientation. A victim of bourgeois religion ("the opiate of the people"), Hilse has been duped into exchanging a measure of social and economic justice in this life for the empty promise of life to come. He is portrayed as a living anachronism destroyed by the very revolution he sought to impede. (3) Hilse represents a basic view of life that Hauptmann himself shared, one of human subjugation by a fate too powerful to be resisted and redemption at the price of prolonged and intense suffering.

That Hauptmann has a predilection for political compromise both in his work and in his life is, by now, beyond debate and may indeed have influenced the ending of *The Weavers*. As has been seen, he also preferred ending his works on a note of ambiguity, and a comparison of earlier drafts of his plays with their completed versions reveals his tendency toward transforming potentially explosive political themes into relatively bland religious ones.

The Marxist view is harder to maintain. Hilse is much more than a one-dimensional religious zealot; he is also the most pragmatic of the weavers and predicts (correctly, as we know from history) that the uprising must fail.

The sheer coincidence of the stray bullet points toward the greater validity of the third interpretation. Later works treated here (and, albeit less strongly, the dramas already treated) indicate a distinctly numinous component of Hauptmann's art. Raised as he was in the atmosphere of Silesian mysticism and himself subject to the temptations of a fundamentalist Christianity during the Lederose period, he could hardly be satisfied with a strictly materialist view of life. Like *The Coming of Peace, The Weavers* is also a commentary on the shallowness of a simplistic alternative between optimism and pessimism. On a political level history supplied a "pessimistic" outcome. On a metaphysical level the radiant character of Hilse, in spite of (or because of?) his death provides a flicker of hope—if only because fate seems to take an active interest in its subjects.

## Hannele

Whereas *The Weavers* was an annoyance to widely varied political interests, *Hanneles Himmelfahrt. Traumdichtung* (*Hannele*) of 1893, managed to affront Marxists, Christians and Naturalists alike. After attending the premiere, the Marxist critic Mehring finally abandoned Hauptmann for his cause with these words: "Never before have we been condemned to witness with our own eyes such a great abuse of such a great talent."[19] From his perspective, the pernicious direction the author had taken with the last act of *The Weavers* was continued and greatly intensified in *Hannele*. The latter play too deals with much suffering and pain—this time in the person of a poor, abused, and dying fourteen-year-old girl. And again, even more blatantly than in *The Weavers*, the emphasis is not so much on provoking social action as it is on arousing compassion and promoting a mystical, Christian stoicism: redemption through pertinacious faith and suffering.

While such a message would hardly be expected to antagonize Christians, the way in which it was presented managed to do just that. In New York City the announcement of an impending production of an English–language version of the play for April 1894 provided Hauptmann with his first American theater sensation and raised his name to a wider American consciousness.[20] Puritan sensibilities were ruffled and censorship was invoked when it was learned that the heroine of the drama was an adolescent girl and that the role would be played by a fifteen-year-old. Although this provided the local guardians of morality (especially the president of the Society for the Prevention of Cruelty to Children and the mayor of the city) with an excuse to prevent the performance, it was the alleged blasphemous nature of the work that had struck a raw nerve. Not only did the figure of Christ Himself appear on the stage, albeit in the form of a mysterious stranger, but His relationship to the girl assumed a naive but indisputable tinge of eroticism. A technical solution to the problem of an underage actress was worked out when the producers substituted in the role the twenty-five-year-old wife of James O'Neill (Eugene O'Neill's celebrated actor–father), but by now the negative publicity had left its mark. The play was performed only twice in this production: once on April 30 for a closed audience of invited critics, men of letters, political dignitaries, clergy, and others whom the producers hoped to win over; and again the next evening for the general public. With the exception of one glowing notice in the *New York Herald* (written by the play's translator) the reviews were almost all bad. The *New York Times* reviewer wrote, "From whatever point of view the piece is regarded, it is not worth one tithe of the fuss that has been made about it in the public press. . . . "[21] And, while the *Tribune* critic grudgingly granted the drama "some poetical phrases . . . some impressive passages," he also complained that much of it was

> no more interesting or dramatic, except possibly to medical students of hysteria, than the delirious ravings of the patients in a clinic. . . . An atmosphere of the strenuous but sentimental piety of the Salvation Army pervaded a considerable part of the play. . . . [It] is not likely to succeed for any considerable length of time, and it ought not to succeed. It may attract audiences of restless sensation-seekers for a few weeks, but it is not a work of genuine merit and it affronts both the verities and sanctities which are still cherished by the people whose influence in this community is for the good.[22]

That such commentary was largely the result of bad advance publicity, the general zeitgeist, and just plain incomprehension is evidenced by the play's rather sudden rehabilitation. The handicap of an inadequate translation was soon pointed out, as was the subtle psychology that tended to go unnoticed by an audience unaccustomed to such finesse on the American stage. Indeed, within a year, the prominent critic William Guthrie was insisting that " 'Hannele,' the little stranger from overseas, who was so inhospitably treated by our New York volunteer censors of the stage, is one of the masterpieces that defy criticism."[23] By 1910, when the actress Minnie Fiske made a final effort to establish an English translation of *Hannele* on Broadway, the accusations of blasphemy and immorality had largely given way to carping about questions of form and style; that is, whether it was a play at all or "only" a poem. (This production closed after sixteen performances.)[24]

More significant, perhaps, than its function as a litmus test for contemporary political and religious attitudes is the change in aesthetic direction that *Hannele* signals. Consisting of only two acts, the play reveals the tragedy of a girl who is forced to live in utter degradation by a brutal, drunken stepfather and tries to drown herself in a freezing village pond. Rescued and then carried to the local poorhouse by the village teacher Gottwald, she spends the short interval before her death hovering between reality and fever-fantasies played out by a succession of actors on the stage.

Surprisingly, but in keeping with Hauptmann's habit of intense personal involvement with his characters, *Hannele* too was inspired by real events. During the Lederose period, while Hauptmann was very much entangled in problems of puberty and fundamentalist religion, his aunt and uncle had bought (as was possible at the time) a poor, sickly, lice-infested girl from her drunken, abusive father and taken her into their home. The author's very personal involvement with the transaction is expressed in his recollection: "I understood that she was intended to replace me" (7:771). A second model for the character of Hannele has been suspected in the thirteen-year-old daughter of a poor widow in Reichenbach whom the author had met on his research trip for *The Weavers* and whom he later occasionally favored with presents.[25]

*Hannele* begins and ends naturalistically. The first scene introduces the audience to the environs of the poorhouse; the last finds the village doctor bending over the girl with his stethoscope and announcing her death. As in Hauptmann's earlier plays, the characters are skillfully and realistically individualized in appearance, speech, and gestures. Although they too are destitute, the regulars of the poorhouse are generally more aggressive and less reputable than the author's Silesian weavers. If the poorhouse symbolizes the world as "vale of tears," that world is indeed a dismal place.

Toward the end of the first act and throughout most of the second, the cold reality of the poorhouse is replaced by the delirious fantasies of the dying girl. As Hauptmann pointed out, "all her visions can be explained on a purely pathological basis.''[26] It is through them and through the strength of her wish-projections (for beautiful clothes, the acceptance of her schoolmates, the love of Gottwald/Christ) that the secret recesses of her soul and the full extent of her suffering are exposed. It is not unrealistic that her dreams abound in references to Christian myth and German fairy tales (Frau Holle, Snow White's glass coffin, and Cinderella's slipper, for example), since these are the elements of her meager culture. And, although it might be argued that Hauptmann trivializes Christianity by intermingling the Grimm brothers with the Bible, this can hardly have been his intention. As in the case of Hilse, realism requires that Hannele's attitudes and beliefs be appropriate to her station. (If there is one area where Hauptmann does compromise, it is with Hannele's language. Unlike the other members of her social class, she speaks with just a trace of dialect—possibly a strategy on the author's part to maintain a greater degree of empathy with his largely middle–class audience.)

In spite of its scrupulously realistic motivation, the drama represents a distinct departure for Hauptmann. The introduction of dreams and/or visions carries him far beyond the strictly naturalistic convention that only palpable, physical reality may be depicted on the stage. By opening the drama to the imagination, he also expands its formal possibilities. Thus it is no coincidence that, near the end, the epiphany of the Stranger blossoms forth in luxurious verse—perfectly acceptable by Neoromantic standards, but anathema to any doctrinaire Naturalist.

## NOTES

1. Quoted by Helmut Praschek in Gerhart Hauptmanns "Weber:" Eine Dokumentation (Berlin: Akademie Verlag, 1981), p. 35.

2. See Praschek, 36.

3. Cf. also Praschek, 36–38.

4. Quoted by Praschek, 106.

5. See Praschek, 44.

6. See Hans Schwab-Felisch, Gerhart Hauptmann: Die Weber (Frankfurt/M.: Ullstein, 1959), pp. 163–75.

7. The most vociferous critic in this category is Peter Szondi. See his Theorie des modernen Dramas, (Frankfurt/M.: Suhrkamp, 1970), pp. 69–73; and Kurt May's opposing view in "Die Weber," in Das deutsche Drama, 2 vols., ed. Benno von Wiese (Düsseldorf: Bagel, 1968) 2:163–65.

8. Hans Rabl, Die dramatische Handlung in Gerhart Hauptmanns Webern, (Halle/S.: Niemeyer, 1928), p. 38.

9. Manfred Brauneck, Literatur und Öffentlichkeit im ausgehenden 19. Jahrhundert: Studien zur Rezeption des naturalistischen Theaters in Deutschland (Stuttgart: Metzler, 1974), p. 51.

10. See Schwab-Felisch, 83.

11. Quoted by Eberhard Hilscher, Gerhart Hauptmann. Leben und Werk. (Frankfurt/M.: Athenäum, 1988), p. 138.

12. Hilscher, 141.

13. Quoted by Peter Sprengel, *Die Wirklichkeit der Mythen: Untersuchungen zum Werk Gerhart Hauptmanns* (Berlin: E. Schmidt, 1982), pp. 101–02.

14. See Sigfrid Hoefert, " 'Gerhart Hauptmann und andere'—zu den deutsch-russischen Literaturbeziehungen in der Epoche des Naturalismus," in *Naturalismus. Bürgerliche Dichtung und soziales Engagement,* ed. Helmut Scheuer (Stuttgart, Berlin, Cologne, Mainz: W. Kohlhammer); pp. 244, 249–50; and Hans Daiber, *Gerhart Hauptmann. Oder der letzte Klassiker* (Vienna, Munich, Zurich: Molden, 1971), p. 76.

15. J. C. Blankenagel, "Early Reception of Hauptmann's 'Die Weber' in the United States," *Modern Language Notes* 68 (1953): 337.

16. Quoted in Blankenagel, 338.

17. Blankenagel, 338.

18. Warren R. Maurer, *Gerhart Hauptmann* (Boston: Twayne, 1982), p. 53–56.

19. Neville E. Alexander, *Studien zum Stilwandel im dramatischen Werk Gerhart Hauptmanns* (Stuttgart: Metzler, 1964), p. 3.

20. See Edith Cappel, "The Reception of Gerhart Hauptmann in the United States" (Ph.D. dissertation, Columbia University, 1953), p. 49.

21. *New York Times,* 2 May 1894, p. 5.

22. *New York Tribune,* 2 May 1894, p. 6.

23. Quoted by Cappel, 49.

24. See Peter Bauland, *The Hooded Eagle: Modern German Drama on the New York Stage* (Syracuse: Syracuse University Press, 1968), p. 15.

25. See Schwab-Felisch, 174–75.

26. See Frederick W. J. Heuser, *Gerhart Hauptmann: Zu seinem Leben und Schaffen* (Tübingen: Niemeyer, 1961), p. 44.

# CHAPTER THREE

# Comedy Is Always Tragicomedy

## *Colleague Crampton*

*Kollege Crampton* (*Colleague Crampton*) had been Hauptmann's first great popular and financial success.[1] Dashed off in two weeks in 1891 after the author was inspired by a performance of Moliere's *Miser* in Berlin,[2] it represents a change in genre and theme: to comedy (to which, henceforth, he is periodically drawn as though seeking relief from the strain of more serious work) and to the problem of the artist versus the claims of society (a recurring preoccupation Hauptmann shared with Thomas Mann, Hermann Hesse, and other contemporaries). On closer inspection, to be sure, this change turns out not to be as abrupt as it first appears. Like its predecessors *Crampton* derives its strength from a wealth of autobiographical material and from the minute depiction of physical and psychological reality. Moreover, *Before Sunrise, The Coming of Peace,* and *Lonely Lives* all contained comic elements—usually associated with servants or members of the lower classes—and all dealt, at least peripherally, with the plight of the creative person and hostile surroundings: Loth and Johannes Vockerat as authors and Wilhelm Scholz as a musician manqué. Finally, like all these plays, *Crampton* contains elements which can only be described as Romantic and which serve to soften the play's harsher, naturalistic contours. Especially noteworthy here is the happy ending: a solution of Crampton's problems that is so sudden and idyllic it bears comparison with the Romanticist Eichendorff's *Aus dem Leben eines Taugenichts* (*From the Life of a Good-for-Nothing*) and with the fairy tales of the brothers Grimm.

As we might expect for a comedy still heavily indebted to contemporary conventions, the plot is more complicated and the characters are more active than in the works mentioned above. Again the opening lines provide a theatrically effective introduction to the protagonist and his predicament. In a scene reminiscent of Kleist's *Der zerbrochene Krug* (*Broken Jug*), Harry Crampton, a professor in an art academy of "a larger Silesian city" (1:263) is awakened by his loyal factotum Löffler into the harsh realities of a new day. As usual he has been drinking heavily the night before, and his students are waiting impatiently for a class in figure drawing to begin. The kind-hearted Löffler has rounded up a poor, decrepit acquaintance to serve as a model, but the professor has never so much as spoken to the man, who is horrified to learn that he is expected to pose in the nude. When he is finally led, resisting, into the classroom, there is an outburst of hilarity among the students. Before he can join his class, Crampton is visited by Max Strähler, a "young, beardless person of not yet twenty years," (1:270) who has come to thank him for his support. In spite of his professor's intercession on his behalf, Max has been dismissed from the academy for neglecting his academic duties. Crampton, who is also about to lose his position, holds a very low opinion of his colleagues as judges of artistic talent. His spirits suddenly rise, however, when he learns of the imminent visit of the reigning Duke Frederick August to the academy. He immediately assumes that the Duke is making the trip to honor him personally, that he will purchase some of his paintings, and that this is sure to signal a turn in his fortunes—by now he has sunk to sign painting in order to support himself and his family.

Unfortunately the meeting with the duke never takes place. He does, it is true, visit the academy but, after paying his respects to Professor Kircheisen, one of Crampton's colleagues, promptly leaves. Crampton, humiliated and in despair, accepts his dismissal and seeks refuge from his creditors (and his own family) in a seedy hotel. Meanwhile his daughter Gertrude, whom Max had met in her father's atelier that morning, has been taken into the Strähler household (her mother has returned home to her people in Thuringia), and Max has promptly fallen in love with her. The young couple sets out to find the professor, but without success. It is only with the help of the practical and prosperous businessman Adolf Strähler, Max's older brother, that Crampton is finally found.

The task remains to rescue him and get him into more civilized surroundings conducive to his work. Max has succeeded in collecting most of the furnishings of his atelier, which had been widely scattered throughout the city by creditors, and in arranging them in their old order, in a room in his brother's house. When he suggests that Crampton move into the new quarters the artist's pride is hurt; and it is only through Max's idea that Crampton be commissioned to do a portrait of Agnes Strähler, Max's sister, that Crampton accepts the invitation and, implicitly, a new life. Max, for his part, receives Crampton's permission to marry Gertrude.

The characters of Crampton and Max Strähler especially, and some of the incidents depicted, hark back on Hauptmann's art school days in Breslau and reflect an idealized vision of that period in his life. At that time Hauptmann, whose mother's maiden name was Strähler, was also a "young, pale, beardless person of not yet twenty years." Like Max he was dismissed from the academy for neglecting his studies, but, unlike him, he was reinstated mainly through the efforts of James Marshall (the fictional Harry Crampton) and Robert Haertel (Professor Kircheisen). Marshall was a type of individual often encountered during this period, a man of talent with a bohemian flair whose alcoholic excess Hauptmann even claims to have had to tone down somewhat for the play.[3] His weakness eventually cost him his position, as did Crampton's. Hauptmann also knew him more intimately than Max knows Crampton. Unlike his fictional counterpart he was an active participant in the professor's nightly revels and came very close to ruining his own life in the process. The eventual rescue of Crampton through the efforts of his student has no factual precedent but may represent something of a wish projection on Hauptmann's part: the acknowledgment of indebtedness and the desire to erase it—if only in the realm of fiction.

Even a brief and incomplete comparison of factual background and finished drama confirms a tendency toward cheerful optimism that contrasts starkly with the earlier works and reveals another side of Hauptmann. The treatment of themes is similarly revealing. The excessive consumption of alcohol, for example, which two years earlier was depicted as one of mankind's worst scourges in *Before Sunrise,* is reduced here to little more than a comic flaw of the type the author had just seen in the play by Molière. While it is responsible for Crampton's difficulties, it is also the source of a great deal of humor since it brings him into environments, situations, and relationships ordinarily considered foreign to a man of his position. It is precisely such confrontations of the unexpected—Crampton wheedling money out of his poor servant Löffler or accepting employment from a house painter while trying to maintain his professional dignity—that provide much of the play's undeniable merriment.

The theme of the artist versus society is likewise exploited largely for comic effect, and, despite Hauptmann's affectionate compassion for his hero, it is a distortion to interpret the play as an illustration of "the dubious position of a bourgeois artist in a class society."[4] His society has rewarded Crampton with a position commensurate with his talents. It is his personal qualities that cause him to lose it, and it is Adolf Strähler, a bourgeois businessman, who rescues him from himself. While the play does bear testimony to Hauptmann's conviction that "there is no comedy which is not a tragicomedy,"[5] insofar as we are shown a basically talented and worthwhile individual brought perilously near a disaster (only to be abruptly and comically snatched from its jaws by a veritable deus ex machina), we must be cautious about accepting Crampton's complaints about the inadequacy of his creative environment at face value. As one critic has noted about the comedy's ending, "There is little reason to believe that Crampton's talent would unfold more productively in his new-found, feather-bedded isolation."[6]

In summary it is safe to say that *Colleague Crampton* shows Hauptmann well on the way toward mastery of that most difficult and seemingly contradictory genre, Naturalist comedy. The play is the marvelously delineated character of Crampton himself, and it is no wonder that the role has been traditionally prized by ambitious actors. The play's most enduring feature, although not its only value, is the humane humor that pervades it; any satirical, political, or even metaphysical overtones it may possess are subordinate to its value as sheer entertainment.

## The Beaver Coat

Written during the time of Hauptmann's legal difficulties over the performance of *The Weavers, Der Biberpelz. Eine Diebskomödie* (1893) (*The Beaver Coat*) slipped by Prussian censorship with remarkable ease. It is unclear whether the censor who dismissed the play as a "miserable concoction . . . without any significant action"[7] was exceptionally stupid or clever. Had the play achieved the notoriety of earlier works, its significance might also have been appreciated sooner. As it was, the first performance received mostly negative reviews; it was performed very infrequently for a number of years; and only after the First World War, when the German public felt a need for some comic relief, did the play come into its own. By the 1920s its qualities were almost universally recognized. Later it survived the bowdlerizations of the Nazi era, and it has now achieved the status of a modern classic, ranked with Lessing's *Minna von Barnhelm* and Kleist's *Broken Jug* as one of the three greatest comedies of German literature. During the 1980s it continued to enjoy exceptional popularity, possibly in part because its liberal audiences still saw in it social and political affinities to their own time.[8]

*The Beaver Coat* is a character comedy that revolves almost exclusively around the unforgettable figure of the washerwoman Mrs. Wolff, who, with great virtuosity and exuberance, manipulates friend and foe alike to her designs. Fiercely protective of her family—consisting of her ineffectual husband, Julius, and two teenage daughters, Adelheid and Leontine—she takes on the Prussian government, as represented by the local head official (*Amtsvorsteher*) Baron von Wehrhahn and his minions, and achieves a complete rout. Although she is responsible for a series of crimes, including poaching and the theft of some firewood and a valuable fur coat from Leontine's employer, the rentier Krüger, she is such a consummate actress and mistress of indirection that Wehrhahn's admiration for her honesty and integrity continues to grow. That her victory is so complete is, however, not entirely her own doing. As a fanatical servant of the Prussian monarchy, the *Amtsvorsteher* is too distracted by what he considers his greater mission—rooting out the democratic and socialist tendencies he suspects in Krüger, and even more in the quiet young scholar and writer Fleischer—to notice what is happening under his very nose.

The comedy, which continues Hauptmann's trend of social criticism, is largely (but not exclusively) a satire on contemporary political conditions. The time is that of the "Septenat struggle toward the end of the eighties" (1:483). This phrase refers to Bismarck's tenacious effort to maintain funding for his peacetime military for an additional seven years and even to get permission to increase its size. Opponents of these measures were treated as enemies of the Reich. Like Fleischer and Krüger they were ruthlessly spied upon and harassed by public officials, who were generally appointed on the basis of social position rather than ability, who placed loyalty to the Crown above all else, and who saw themselves as representatives of the Kaiser himself.

Hauptmann's exposure to these conditions was direct and personal. During his stay in Erkner he encountered the people and many of the events depicted in his comedy. Like the twenty-seven-year-old Fleischer, he was a young, liberal outsider of precarious health whose mail (for example, the socialist periodical *Die neue Zeit* [*The New Age*]) had attracted the attention of Oskar von Busse, the prototype of Wehrhahn. It was to the self-inflated von Busse, who, like Wehrhahn, proclaimed himself the local "king," that Hauptmann, like the barge owner Wulkow of the play, reported the birth of a child and to whom, like Adelheid, he brought a suspicious bundle of clothing he had found in the forest. In Erkner he heard about the theft of a fur coat and found the models for Krüger (his landlord, Nikolas Lassen); for Motes, Wehrhahn's most zealous spy and informer (a fellow tenant named Haché); and for the Wolff family. Mother Wolff was inspired by Marie Heinze, the author's own laundress, and her daughter Ida served as a maid in the Hauptmann household (as does Leontine in Krüger's). Although Mrs. Heinze was no thief and later came to resent the author's portrayal of her as one, she shared Mrs. Wolff's strongly matriarchal proclivities.[9]

For Hauptmann the essence of drama lies in "meetings . . . relationships . . . it lies in the movements of human beings with each other, and around each other, and against each other."[10] Action, as he also wrote, derives from character: "If one presupposes certain characters, then they necessitate a certain action, i.e., movement" (11:757). With this in mind it would appear appropriate to examine a bit more closely the characters of *The Beaver Coat* and their relationship to each other.

The "thieves" group includes Mrs. Wolff, her husband and children, and Wulkow; while the "law" is represented by Wehrhahn, Mr. and Mrs. Motes, the scribe Glasenapp, and the bailiff Mitteldorf. On one level, the Wolffs reflect the general social, moral, intellectual, and cultural climate of the period during which the play was written. Matriarchal to a fault (not uncommon for families at the lower end of the socioeconomic scale), the family shares none of the symptoms of grinding poverty encountered in *The Weavers*. And, although keenly aware of social and economic inequities, Mrs. Wolff does not see herself as a member of the proletariat, takes no personal interest in socialism, and is quite content to compete in the pervasive struggle of rampant, Darwinian capitalism around her. Like the so-called "founders" (*Gründer*) typical of the period following the Franco-Prussian War, she has obsessive and straightforward ambitions: material and social advancement for herself and her family. Like the *Gründer,* too, she is not fastidious about the means of attaining her goals, and she is quite persuasive in convincing herself that ends justify means. "We are not thieves," (1:520) she tells her skeptical daughter Adelheid (who sees the evidence of theft all around her) and, in the next breath, admonishes her to "learn your Bible quotations" (1:520). Religion has lost its power to constrain from wrongdoing, ethics are situational, and morality is for those who can afford it.

By his choice of crimes Hauptmann, of course, tempers the severity of Mrs. Wolff's offenses and thereby makes them more appropriate to comedy. Historically the ownership of the natural products of forest and stream (wild game, wood, beaver) was a matter of protracted dispute in Germany between peasants and landowners, and the former tended to dismiss such thefts with the phrase "milking the green cow."[11] Be that as it may, the theft of an expensive fur coat clearly oversteps the line between misdemeanor and serious criminality and presages the detestable behavior of Mrs. Wolff when we again encounter her in *Der rote Hahn* (*The Conflagration*), Hauptmann's sequel to *The Beaver Coat*. Although she justifies the theft with the argument that one big "score" will help pay off the mortgage on their home and even permit adding a few rooms for summer guests, thus increasing the family income, it is also clear that she revels in her success in deceiving the law, that her crimes are escalating excitingly but dangerously, and that her effort to purchase social respectability through crime will eventually exact its price on her and her family.

Cold-blooded manipulation of others for one's private ends is not an endearing trait, but when Hauptmann has Mrs. Wolff direct it against her natural enemies Wehrhahn and Motes, he can still count on the audience to condone her methods. To take just one easily overlooked example, by the end of the play she manages completely to neutralize Motes, Wehrhahn's informer, and in so doing deprives the *Amtsvorsteher* of his strongest ally. In act 1 Motes and his wife are aware of the family's poaching activities and successfully blackmail Mrs. Wolff into not demanding the return of money they owe her and in supplying them with bread and eggs. By the third act she has discovered that Motes has been trying to incite one of her acquaintances, a Mrs. Dreier, to commit perjury against Fleischer in order to convict him of crimes against the state. Informed of this by Mrs. Wolff, Fleischer investigates the matter (albeit reluctantly) and, by the last act, he and Krüger have obtained a signed statement from Mrs. Dreier and with it a potent weapon against further political persecution. While there may have been an element of altruism vis-à-vis Fleischer and Krüger in this intrigue, the statement implicating Motes in a serious crime also frees Mrs. Wolff from continued blackmail without in any way revealing her hand in the matter or reducing her standing with Wehrhahn.

Although the relationship with Fleischer allows Hauptmann to add a sympathetic note to Mrs. Wolff's character (little Philip, his son, brings out her motherly qualities and leads to the touching revelation that she had a son who died), the suspicion remains that even here she may be acting—at least partially—from self-interest. Having decided that Adelheid should enrich the family with a stage career, she is ever alert for opportunities to further her plan. And, although the girl is hilariously unqualified for such a career by virtue of her speech (the Berlin dialect), education, and general demeanor, Mrs. Wolff is aware of Fleischer's connection to local literary circles and, vaguely, to the theater itself; his brother is a theater cashier, a gratuitous touch by Hauptmann unless the intention is to make suspect what appears on the surface to be a perfectly harmless and straightforward relationship.

Mrs. Wolff's duplicity even with "friends" comes out more strongly (and humorously) in her relationship to Krüger. To be sure, with his excessive demands on Leontine, Krüger does exemplify the harsh relationship between masters and servants quite legally prevailing at the time, but this hardly justifies outright theft. The temporary falling-out between Krüger and the

Wolffs, occasioned by Leontine's refusal to bring in a load of firewood from the street late at night (thus making it a tempting target for "thieves") is gradually but skillfully mended by Mrs. Wolff herself. At one point she brazenly challenges Krüger directly with the question "Did I perhaps steal your wood?" (1:514), and the final reconciliation amounts to a veritable love fest. He is so taken by her feigned aura of integrity that he rehires her to do his family laundry and accepts Leontine (whose presence in his household also provided the intelligence for the theft of the fur coat) back into his home at a salary higher by a third than he paid her before. Typically, Mrs. Wolff accepts his largesse with tears of emotion in her eyes.

Manipulating her husband Julius is no challenge for our heroine, given his naive nature and limited intelligence, and she does so almost disdainfully by appealing to his fatherly instincts, casting aspersions on his manhood, and, for crucial actions like the theft of the coat, plying him with alcohol before giving him his marching orders.

In the daughters Leontine and Adelheid, Hauptmann shows the effects not only of heredity and environment but also of the suspect morality of a family (or society) whose motto seems to be "Do as I say, not as I do," and in which appearance takes precedence over substance. Having recognized that culture and education (*Bildung*) attach to that class to which she aspires, Mrs. Wolff seeks to improve her status with the same direct means she uses to acquire wealth or, for that matter, religion ("learn your Bible quotations"). That the path will not be easy is implied by the way Hauptmann has her speak to her daughters—for example when she remarks about her husband, "you see he ain't learned no culture" and continues, "that wouldn'ta been no different with you neither if I hadn'ta raised you educated" (1:491). Of the two, Adelheid takes more clearly after her mother. She too is quick-witted, a born liar, and a formidable actress. Unfortunately, although she is only fourteen, "the expression in her eyes betrays early corruption," (1:489) and, to her mother's dismay, she keeps company with an ex-convict, "a real pimp" (1:489) named Fielitz.

Mrs. Wolff's opponents (unequal because they vastly underestimate her) are Wehrhahn and the characters clustered about him as representatives of the "law." Wehrhahn himself is a quintessential Prussian official of the time who sees his office as a "sacred calling" (1:533), which entitles him to treat the petitioners who appear before him with the haughty disdain of a proxy-monarch. Although he is not without positive traits and even a touch of the tragic, (in keeping with Hauptmann's view that there are no unmitigated villains) his scheming and acting ability, on which he obviously prides himself,

are too intellectually contrived to be as effective as Mrs. Wolff's more instinctive manipulations. A congenital subordinate (*Untertan*) to the Crown,
with the ideé fixe that the enemies of the realm are everywhere, he has surrounded himself with sycophants to do his unsavory bidding. They include
the scribe Glasenapp, who excels at transforming himself into a virtual caricature of his boss, and the more dangerous informer Motes, who also belongs (a nice touch) to a "society for the breeding of pointer dogs," (1:508)
of which Wehrhahn's brother-in-law is a member. Perfectly harmless, on the
other hand, is bailiff Mitteldorf, who, like Julius Wolff, contributes a more
purely farcical element to the play. Slow of speech and mind, and with a diminutive attention span, this impoverished father of eleven is in the habit of
fleeing to the local tavern to escape the tongue—lashings of his wife and to
drown his considerable sorrows. The comic high point of his role occurs at
the end of the first act when Mrs. Wolff enlists his help in preparing a sled for
the theft of Krüger's firewood and hands him a lantern to light the way as she
and Julius set out to commit the crime.

In a 1937 discussion of *The Beaver Coat,* Hauptmann remarks that it is
"completely a child of Brandenburg soil (*Kind der märkischen Erde*)" and
goes on to claim that "only Berlin with its witty dialect could produce a German Aristophanes" (11:1156). This juxtaposition of modernity with antiquity
goes a long way toward characterizing the play. Like *Colleague Crampton,*
but more daringly, *The Beaver Coat* combines convention and innovation to
achieve a form of Naturalistic comedy. While still largely adhering to the
classic unities of time and place, because he believed that they contribute to
the "logic, condensation, concentration, economy, [and] architecture"[12] of a
work, and not averse to traditional forms of exposition (as exemplified especially by the first act), Hauptmann was undoubtedly influenced—particularly
in the fine art of comic characterization—by such predecessors as Kleist and
Molière.[13] Where he broke with the older tradition was in his insistence on a
stringent realism that would persuade an audience that what it was seeing on
the stage could as easily be seen in real life. Not only did this approach eliminate such obstacles to credibility as the traditional asides spoken by the actors to the audience; it also greatly inhibited the creation of elaborate
intrigues of the Molière variety. Instead of complicated plots, Hauptmann
stressed the complex psychology of human relationships.

This is not meant to imply that even his characterizations are completely
divorced from tradition. As Fritz Martini has pointed out, most of the characters in *The Beaver Coat* transcend their real—life models and partake also of
a venerable tradition of stock types. Thus Mrs. Wolff, the clever and sover-

eign subjugator of all problems and threats that confront her, is a variant of the picaresque servant; Wehrhahn an offshoot of the *miles gloriosus;* Mitteldorf of the *Dümmling* (simpleton) tradition; and Krüger, the irritable and outspoken old man whose hearing problem leads to comic misunderstanding, a specimen of *senex iratus.*[14] Indeed, only Fleischer represents a significant exception to this rule. An obvious stand-in for the author, he falls into that more specifically Hauptmannian category of the outsider whose presence catalyzes the action.

The possibility of another, more contemporary, influence on *The Beaver Coat* should at least be mentioned in passing: the writings of Friedrich Nietzsche. As Oberembt has convincingly argued, Mrs. Wolff's "philosophy" reflects a Nietzschean outlook, and the drama depicts the "battle of the exception with the rule,"[15] the struggle between an exceptional individual and her mediocre opponents. The amoral, vital "carnivorous animal" (*Raubtier*) enjoys an advantage over the decadent bureaucrat, or, as Nietzsche sums it up, "the [contemporary] European disguises himself in morality, because he has become a suffering, sickly, crippled animal, that has good reasons to be 'tame,' because he is almost a freak, something incomplete, weak, clumsy. . . . "[16] As compared with the one-eyed Motes, the diabetic Fleischer, Wehrhahn and his monocle, Krüger with his hearing impairment, Wulkow and his rheumatism, or the dim-witted Mitteldorf, Mother Wolff does indeed seem the embodiment of Nietzsche's healthy *Raubtier.*

Using much the same evidence it is also possible to argue with Oskar Seidlin that *The Beaver Coat* represents a depiction of the theme of matriarchy—a precursor of Hauptmann's novel *Die Insel der großen Mutter* (1924) (*The Island of the Great Mother*). Seen from this perspective Mrs. Wolff represents a kind of Ur-mother, acting spontaneously from a great female collective unconscious and brushing aside all interference from the inferior, weak-kneed males surrounding her. That Hauptmann was strongly attached to this theme seems clear. In his own family his mother reigned supreme, and he admits in his autobiography that his entire childhood was spent under the influence of matriarchy. Whether because of such conditioning or for other reasons entirely, his works do show a predilection for strong women and weak men. On the other hand, none of the other female characters (not even Adelheid) approaches Mrs. Wolff's forceful vitality in pursuing her goals, so even among women she remains an exception (a sad exception at that, when we consider the fate which overtakes her in *The Conflagration.*)

Its modern, specific setting on the outskirts of Berlin notwithstanding, there is also something decidedly archetypal about the humor of Hauptmann's comedy. "In *The Beaver Coat* and *The Conflagration*," he later remarked, "I reached, unintentionally, into the area of mimic folk humor."[17] Indeed, this portrayal of the "life struggle of a washerwoman" (6:885–86) depends for much of its success on humor of a fairly basic variety. In addition to the inherently funny struggle between the slow-witted and foolish with the quick and clever, or the comic role reversal of the weak and ineffectual male pitted against the strong, enterprising woman, Hauptmann spices his comedy with touches of unmistakably cruel, atavistic humor. Thus, for example, Mitteldorf's pathetic situation (poverty, eleven children, fear of his wife, escape into drunkenness, and the like), Krüger's deafness-induced misunderstandings, or Wehrhahn's remark apropos Fleischer's diabetes ("let him sweat syrup if he feels like it" [1:505]) are at once funny and cruel and remind us of Hauptmann's conviction that the comic and tragic are invariably found in close proximity to each other, and that every true comedy is really a tragicomedy.[18]

The archetypal ambience of the play is further enhanced by a profusion of animal images and references.[19] As Furst has noted, "the recurrent imagery of Naturalist writing is drawn from the animal world, and its vocabulary . . . abounds in the 'law of claw and fang.' "[20] For Hauptmann, as for such different authors as Jean Paul or Hermann Hesse, humor seems to function as a palliative for the pain of an inherently cruel existence. In a revealing passage he juxtaposes his susceptibility to humor with a rather dark view of humanity expressed in animalistic terms. "You wonder," he asks,

> that I laugh and am cheerful? It is just that I have a talent for vegetative joys. As soon as I consider— . . . or more accurately: as soon as someone brings me to my senses—for example, with the question "What do you think about the possibility of a happier future for mankind?", I will answer without hesitation: 'Humanity is a tenacious but fatally wounded prey. It sweats—runs—collapses, continues bleeding, runs, because it hopes or is hunted, and again collapses. Perhaps it can't die before sunset.[21]

That *The Beaver Coat* continues the archaic tradition of "animal comedy" is also suggested by the blatantly significant names of the principal antagonists. As would be typical for much earlier German comedy, von Wehrhahn is almost completely expressed by his name. The *von* identifies him with the frequently ridiculed (as excessively intermarried, not-too-bright) Prussian nobility, while the *Wehr*-component suggests the man's defensive, conservative political stance. More telling (and humorous) is the second component of this richly evocative surname. A *Hahn* is, of course, a cock or rooster and expresses the posturing and crowing (in an "almost falsetto" [1:504] tone of command) of the vain cockalorum *Amtsvorsteher*. In Wehrhahn the proud eagle of the Prussian coat of arms has been reduced to a thoroughly domesticated barnyard fowl which is no match for a wild and free carnivorous "wolf in sheep's clothing" (1:533) embodied in the name of Mrs. Wolff, especially when Wehrhahn insists on reserving that role for the innocent Fleischer. Intensifying the piquancy of the unequal combat for readers and audiences is the familiar folkloristic tradition associated with the animals in question. To take just one example, in the old fable of *The Rooster and the Pearl* the rooster appears as a self-inflated ignoramus who judges according to his own petty criteria and fails to recognize the true nature of things under his very nose—as does Wehrhahn, of course, in his dealings with Mrs. Wolff.[22] The wolf, on the other hand, frequently epitomizes the defiantly undomesticated forces within the human animal (this occurs also in Hermann Hesse's *Steppenwolf*)—the id in Freud's terminology. For Hauptmann, as for Freud and Nietzsche, civilization exacts a debilitating sacrifice from its victims, so that the barnyard "fowl" and "sheep" of this world are a poor match for its "foxes" and "wolves."

Turning briefly to some of the more formal aspects of *The Beaver Coat*, the reader is first forced to notice how absolutely impervious it is to adequate translation. Beyond such obvious problems as puns and wordplay, Hauptmann not only sticks to his usual practice of individualizing his characters by providing them with their own distinctive linguistic "tone" and speech rhythm, but—with the exception of Fleischer—has them labor under the comic burden of a potpourri of dialectal inflections as well. The result—especially when several characters try to speak at the same time—is a delightful Babel with the serious undertone evoked by that name: the ultimate futility of human attempts at clear, precise communication.

Although hardly the only one of Hauptmann's formal innovations, the comedy's ending, a bold departure from the inviolable tradition that the guilty must be punished and justice served, caused the most consternation among the author's contemporaries. That Mrs. Wolff escapes punishment and will, presumably, continue in her wicked ways focuses attention on the relativity of legality (who is the greater "criminal," she or the tyrant Wehrhahn?) and introduces an element of reality into the plot (real criminals are not always caught). Indeed, given the nature of the protagonists, the satirical tenor of the play, and the naturalist requirement that art must mirror reality, Hauptmann's solution now seems inevitable.

## The Conflagration

It seems to be an aesthetic rule of thumb that sequels, because they are often only motivated by the effort to repeat an earlier success, are rarely satisfactory. In *Der rote Hahn. Tragikomödie* (*The Conflagration: A Tragicomedy*) Hauptmann continues the story of Mother Wolff but, perhaps in accord with perfectly sound social, political, and psychological motivations, changes her into a crabbed, morose, and debilitated old woman, devoid of the inimitable charm and vitality that had made her one of the most unforgettable characters in all of German literature. Again the setting is "somewhere near Berlin," but the time is that of "the struggle over the Lex Heinze" (2:11), a political allusion to the virulently repressive Prussian attempts at censorship at the turn of the century. Although Mrs. Wolff is presumably still living in the same village that she had lived in at the end of *The Beaver Coat*, the place and cast of characters have changed profoundly during the decade that separates the action of the two plays. Von Wehrhahn is still around as the *Amtsvorsteher*, though he has been so subdued and changed as to be hardly recognizable (for example, he now speaks in a much more pronounced Berlin dialect), and Leontine and Glasenapp have also been retained. More telling still are the changes in the social and political climate. No longer do we have the impression of a relatively idyllic village life; the encroachment of Berlin and the dubious morality associated with this ominous metropolis have become more pronounced, and the imperialism and hyper-capitalism of the era of Wilhelm II have produced a hardbitten, unscrupulous generation of speculators who reject any concession to compassion as inimical to standard business practice.

These changes are especially evident in what remains of the Wolff family. The formerly proud matriarch is, by her own confession, "no longer a Mother Wolff" (2:15). Her husband Julius has died and—horror of horrors—she has married the "lousy shoemaker Fielitz" (1:489), the ex-convict/pimp against whom she had warned her daughter Adelheid ten years earlier. Leontine, in her late twenties and in danger of becoming an old maid, is the object of erotic attentions from a married man, a blacksmith with the suggestively phallic name Langheinrich (long Henry), while Adelheid has married an unscrupulous builder named Schmarowski (compare the German word *Schmarotzer* = parasite). The central episode, and the one reflected in the play's title, seems to have been inspired by a visit Hauptmann made in 1894 to the community of Kagel, near Berlin, where the local fire chief told him of an increasingly common practice in which property owners set fire to their own buildings in order to defraud insurance companies.[23] (The colorful term "red rooster" appears to derive from the resemblance of flames to the coxcomb of a rooster.)

Although she has by now achieved financial security and bourgeois respectability, Mrs. Fielitz—whether from force of habit or hubris—cannot resist the temptation to continued criminality. With the help of her husband, she rigs a device that will set fire to her empty house while she and Fielitz are in nearby Berlin. The plot is outwardly successful, and she collects seven thousand marks in insurance money intended for investment in the building speculations of her son-in-law, Schmarowski. Although the crime is less than perfect (Langheinrich has found a piece of fuse from the incendiary device and is in a position to blackmail her), Mrs. Fielitz manages to encourage Wehrhahn in his suspicion that the arson was committed by Gustav Rauchhaupt (whose name, literally translated, means smoke-head), the mentally retarded son of a former local gendarme. Compounding her guilt with a display of cynical hardheartedness, she suggests to the father that his harmless son will be better off committed to an insane asylum for his "crime," where he will at least have three square meals a day. She dies a short time later in the presence of her husband, who scarcely seems to notice her demise.

Together with a great deal of peripheral talk, which also conveys the zeitgeist of the era (its capitalist excess, religious hypocrisy, and anti-Semitism, among other characteristics), the play depicts, in the sad decline of Mrs. Fielitz, a rampant materialism that results in an increase in selfish criminality and a concomitant deterioration of humane values. As Schrimpf and Seidlin have suggested, matriarchy has failed in the new violent environment and been replaced by a harsher patriarchy.[24]

While there is at least one obvious problem—the heroine's upward material advancement has done nothing to enhance the authentic quality of her life—it is, nevertheless, easy to see why *The Beaver Coat* and *The Conflagration* should have attracted the attention of contemporary and later Marxists. Again Brecht is a case in point. In 1951 he reworked and combined the two plays for a six-act production by his Berliner Ensemble. In a letter to Berthold Viertel he expressed his intentions and, simultaneously, a basic difference between Naturalism and Marxist ideology: "We decided to trust Hauptmann completely insofar as his art of observation was concerned (i.e., we investigated the significance of the smallest details and retained them if at all possible). Less trustworthy, however, was his knowledge of the historically essential. We had to bring the workers' movement (social democracy), which Hauptmann almost completely overlooks, into the picture."[25] The changes Brecht undertook, with the intention of stressing the role of the workers' movement and the view that social conditions must be directed through organized, political effort, failed to "rescue" the works for Marxism. Instead of living drama the end result was such a humorless, politicized, and contrived *Lehrstück* (didactic play) that Hauptmann's heirs promptly withdrew permission for further performances.[26] That Brecht's preoccupation with Hauptmann may not have been a complete loss, however, is suggested by the fact that the figure of his own memorable female character, Mother Courage, seems to owe a great deal to Mother Wolff.[27]

## NOTES

1. See Peter Sprengel, *Gerhart Hauptmann, Epoche-Werk-Wirkung* (Munich: Beck, 1984), p. 123.

2. See H. D. Tschörtner, *Ungeheures erhofft. Gerhart Hauptmann—Werk und Wirkung* (Berlin: Der Morgen, 1986), p. 159.

3. See Carl F. W. Behl, *Zwiesprache mit Gerhart Hauptmann: Tagebuchblätter* (Munich: Desch, 1949), p. 39.

4. Eberhard Hilscher, *Gerhart Hauptmann. Leben und Werk* (Frankfurt/M.: Athenäum, 1988), p. 147.

5. See Hans-Egon Hass and Martin Machazke, eds. *Gerhart Hauptmann: Sämtliche Werke*, 11 vols., (Frankfurt/M.: Propyläen, 1966–74) 6:792. See also Karl S. Guthke, *Geschichte und Poetik der deutschen Tragikomödie* (Göttingen: Vandenhoeck & Ruprecht, 1961), p. 256.

6. John Osborne, *The Naturalist Drama in Germany* (Manchester: Manchester University Press; Totowa N. J.: Rowan & Littlefield, 1971), p. 140.

7. Bernhard Zeller, ed., *Gerhart Hauptmann. Leben und Werk: Eine Gedächtnisausstellung des Deutschen Literaturarchivs* (Stuttgart: Turmhaus-Druckerei, 1962), p. 86.

8. For a more detailed history of the reception of *The Beaver Coat* by German audiences, see Gert Oberembt, *Gerhart Hauptmann: Der Biberpelz* (Paderborn, Munich, Vienna, Zurich: Schöningh, 1987), pp. 155–85.

9. See Oberembt, 15.

10. Martin Machatzke, ed., *Die Kunst des Dramas: Über Schauspiel und Theater* (Frankfurt/M.: 1963), p. 203.

11. Oberembt, 105.

12. Machatzke, *Kunst des Dramas*, 36–37.

13. Cf. Ludwig Büttner, "Gerhart Hauptmann: Der Biberpelz," in *Europäische Dramen von Ibsen bis Zuckmayer*, ed. Ludwig Büttner (Bonn: Diesterweg, 1961), pp. 60–62.

14. See Fritz Martini, "Gerhart Hauptmanns 'Der Biberpelz:' Gedanken zum Bautypus einer naturalistischen Komödie," in *Studien zur Literatur und Kunst seit der Jahrhundertwende*, ed. Renate Heydebrand and Klaus Günther Just (Stuttgart: Metzler, 1969), pp. 97–100.

15. Oberembt, 135.

16. Quoted by Oberembt, 57.

17. Machatzke, *Kunst des Dramas*, 219.

18. See Martini, 90.

19. See Oberembt, 136–40.

20. Lilian R. Furst and Peter N. Skrine, *Naturalism* (London: Methuen, 1971), p. 16.

21. Quoted by Oberembt, 138.

22. Oberembt, 138.

23. See Carl F. W. Behl and Felix A. Voigt, *Chronik von Gerhart Hauptmanns Leben und Schaffen* (Munich: Bergstadtverlag, 1957), p. 41.

24. See Warren R. Maurer, *Gerhart Hauptmann* (Boston: Twayne, 1982), p. 72.

25. Quoted by Tschörtner, 284–85.

26. Tschörtner, 286.

27. See Herbert W. Reichert, "Hauptmann's Frau Wolff and Brecht's Mutter Courage," *German Quarterly* 34 (1961): 439–48.

# CHAPTER FOUR

# History—Folklore—Legend

*Florian Geyer*

Although often controversial, Hauptmann's dramas from *Before Sunrise* through *The Beaver Coat* were generally well received and seemed to indicate a close rapport between author and audience. *Florian Geyer. Die Tragödie des Bauernkrieges* (1896) (*Florian Geyer: The Tragedy of the Peasants' War*) was a dismal failure when it was first performed and provided its author with a humiliating lesson on the limitations of his popularity.

To the reader without an intimate knowledge of German history, the failure is not surprising. Hauptmann's intent is a tour de force application of the principles of Naturalism—especially as they relate to the accurate reproduction of realistic language—to an historical subject matter from the sixteenth century. In addition to immersing himself in the history of the period in question, as he had already done for his much more contemporaneous *The Weavers*, this meant the laborious acquisition of a virtually new language. And while one cannot help admiring the philological assiduity with which he plundered archaic folksongs, chronicles, and authors for suitable linguistic material,[1] one can also not help questioning the practicality of the approach. On the one hand the written sources (some from a century after the event) give a very inadequate idea of the language as it must have been spoken at the time; on the other, instead of making a difficult and complex material more accessible to the reader or theatergoer, the esoteric language imposes yet another burden upon an already sorely tried audience. In a play that demands emotional empathy for its success, an unintended estrangement is interposed between audience and performance. The overall impression is of a tableau of epic breadth (302 pages in the first edition) and dramatic laxity whose more than sixty-five speaking roles must tax the retentive powers of even the most dedicated viewer.

In general outline the drama follows historical events. It begins with a prologue that reviews the causes of the peasants' rebellion in 1525, especially their demands for a free choice of spiritual leader for each congregation, the removal of the tithing requirement, and the abolition of serfdom. The five-act drama follows the changing fortunes of the revolt when these claims are rejected out of hand by the nobility and is particularly concerned with the fate of its little–known leader, Florian Geyer. Hauptmann depicts Geyer in an ambiguous and therefore all the more human light. He is a knight who joins the peasants as a moderating force but without losing sight of the aims and ideals of his own class. He would restore the emperor's former powers, separate Church and State, and recapture the glory of knighthood as it flourished under Barbarossa. At the same time he stresses, "I am a peasant and nothing but a peasant!" (1:622). In a dispute with his much more celebrated contemporary Götz von Berlichingen, he calls for the destruction of the castles of the nobility, supports the taking of nine Franconian cities, and in the end, before he is killed by a soldier of their service, rejects a reconciliation with his noble compatriots.

The "black knight" Geyer is a patriotic idealist surrounded by individuals—peasants and nobles alike—who place their often petty personal concerns above the good of the nation. This central theme is most graphically depicted at the end of the first act when the hero, in his struggle with Götz for leadership, invites his followers to plunge their daggers into a chalk circle on the church door in Würzburg. Whereas most of them choose personal enemies for symbolic death, Geyer stabs the door with the most memorable line of the play: "Into the center of the heart of German discord!" (1:629).

It is this theme of petty discord, which Hauptmann raises to an almost archetypal flaw of German national character, that contributed to a short but intense revival of the drama between the world wars, when audiences were susceptible to perceived parallels with their own situation. During the First World War they had discovered that heroism and defeat need not exclude each other, and in the death of the besieged hero, who succumbed to a shot from ambush, many saw a parallel with their own situation: a nation with many victories on the battlefield, stabbed in the back by the terms of the Treaty of Versailles.

The Nazi era, with its own emphasis on a single strong leader, revived interest for a short time. In 1944 the 8th SS Cavalry Division was established under the name "Florian Geyer," and now, for the first time, the name insinuated itself into a wider German consciousness. After the war, of course, the Nazi interest became a source of embarrassment, and Brecht denigrated the drama as Hauptmann's "most fascistic"[2] work. Today it tends once more to be relegated to the category of historical interest—in all nuances of that designation.

## The Sunken Bell

In a bitter comment on the public failure of *Florian Geyer,* Hauptmann remarked, "German national sentiment is like a cracked bell. I struck it with my hammer but it didn't resound."[3] In an effort to "wipe out the Geyer disgrace,"[4] his next work, *Die versunkene Glocke. Ein deutsches Märchendrama* (1897) (*The Sunken Bell: A German Fairy Tale Drama*), was to be a radical new departure, which, while still retaining a few naturalistic touches, was more closely aligned with the latest literary trend in Germany: a transition from broad sociopolitical themes to a concern with the more intimately personal problems of the creative artist. One of the earliest examples of Neoromanticism, *The Sunken Bell* is a confessional verse drama in which, to a greater extent than in his earlier plays, Hauptmann bares his soul and gives a prominent role to eros.

Too sentimental, and overladen with a veritable fricassee of late nineteenth–century ideas and philosophical and literary allusions for today's audiences, *The Sunken Bell* nevertheless soon became an enormous international success—in spite of the added difficulty inherent in translating its often embarrassingly bad verse. As far away as in Japan phonograph records of songs attributed to the Nickelmann and Rautendelein characters were lucratively marketed,[5] and for many older Americans it remains the first play that comes to mind when Hauptmann is mentioned.

While the European premiere of the new play signaled a diminution of interest in Naturalism (although much of Hauptmann's best work was to continue, more or less, in that vein), America had not yet discovered a taste for the movement and, at any rate, preferred light entertainment and spectacle to sociopolitical and cultural edification. Performed more than twice as often as Hauptmann's other plays, it was sufficiently nebulous to permit a wide range of genteel speculation regarding its meaning, and the vestiges of Naturalism still remaining in the original virtually disappeared in translation. First produced in German by Heinrich Conried at his fine Irving Place Theatre in New York and on tour in 1897 and 1898, the English translation, by Charles Meltzer, attracted considerable attention in productions in such major American cities as Baltimore, Boston, Chicago, Milwaukee, Philadelphia, Pittsburgh, St. Louis, and Washington, where it was lauded by critics for its power and significance as serious drama; for a perceived kinship with Goethe and his *Faust;* and for its "charm," specifically the beauty of its poetry and its ineffable fairy–tale atmosphere. From an artistic standpoint, Conried's production, featuring a distinguished German cast headed by the legendary Agnes Sorma, appears to have been the most successful presentation of any of Hauptmann's works in America.[6] From the perspective of widespread popularity, however, credit is due to the more blatantly commercial E. H. Sothern-Julia Marlowe repertory company, which introduced the author to

Broadway and the above-mentioned cities during the 1889-90 and 1906-07 seasons. Although much of the attention was focused on the star (Marlowe) and spectacular stage effects (such as rising steam, colored lighting, and a green rubber mask for Nickelmann), with the play itself sometimes the object of critical abuse (it was called, for example, "a dreary, foggy, purile exposition of the discontent that is naturally sequent on an ill-assorted marriage"),[7] the overall reception was positive. Thus Henry Austin Clapp, the dean of Boston reviewers, directed his censure mainly against the inadequacies of unsophisticated American audiences, concluding that "the mental level of dramatic work [in the United States] is generally so low that a change of this sort has an ineffably tonic and soul-stirring value."[8] And Weisert, in his detailed discussion of the reception of the play in America, perhaps best summarized its importance in these words: "The fact remains that during the first decade of this century plays like *The Sunken Bell* could be put on in America with some hope of artistic and financial profit. Hauptmann's play did its share to bring about that situation."[9]

In addition to being a new artistic departure, *The Sunken Bell* is interesting as a rather transparent self-portrait of its author. In the character of bell founder Heinrich, Hauptmann expresses his own doubts as an artist (exacerbated by the failure of *Florian Geyer*), his domestic problems, and his hopes and spiritual aspirations. The decade of 1894 to 1904 was at once one of the most tumultuous and most productive of his long life. Hauptmann's roman à clef, *Buch der Leidenschaft* (1929) (Book of Passion), if read with the realization that it is a subjective account which tends to put the largely autobiographical hero (Titus) in a favorable light, is helpful as an outline and description of the author's emotional travails during this period. The problems began on the evening of November 14, 1893, during the German premiere of *Hannele* and a chance encounter with the aspiring young violinist and actress Margarethe Marschalk. Although he had known her casually since 1889, when she was only fourteen, he now fell passionately in love with her. A virtual antipode to his wife Marie, Margarethe was much younger, more cheerfully energetic, and something of a tomboy who shared not only her lover's cultural enthusiasms but also his interest in such outdoor sports as hiking, ice-skating, and skiing. When Marie found out about her rival, Hauptmann, who considered himself both reasonable and progressive in such matters, suggested a ménage à trois. As one might have expected from her conservative religious background, however, Marie would have none of this. As Käthe Vockerat had only threatened to do in *Lonely Lives* under similar circumstances, she packed up and fled with her three sons to America, going to the household of Alfred Ploetz, who had settled in Meriden, Connecticut. If the intent was to shock some sense into her wayward spouse, the plan seemed to work. After much tragicomic commotion, during which he even considered suicide, Hauptmann followed in hot pursuit on the steamer Elbe and was reunited with his family in early 1894. While in the United States he found time to work on *Der Mutter Fluch* (The Mother's Curse), a preliminary study for *The Sunken Bell*, and—by sheer coincidence—he became involved in the theater scandal over *Hannele*. He was present at the meeting at City Hall in New York to hear the mayor of that city condemn his work as offensive to "the decent sense of the community,"[10] and this, plus other sobering experiences during his stay, added a touch of ambiguity to the largely positive image of America he had had before the trip. In the novel *Atlantis* (1912), another roman à clef that rather impressively chronicles his stormy sea voyage to the United States (and attracted considerable attention at the time for the way in which it seemed to have anticipated the *Titanic* disaster), Hauptmann portrayed the darker side of "Americanism" (its puritan self-righteousness, cultural backwardness, and capitalistic excess) as he recalled it from his visit.

Shortly after the family's return to Europe Marie separated from her husband and moved with the children to Dresden. Hauptmann, maintaining two expensive households, began to travel openly with Margarethe. In 1900 she bore him a son, Benvenuto, and the next year they moved into a just completed mansion in Agnetendorf (Jagniątkóv in present day Poland). Hauptmann's divorce from Marie and marriage to Margarethe took place in 1904.

The decade had been a difficult one for Hauptmann in other respects also. His health continued to be a problem. The death of his father in 1898 was followed by that of his oldest brother, Georg, the next year; and the smoldering enmity of his brother Carl (which culminated in a spectacular row, reminiscent of the one in *The Coming of Peace*, during Christmas of 1897) became increasingly unbearable. A moderately successful and talented author in his own right, Carl had long been considered the most promising hope of the family. He found it difficult to adjust to the role of second fiddle and tended to see Gerhart's efforts at reconciliation as condescending. Perhaps the mood that Hauptmann found himself in during this most difficult of periods is that expressed by his alter ego, Titus, in *Das Buch der Leidenschaft* (The Book of Passion) when he remarks, "I can see that in my internal, as well as in my external, life I have lost the reins," (7:355) or again when he reverts to the image of the bell: "Nothing resounds in me any longer or, as much or as little, as with a bell that has cracks" (7:355).

This mood of personal and creative despair also permeates *The Sunken Bell*. It opens with a fairy–tale scene by a well and the introduction of the beautiful water sprite Rautendelein ("half child, half maiden: [1:761]); the merman Nickelmann (with the "brekekekex" trademark of Aristophanes' *Frogs*); and the jealous, malicious Waldschrat (an oversexed, pipe-smoking forest sprite—possibly an unflattering portrait of brother Carl).[11] The latter boasts of having broken Heinrich's wagon as he was hauling his finest bell to the top of a high mountain, where it was to be installed in a chapel. That the bell has fallen down into a lake Heinrich construes as a divine censure for his creative inadequacy. Wounded in the fall himself and despairing over an existence made onerous by his failure to achieve his artistic ideal, he confesses: "I am dying; that is good. God means well. . . . My work was bad; the bell . . . which fell down, was not made for the heights, to awaken the echo of the mountain peaks" (1:801). Roused from his depression by the enchanting Rautendelein, he leaves his wife Magda and their two sons to enter her magic realm and try again to create his perfect masterpiece. As a "pilgrim of the sun," (1:826) half mortal, half divine, he competes with the gods in fashioning a bell that will surpass all those of the mortal world. But this too comes to naught. Drawn back to the valley by his conscience, he is reviled by the doctrinaire Christians and learns that his long-suffering wife has died. Again he scales the heights, but the magic potion he drinks to regain Rautendelein and his superhuman creative prowess also brings death. His dying words—"the sun . . . the sun is coming!—The night is long" (1:869)—are paradigmatic for the ambiguity of the entire play.

*The Sunken Bell* is an early and extravagant example of Hauptmann's tendency toward a syncretism in which religious, philosophical, and literary ideas and reminiscences are mixed together in almost helter-skelter fashion. It has been linked to Arnold Böcklin's paintings; Goethe's *Faust* (the title character's first name is also Heinrich); the Grimms' fairy tales and Silesian folklore; Ibsen's *Peer Gynt, Brand, Lady from the Sea,* and the epic poem *On the Heights* (with which it shares a surprising number of significant themes and motifs); Friedrich Fouqué's *Undine;* Eduard Mörike's *Orplid;* Richard Wagner's *Nibelungen;* various works by Nietzsche with which Hauptmann was demonstrably familiar; the verse drama *Erlinde* by Goethe's grandson Wolfgang Maximilian von Goethe; ideas from the utopian philosopher Thomas Campanella; the Germanic *Edda;* and various other alleged sources.[12]

Not surprisingly, this potpourri of possible sources also would yield a multiplicity of themes. Although clothed in a fairy-tale atmosphere, replete with sprites, elves, and malicious dwarfs, *The Sunken Bell* is also a social drama, of a kind popular at the time, of a man caught between a demonic woman and a bourgeois woman. (One wonders about the state of mind of Marie and Margarethe as Hauptmann dictated different parts of the play to each of them in turn.)[13] It is furthermore both a religious drama and an exploration of the nature and significance of artistic creativity. As the former, it dwells on a problem to which Hauptmann returned again and again: the conflict between paganism (symbolized here by a veritable cult of the sun, but one also expressed in the author's personal life) and the inhibitions and limitations imposed on "natural man" by the strictures and inhibitions of an ascetic Christianity. Similarly, in its artisan bell founder Heinrich, the play raises questions about mere craftsmanship versus a higher art in which the artist must transcend formulae and rules and expose himself to vital, sensual, Dionysian forces if he hopes to succeed. Finally, it even suggests the bleaker Faustian question as to whether human beings can ever match their aspirations with the perfection required for their satisfaction. As the Wittichen character informs Heinrich in her brutally direct manner near the end of the play, "One can say this: You were a straight sprout, / strong, but not strong enough. You were called, / but a Chosen One you were not" (1:861).

## Henry of Aue

*Der arme Heinrich: Eine deutsche Sage* (1902) (*Henry of Aue: A German Legend*) can best be described as a dramatic poem in modern German and in symbolic form that portrays its author's recovery from a severe case of mid-life crisis; Hauptmann was forty years old when he completed it. The autobiographical problems are very similar to those that helped inspire *The Sunken Bell* (separation from his first wife, the failure of *Florian Geyer,* the death of his father and oldest brother, his own illness and depression), but the vehicle he chose for expressing them was a radically reworked version of a famous medieval epic, Hartmann von Aue's *Der arme Heinrich* (circa 1190). Considering the attendant circumstances, the choice is not surprising. Hauptmann's historical studies had enabled him to feel comfortable with the distant German past, and throughout the nineteenth century his work had received increasing attention. As a boy the author had been deeply moved by an early manifestation of this interest, Adalbert von Chamisso's popular ballad of 1839; and Henry W. Longfellow's treatment of *The Golden Legend* (1851), when it was translated into German, spawned a plethora of works on the theme.[14] And while it is probably ill-advised to relate Hauptmann's drama too directly to Longfellow (he later denied any knowledge of the American's work either in the original or in translation),[15] Longfellow's role in popularizing the material, and thus making it a tempting choice, cannot be completely ignored.

Hauptmann's plot describes the Job-like progression of a nobleman who, having led a rich and full life, is suddenly stricken by leprosy, depression, and metaphysical doubt. Unlike Hartmann's Heinrich, Hauptmann's hero fails to comprehend his affliction as punishment for a godless life and withdraws into a lonely cave with his sufferings. Eventually, during the course of four acts, his existence reaches such a nadir that, like Hartmann's protagonist, he is tempted by an extreme, pagan cure: the willing sacrifice of a young girl for her life-sustaining blood. Just as the knife is about to be plunged into the victim's pale, nude body, he has a change of heart and prevents the sacrifice, whereupon he is miraculously cured. Returning from Salerno, where the sacrifice was to have taken place, Heinrich marries his "little bride" Ottegebe, and the only agony she will henceforth endure is the "sweet death" (2:181) of his embrace.

Among the most important deviations from Hartmann are the personality of Ottegebe and the nature of Heinrich's religious crisis. In some respects Ottegebe is a Hannele rediviva. "An anemic child at the edge of puberty," (2:80) she is the illegitimate daughter of a penitent priest, and very early she has conceived an unhealthy infatuation for her father-figure Heinrich. Her motive in offering herself to be sacrificed has little in common with the caritas of her Hartmannian prototype but is compounded of inferiority feelings, a desire for sainthood, and eros. The catharsis that occurs in Salerno affects her as well as Heinrich; her love is exalted by the ordeal and she becomes a worthy partner to her spouse.

Heinrich also differs markedly from his earlier counterpart. Hartmann's hero is healed in accord with orthodox Christian belief for having recognized and repented his sin. Hauptmann confronts us with a more ambiguous situation. Here suffering is imposed upon an innocent man by an inscrutable God suspected of pursuing him for His own sadistic pleasure. Heinrich's recovery is just as inscrutable. Although he credits God with striking him with three "rays of Grace," (2:116) his enlightenment is also the result of an intense suffering that elevates him above the banalities of ordinary existence and makes him receptive to the recuperative powers of love. Metaphysics and psychology are inextricably conjoined, and this lessens the cogency of the criticism sometimes voiced that the psychological basis of Ottegebe's infatuation and the miracle ending of the play are not compatible.[16]

*Henry of Aue* signals a new artistic and personal conviction for Hauptmann: that the enjoyment of intense human love can have the force of redemption. He can finally exclaim with his hero, "I am free of the spell! / Let my falcons, my eagles, rise again!" (2:181).

## NOTES

1. See Hermann J. Weigand, "Auf den Spuren von Hauptmanns 'Florian Geyer," *PMLA* 52 (1942): 1160-95; and 53 (1943): 797-848.
2. Quoted by H. D. Tschörtner, *Ungeheures erhofft. Gerhart Hauptmann—Werk und Wirkung* (Berlin: Der Morgen, 1986), p. 281.
3. Carl F. W. Behl and Felix A. Voigt, *Chronik von Gerhart Hauptmanns Leben und Schaffen* (Munich: Bergstadtverlag, 1957), p. 42.
4. Bernhard Zeller, ed., *Gerhart Hauptmann. Leben und Werk: Eine Gedächtnisausstellung des Deutschen Literaturarchivs* (Stuttgart: Turmhaus-Druckerei, 1962), p. 108.
5. See Kurt Lothar Tank, *Gerhart Hauptmann in Selbstzeugnissen und Bilddokumenten* (Reinbeck b. Hamburg: Rowohlt, 1959), p. 47.
6. Cf. Walter A. Reichart, "Gerhart Hauptmann's Dramas on the American Stage," *Maske und Kothurn* 8 (1962): 226.
7. Quoted by Edith Cappel, "The Reception of Gerhart Hauptmann in the United States" (Ph.D. dissertation, Columbia University, 1953), p. 273.
8. Quoted by John Weisert, "Critical Reception of Gerhart Hauptmann's 'The Sunken Bell' on the American Stage," *Monatshefte* 43 (1951): 223.
9. Weisert, 234.
10. Quoted by Frederick W. J. Heuser, *Gerhart Hauptmann: Zu seinem Leben und Schaffen* (Tübingen: Niemeyer, 1961), p. 20.
11. See Jean Jofen, *Das letzte Geheimnis: Eine psychologische Studie über die Brüder Gerhart und Carl Hauptmann* (Bern: Francke, 1972), pp. 222-23.
12. For an extensive catalogue of these alleged sources see Warren R. Maurer, *Gerhart Hauptmann* (Boston: Twayne, 1982), p. 142; and Peter Sprengel, *Gerhart Hauptmann. Epoche–Werk–Wirkung* (Munich: Beck, 1984), p. 156.
13. See Tank, 32.
14. See Walter A. Reichart and Philip Diamond, "Die Entstehungsgeschichte des 'Armen Heinrich,'" *Gerhart Hauptmann Jahrbuch* 1 (1936): 84 n. 53.
15. Reichart and Diamond, 84.
16. See Sigfrid Hoefert, *Gerhart Hauptmann* (Tübingen: Metzler, 1974), p. 39.

# CHAPTER FIVE

# Suffering Artists

## Michael Kramer

Although its early reviews were mixed—some professional critics were disturbed by what they considered the undramatic nature of its last act— *Michael Kramer* (1900) was enthusiastically hailed by such future greats as Thomas Mann, Rainer Maria Rilke, James Joyce, and even Bertolt Brecht.[1] "How I loved that last act with Arnold Kramer's coffin in the glow of the candles, when death has transfigured and elevated that ugly man,"[2] Mann recalled later, and for Rilke the drama had the force of revelation. Writing in 1900 he commented, "In my opinion this *Michael Kramer* is the greatest [work] that Hauptmann has thus far achieved; a masterpiece that . . . one will perhaps only understand and cherish decades from now."[3] Shortly afterward he dedicated his own *Buch der Bilder* (1902) (*Book of Pictures*) to Hauptmann, explaining to him in a letter that his intention was "to somehow summarize my gratitude for *Michael Kramer* and in this way to conjoin with the best and the dearest that the last years have given me."[4] Joyce, a lifelong admirer of Hauptmann, translated the play into English in 1901 and, in so doing, all but memorized it. Its influence has been detected in "The Dead" (*Dubliners*), in *Ulysses*, in an essay on William Somerset Maugham read before the English Literary and Historical Society in February 1902, and in Joyce's concept of literary epiphanies.[5] In 1938, with the help of Ezra Pound, a mutual acquaintance, he managed finally to obtain an autographed copy of *Michael Kramer* that Hauptmann inscribed, "Never has this book had a better reader than James Joyce."[6]

In retrospect it is easy to speculate about what might have attracted these authors, each at the beginning of his career, to Hauptmann's work. The poignant struggle and failure of a talented young artist would, of course, have had some fascination for all of them, while individually they could also focus on aspects of the drama that they must have found especially congenial: Rilke, for example, on the expressed proximity of art and religion or on the description of the artist as obsessive craftsman; Mann on the problem of the artist in a bourgeois society; and Joyce on the conflicts of a young artist with his family, on Hauptmann's "epiphanies" as suggested by the dithyrambic monologues of Michael Kramer beside his son's bier, or on the sudden illumination hinted at by the Lachmann character when he remarks, "I'm not at all depressed. I've just glanced back again, and noticed that I'm actually not living at all anymore" (1:1153).

Except for the third act, which takes place in the rough environs of a restaurant frequented by a steady clientele of middle–class philistines, there is very little overt action in the play. Instead the audience is gradually but intimately exposed to the inner life of a handful of characters: the paterfamilias Michael Kramer, who is a painter and art teacher; his family; and several others who have, for one reason or another, been drawn into his circle. With the possible exception of the restaurant regulars, everyone is unhappy. The titular hero, like Dr. Fritz Scholz of *The Coming of Peace*, is married to a pedestrian, whining woman with little apparent understanding of his aspirations. He suffers from the knowledge that his talent is inadequate to the attainment of his exalted ideals, and the resultant dissatisfaction has poisoned the lives of Arnold and Michaline, his grown children. Of the two Michaline has suffered least because, since she is a woman, her father expects less from her and also perhaps because she is better able to transmute adversity into strength than her younger brother. She too is a painter and ekes out an existence by giving art lessons to other unfortunate young women while watching life pass her by. Instead of resisting her father she has submitted to his expectations and now finds herself a somewhat masculine young woman rapidly approaching spinsterhood who indulges only in such relatively decorous vices as smoking cigarettes. (Apparently named after her father, she is indeed her father's child.)

Although he appears relatively infrequently on stage, Arnold is the focus of the family's problems and of Hauptmann's attention. He is described as "an ugly person with black, fiery eyes behind eyeglasses, dark hair and traces of a sparse beard, with crooked, somewhat stooped posture. His facial complexion is dirty pale" (1:1123). This long-awaited son has been burdened with Michael's own unfulfilled ambitions since before his birth and was raised between an indulgent mother and a perfectionist father who still punished him physically when he was fifteen. Although the elder Kramer prefers to see in his son a rare artistic genius and is perpetually affronted by Arnold's stubborn refusal to apply his alleged God-given talent, the real nature of that talent is difficult to evaluate, given the father's exaggerated hopes and the son's refusal to exercise it—except as a weapon, in the form of caricatures, against his philistine tormentors. Instead of subscribing to his father's work ethic he idles away his days and spends his nights in pursuit of Liese Bänsch, a pretty but otherwise quite ordinary barmaid with whom he has become hopelessly infatuated. When his situation becomes unbearable and he pulls out a revolver to threaten his tormentors in the Bänsch restaurant, they disarm him, chase him into the street, and pursue him toward the river. By the next morning he has drowned himself, and the last act is largely given over to Michael Kramer's somber panegyric.

In addition to the Kramer family and Liese Bänsch, there is one other character who deserves special mention: Ernst Lachmann. He is an outsider of the type we are familiar with from Hauptmann's earlier works, but his function seems less that of a catalyst to the action than to provide Hauptmann with yet another voice with which to illuminate the problematic calling of art. A friend of the household and an admiring former student of Michael Kramer, he too is trapped in a mésalliance with a shallow wife. For him too life has not turned out as he had hoped. Unable to support his family with his painting, he has turned to hack writing to make ends meet. Now that it is too late, he appears to regret having missed the opportunity for a life with Michaline and, at one point, playfully but ruefully asks her to marry him.

Like *Colleague Crampton* and the later comedy *Peter Bräuer* (1921), *Michael Kramer* reflects Hauptmann's art school days at a time when he was unable to decide whether to devote himself to sculpture or to literature. The biographical correspondences between the characters and their real-life models have been too thoroughly documented elsewhere[7] to require extensive discussion here. It is enough to say therefore that Michael Kramer is a composite figure with traits borrowed from at least three people: Albrecht Bräuer, one of Hauptmann's art professors in Breslau, who, like his fictional counterpart, spent years working on an unfinished portrait of Christ; Gerhart's own fastidious and emotionally distant father; and, in some of his views, the author himself. Arnold Kramer is a veritable portrait of the artist as a young man, as Hauptmann remembered himself from the early eighties. Like Arnold he had considered himself physically unattractive and had suffered from low self-esteem, feelings of rejection, and thoughts of suicide. Like him also he had led a dissolute life on the verge of self-destruction while trying to persuade himself that he would take revenge on his tormentors and gain the love of a beautiful woman through the creation of masterpieces. Lachmann was inspired by an artist friend, Hugo Ernst Schmidt (to whose memory the drama is dedicated), while Arnold's mother and Michaline are reminiscent of the author's own mother and sister.

Of the three most prominent themes—the father-son conflict, the problematic nature of the artist in society, and the metaphysical confrontation with death—the first and least significant is familiar from *The Coming of Peace* and has been touched upon above. Its central message here seems to be that it is morally irresponsible and dangerous to burden one's progeny with one's own unfulfilled ambitions.

More important is the preoccupation with art in *Michael Kramer*. Rather typically it is the plastic arts (here painting) rather than literature which attract Hauptmann as a vehicle for his thoughts and ruminations in this area. Not only had his art school days provided him with a lively milieu and interesting characters, but they had also presented him with a dilemma—the painful choice between literature and art as a profession—which he never completely overcame. In a revealing, if hardly modest, remark he once confessed, "I feel that, as a sculptor, I would have achieved Rodin's greatness," and then, with a touch of regret, admonished himself, "Transfer your greater gift (sculpture) to your lesser one: the art of words."[8] Rilke, appreciative of Hauptmann's plight, consoled him with an argument he must have relished. In a 1903 letter he assured him that *"only* plastic art exists and he who possesses his art completely possesses art in its *entirety*. Nothing, dear Gerhart Hauptmann, has 'atrophied' in you—you are a sculptor. . . . The tool you abandoned as a youth isn't rusting. Chisel and mallet and pure stone still exist deep within you. And everything lives and enters willingly into the form that you later prepared for yourself."[9]

In addition to the plastic arts, Hauptmann also had a life-long attraction to music. Just as the music of Mozart and Wagner left its indelible mark on Hermann Hesse and Thomas Mann respectively, Hauptmann (as in his remarks on *The Coming of Peace*) saw an affinity between his work and that of Beethoven. Not only does Beethoven's death mask serve as a kind of tangible leitmotif in *Michael Kramer*—reaching its apotheosis in the final lines when, Hamlet-like, Michael Kramer holds it in his hand and muses on the conundrum of human existence—but critics have frequently found themselves reverting to musical imagery in an effort to express the essence of the play. Thus Wolfgang Witkowski describes the work as "a tragic symphony, a music heavy with fate," and Karl S. Guthke speaks of the "oratorio-like requiem" of its ending.[10]

Whether we resort to the use of such terms as classic and romantic, Apollonian and Dionysian, bourgeois and bohemian, or even Schiller's naive and sentimental to describe them, it is clear that Michael Kramer and his son represent two very different types of artists manqué. Recognizing his own lack of genius, Michael Kramer subscribes to a personal philosophy of dogged persistence, sacrifice, and suffering in the hope that these will suffice for the creation of one great masterpiece. For him, indeed, "art is religion," (1:1135) and the fact that he has chosen Beethoven as his patron saint and a portrait of Christ for his magnum opus is consistent with his outlook. His tragedy lies in the disproportion between his intention and the ability to realize it and, worse still, the painful awareness of this disproportion. Arnold's situation is different. He is the embodiment of that belief, especially prevalent around the turn of the century, that artistic talent is accompanied by neurosis and abnormality, combined with the familiar notion, as old as Goethe's Werther, that it is tragic to possess great artistic sensibility without the conviction or stamina to express it adequately in liberating, creative work. The ideal, of course, would be a combination of the two types of artists, but even Michael Kramer finally seems to sense that that combination is exceedingly rare and that life, love, and a tolerance for otherness must, in the final analysis, take precedence over even the greatest art.

Another aspect of the "artist problem" that *Michael Kramer* has in common with the work of some of the contemporaries of Hauptmann is that of the love-hate relationship between artist and bourgeoisie, the artist as outsider attracted to the "normalcy" of the bourgeois world but unable to find happiness in it. Of the three principal male characters, Michael Kramer and Lachmann have already married bourgeois women with no understanding for their aspirations, while Arnold, in his infatuation for Liese Bänsch, seems bent on making the same mistake. This artist/bourgeois dichotomy has come to be identified with Thomas Mann's *Tonio Kröger* perhaps more strongly than with any other work, and, in spite of differences in temperament, Arnold Kramer has much in common with Mann's hero. In *Tonio Kröger* the split is between the healthy, blond, blue-eyed innocents Hans Hansen and Ingeborg Holm, whom Tonio loves with intense, unrequited passion, and the clumsy, unattractive, but sensitive Magdalena Vermehren, who, to his dismay, is attracted to him. In *Michael Kramer* the equivalents for Arnold are the pretty, empty-headed Liese on the one hand and, on the other, the poor, "somewhat deformed" (1:1164) girl he had never paid attention to, who had taken up painting because of him and who expressed her secret love through an expensive floral arrangement for his funeral. Even the names Tonio Kröger and Arnold Kramer would seem to symbolize the dilemma of their bearers as they are torn between art and life. Both Kröger and Kramer are common, unpretentious names, derived from occupations and easily associated with middle-class virtues, while the names Tonio and Arnold both express an artistic component: Tonio because it is an exotic, southern name inflicted on the north German character by his artistically inclined mother, and Arnold because it appears to have been chosen in homage to the enormously respected nineteenth–century painter Arnold Böcklin, idolized by Arnold's father.[11]

While we may tend to categorize *Michael Kramer* as an artist drama, Hauptmann and his admirers would hardly have been satisfied with such a limited appreciation. The last act, which is largely devoted to a preoccupation with death, made an exceptionally strong impression on contemporaries, and there is considerable evidence that the inspiration for the play came from Hauptmann's intimate personal experience with this subject. At 9:00 AM on August 20, 1898, he had recorded his thoughts while sitting beside the bed of his dying father: "Life contains everything, including death, but death is the mildest form of life. When, on the eighteenth of August, between six and seven o'clock, father suffered a severe attack of cardiac asthma, I longed for him to attain this mildest form of life. From now on, as long as the light of my intelligence still glimmers, I shall no longer be able to fall victim to an error concerning the nature of death. There is nothing that is slandered worse than death—unless it be life!"[12] Anyone familiar with *Michael Kramer* will immediately recognize the close proximity of these thoughts to those expressed by the elder Kramer and notice the verbatim anticipation of the work's most memorable line: "Death is the mildest form of life" (1:1172). As Kramer explains, "death . . . points out into the sublime. You see, one is bent down. But that which condescends to bend us down is, at the same time, splendid and monstrous. We feel that then, we almost see it, and listen: then one becomes—great; through suffering" (1:1168-69). Here we have Hauptmann's philosophy of suffering and redemption in its most concise and explicit form.

## Gabriel Schilling's Flight

Almost from the time he wrote it, Hauptmann displayed a certain reticence about exposing *Gabriel Schillings Flucht* (1906) (*Gabriel Schilling's Flight*) to a wider public. Aware of the intimate nature of the work, he was reluctant to "place it on the roulette table of a premiere" (2:404) and did not bother publishing it until 1912. With the exception of its wonderfully evoked seascapes, time has not been kind to this drama, and it contains melodramatic scenes likely to provoke patronizing smiles from a modern audience.

Like *The Coming of Peace, Lonely Lives, The Sunken Bell,* and *Michael Kramer,* with which it has much in common, *Gabriel Schilling's Flight* is a variation on that popular fin de siècle theme of art versus life, replete with the familiar corollary that art and sickness go hand in hand. Schilling, a painter, has been all but incapacitated by his entanglement between two women: a whining, pedestrian wife, Eveline; and a more demonic, vampiric Slavic mistress, Hanna Elias. His only artistic accomplishment in recent years is the saccharine portrait of the sickly child alleged to be his son by Hanna, and he has taken refuge on a tiny island in the Baltic sea. Having finally distanced himself from the two women, he hopes that the glorious ocean atmosphere and uncomplicated friendship of Ottfried Mäurer, a sculptor who promises to take him on a trip to Greece the following year, will regenerate both his health and his creativity. Unfortunately, Anna has discovered his whereabouts and followed him to the island. With her all his old doubts and troubles return, and he suffers an attack of an unidentified but serious malady. When his physician also summons Eveline to her husband's side, the resultant strife between the rival women is too much for poor Schilling and he undertakes his last flight: into the depths of the sea.

A contrasting plot strand involves the portrayal of the "healthy" artist, Mäurer, who has the strength (or brutality) to keep his personal and artistic lives scrupulously separated. Like Schilling, he finds himself between two females—an exuberant young girl with the appropriate name Lucie Heil (*Heil* = healthy, sound) and Hanna's teenage Russian companion, Fräulein Majakin. In contrast to Schilling, however, he avoids marriage as a matter of principle and concentrates on the sensual aspects of his relationships. Lucie sums up his attitude toward women and art succinctly when she informs her rival, "Don't think that Mäurer is a man like Schilling! Mäurer takes—one, two, three—what he wants and then goes and makes his statues. Beyond that he has no scruples" (2:466).

The autobiographical aspects of *Gabriel Schilling's Flight* can be quickly summarized. Hauptmann's fascination with the problem of a man between two women is no longer a novelty, and, in spite of the fact that the male protagonists were apparently modeled after real artists (Schilling after Hugo Ernst Schmidt and Mäurer after Max Klinger)[13] we can safely assume that they also served as repositories for Hauptmann's own ideas, feelings, and desires. Beyond this is the fact that the play is also a celebration of the author's beloved island of Hiddensee, to which he kept returning over a period of some sixty years and on which he was buried in 1946.

It is Hauptmann's fascination with the sea, nourished by his productive vacations to Hiddensee and several difficult ocean voyages, that provides a welcome counterpoint to Schilling's maudlin problems. The omnipresent sea is both setting and all-pervasive symbol. Its immensity and "magic brightness" (2:465) keep human events in perspective. Even the matter-of-fact Mäurer is overcome in its presence with the feeling "that behind this visible world another is hidden" (2:440).

For Schilling the sea assumes a mythic significance superior even to his attraction for Greece as a spiritual home, and his flight to the demonic solace of its waters is foreshadowed throughout the play. "We come from there, there we belong," he tells Mäurer, who replies humorously, "water thou art, and water thou shall become!" (2:418). He dreams that his soul has entered an eel, admires the island for its beauty as a last resting place, and has a vision of his own funeral procession. The most ambitious symbol, however, is a painted ship's figurehead that has washed ashore from the wreck of a Danish ship which went down with all hands aboard. In this strangely attractive female figure Hauptmann tried to embody the main elements of his drama: art; the invisible world of the dead, which sends out emissaries to the living; and the destructive force of passion—the strong resemblance between the somnambulistic wooden mermaid and Hanna Elias, who wears poppies in her raven hair, is hardly accidental.

Brought together in this way, the elements of *Gabriel Schilling's Flight* represent a virtual embodiment of the zeitgeist around the turn of the century. Art, love, and death are the special preoccupation of Neoromantic literature; water, marine imagery, polychromatic sculpture, and faintly decadent mermaids the recurring motifs of *l'art nouveau*.

## NOTES

1. See H. D. Tschörtner, *Ungeheures erhofft. Gerhart Hauptmann—Werk und Wirkung* (Berlin: Der Morgen, 1986), p. 280.

2. See Bernhard Zeller, ed., *Gerhart Hauptmann. Leben und Werk: Eine Gedächtnisausstellung des Deutschen Literaturarchivs* (Stuttgart: Turmhaus-Druckerei, 1962), p. 129.

3. Quoted by Helmut F. Pfanner, "Deutungsprobleme in Gerhart Hauptmann's 'Michael Kramer,'" *Monatshefte* 62 (1970): 53.

4. See Zeller, 130, and Carl F. W. Behl and Felix A. Voigt, *Chronik von Gerhart Hauptmanns Leben und Schaffen* (Munich: Bergstadtverlag, 1957), p. 51.

5. See Hugo Schmidt, "Hauptmann's *Michael Kramer* and Joyce's *The Dead*," *PMLA* 80 (1965): 141–42.

6. Schmidt, 141.

7. For autobiographical details see Charles R. Bachmann, "Life into Art: Gerhart Hauptmann and *Michael Kramer*," *German Quarterly* 42 (1969): esp. 386-89.

8. Quoted by Peter Sprengel, *Die Wirklichkeit der Mythen: Untersuchungen zum Werk Gerhart Hauptmann* (Berlin: E. Schmidt, 1982), p. 62.

9. Sprengel, 62.

10. Zeller, 132; and Karl S. Guthke, *Gerhart Hauptmann: Weltbild im Werk* (Munich: Francke, 1980), p. 102. See also Philip Mellen, "The Beethoven Death Mask in Gerhart Hauptmann's *Michael Kramer*," *Germanic Notes* 14 (1983): 18–20.

11. See also Warren R. Maurer, "Gerhart Hauptmann's Character Names," *German Quarterly* 52 (1979): 467.

12. Quoted by Philip Mellen in "A Source of Hauptmann's Michael Kramer," *Germanic Notes* 17 (1986): 35.

13. See Behl and Voigt, *Chronik*, 58, and Eberhard Hilscher, *Gerhart Hauptmann. Leben und Werk* (Frankfurt/M.: Athenäum, 1988), p. 251.

# CHAPTER SIX

# Variations on Motherhood

## *Drayman Henschel*

When *Fuhrmann Henschel* (*Drayman Henschel*) premiered in 1898, even Hauptmann's friend the director Otto Brahm had trouble understanding the heavy dialect in which it was written and prevailed upon the author to provide a version more easily understandable by non-Silesians.[1] It was this (some would say inferior) revised version that introduced a series of realistic dramas that show Hauptmann at the height of his abilities and have come to be considered by many of his admirers as typical of his very finest work.

Henschel, the title character, is introduced in the first act. He is a large, amiable, physically robust forty-five-year-old who, by dint of honest hard work and self-reliance, has developed a successful transport business that he runs from his home in the basement of the Gray Swan spa hotel. Gradually, but with increasing momentum, his fortunes are reversed in a Job-like decline. By the beginning of the second act his sickly wife has died, but not before extracting from Henschel the seemingly innocuous promise that he will not marry their much younger housemaid, Hanne Schäl. The promise turns out to be harder to keep than Henschel had imagined. He needs someone to care for his daughter Gustel while he is on the road, and, although it is mostly suggested by subtle touches, the sexual aura exuded by Hanne proves difficult to resist. Hanne is a selfish young woman with promiscuous instincts and a disreputable past; although she foolishly insists on denying the fact (which everyone knows anyway), she has a six-year-old illegitimate daughter whom she has callously left in the hands of her drunken father in a nearby village. And, while she succeeds in persuading Henschel to marry her, the respectability that she hoped to acquire is soon compromised by her inability to resist her baser instincts. Among her other transgressions (for example, she is responsible for the dismissal and sad decline of Hauffe, Henschel's long-time faithful employee, and is suspected of contributing to the death of little Gustel by her neglect), she blatantly deceives her husband with the rascally waiter George. When Henschel finally discovers what everyone around him already knows, it is a final blow to his ego and self-respect. Suffering insomnia and pursued by the apparition of his first wife, he accepts the consequences of having broken his promise and kills himself.

Such a bare-bones outline of the main plot of *Henschel* glosses over the psychological nuances of the main characters; ignores some of the lesser, equally well conceived ones entirely; and suggests a melodramatic element that, if it exists at all, is so skillfully modulated as to go unnoticed when the drama is well performed. Again the key to Hauptmann's success, aside from his unique and by now sovereign control of his talent, lies in his empathy with the human condition and in his sensitivity to historical, regional, and social circumstances. Set in the 1870s the play is saturated with personal childhood reminiscences. The Gray Swan is an easily recognizable stand-in for the Prussian Crown Hotel operated by Hauptmann's father. Its ground floor, containing the Henschel home and the not very respectable tavern of the has-been actor Wermelskirch and his family, correspond respectively to the peasant quarters of drayman Krause's household in which Hauptmann had felt so pleasantly at home as a child and to a similar drinking establishment also leased by an ex-actor. Even some of the events depicted in the play derive from real life. Siebenhaar, the ineffectual owner of the hotel who loses it to creditors, resembles Robert Hauptmann in such externals as his fastidious grooming and the nickel-plated rims of the glasses he wears. (The name Siebenhaar [seven-hair] seems to be a blatant allusion to the elder Hauptmann's baldness.) Like Siebenhaar, Robert also lost his hotel to creditors in 1877 and was reduced to running the train station refreshment room in Sorgau. Another, more central, strand of the action apparently derived from stories about Hauptmann's grandfather's marriage to a younger housemaid who, like Hanne Schäl, mistreated her own illegitimate child.[2]

At first glance *Drayman Henschel* may appear to be little more than a conventional social drama. Among its more obvious themes is that of the Ibsenian "marriage lie" combined with the prejudicial notion, popularized by Strindberg and others, of the erotically destructive female and featuring such recurring Hauptmannian preoccupations as that of the weak man between two women and the victimization of children used and abused as pawns in such conflicts. A comment by Thomas Mann to the effect that the drama is an "Attic tragedy in contemporary, realistic form,"[3] however, suggests overtones of grandeur and metaphysical profundity not usually associated with the pragmatic depiction of socioeconomic problems. Especially toward the end, the play takes on the character of a fate tragedy in which the almost casual misstep of a hero is inexorably punished. Being a simple, superstitious man, Henschel perceives fate in terms of omens and apparitions. Brought low by suffering, he acknowledges: "Indeed I'm guilty of everything; I know I'm guilty" (1:993). But, in his view, fate had singled him out even before the death of his wife and his calamitous second marriage. Simple events—a fine walking stick broken accidentally; an accident in which he ran over and killed his favorite dog with his freight wagon; the death in rapid succession of his best horses—he now sees as portents, and concludes: "But no, a snare was set for me, and I just stepped into that snare" (1:993). When asked by Siebenhaar who it was who set the snare for him he replies cryptically: "Maybe the devil, maybe another. I've got to strangle, that's for sure" (1:993). If we should speculate as to who is meant by this mysterious "other," we might certainly consider God a prime suspect. The idea of a malicious, sadistic God was hardly foreign to Hauptmann, although some of his Friedrichshagen acquaintances (Stanislaw Przybyszewski, for example) were more strongly attracted to an overt satanism than he seems to have been.

Tormented by the apparition of his dead wife and thoroughly initiated into the "metaphysics of suffering"[4] involving a guilt that is more existential than personal, Henschel accepts the sentence fate has dealt him. He walks calmly into the next room—and is found dead there a short time later by Hanne.

### Rose Bernd

For German actresses the title role of *Rose Bernd* (1903) has been much coveted, and the play itself is consistently ranked among Hauptmann's best by both popular critics and literary scholars. Like *Drayman Henschel* it is a tragedy of unbridled eros. In contrast to Hanne Schäl, however, the robust young peasant woman Rose Bernd is the victim of the pungent sexuality she exudes and of the men she attracts.

The five-act play opens on a sunny Sunday morning in May, during the course of which Hauptmann, with skilled dramatic economy, introduces the main constellation of characters and sets the action moving inexorably towards tragedy. Rose and her married lover, the prosperous landowner Flamm, appear flushed and disheveled from an assignation in the bushes beside a country lane. From their behavior it is obvious that there is genuine affection between them, but the situation is complicated by class difference and (much as in *Henschel*) by the fact that Flamm's wife is an invalid who—although wiser and morally superior to her husband—cannot satisfy his sexual desires. Because Rose has been persuaded by her pious, widowed father to marry the sickly and unprepossessing bookbinder Keil (a Pietist who appears to cling to religion in compensation for his worldly shortcomings), she must break off her relationship with Flamm, who is very reluctant to let her go. Unfortunately the final tryst had a secret witness: Arthur Streckmann, a married, "brutally handsome" steam engine operator who roams the countryside helping the estate owners with their thrashing while seducing their female help. Streckmann, who has had his eye on Rose for some time, exploits the opportunity to blackmail her. Threatening to dishonor her before her father, her betrothed, and the community by exposing her relationship to Flamm, he forces himself upon her. On a hot August afternoon, in the presence of farm workers and Keil and Rose's father, who are busy haying, the situation comes to a head. Streckmann, who has been drinking, is drawn into making derogatory remarks which Keil sees as impugning the honor of his bride-to-be. Drawn into a fight with his much stronger rival, Keil loses his left eye. Bernd, unaware that his daughter is pregnant with Flamm's child, insists on restitution for his future son-in-law and takes the matter to court. During the proceedings that evolve, Rose—out of a deep sense of shame—denies having had a relationship with either Flamm or Streckmann, in spite of the fact that both have made sworn statements to the contrary. Flamm, having misconstrued Rose's relationship to Streckmann, now turns against her, and only his crippled wife understands her situation and promises to stand by her and care for her child when it is born. By the last act, which is set in the austere Bernd household, Rose's mental state has deteriorated. Keil, mellowed by his own suffering, recognizes the true state of affairs but nobly offers to take Rose and her infant away with him to a different part of the country where they can begin a new life. But Bernd, not as perceptive as Keil and worried that his position as a church elder may be jeopardized, insists on a continued legal battle to clear his daughter's name. Only when Keil explains the situation does he break down. But it is too late. Rose comes out of her room and confesses to a policeman who has come to serve her a further summons, "I have strangled my child with my hands!!" (2:258). The policeman rejects the confession as distraught fantasy, but Keil realizes that it is true and the play ends with his words: "The girl . . . how she must have suffered!" (2:259).

*Rose Bernd* reflects a complex congruence of Hauptmann's personal and literary experiences. To begin with, there were the repercussions of his continuing marriage crisis. (Divorce proceedings were initiated during the writing of the play.) Like Flamm he had found himself torn between a sickly wife and a much younger mistress with whom he had an illegitimate child, this at a time when the stigma resulting from such behavior was still strong. Having recently moved to the Villa Wiesenstein near Agnetendorf in Silesia, he was also making a conscious—and, in retrospect successful—effort to incorporate the language of the area, its character types, and the beauty of its distinctive atmosphere and landscape in his new work. Memories of his experiences as an agricultural apprentice with his aunt and uncle Schubert contributed not only to a realistic portrayal of local religious customs and attitudes of his characters but also to the depiction of the gradual incursion of technology into rural Silesian communities. (Uncle Schubert, like Streckmann, had owned a steam engine with which he roamed the countryside contracting threshing jobs on agricultural estates.) Finally, and most directly related to *Rose Bernd,* in April of 1903 Hauptmann served as a juror in nearby Hirschberg in the trial of a female agricultural worker accused of infanticide. Although he succeeded in moving his fellow jurors to an acquittal, the public prosecutor's office rejected his "poetic approach" and retried the case later without him. Significantly, by the second day of his jury duty, he was already at work on the drama.[5]

While the direct impetus for writing *Rose Bernd* was personal, the drama also reveals numerous literary influences. Most significantly it represents a late stage of two literary traditions that had flourished in German literature since the eighteenth century and had always shown a natural tendency to merge: middle-class tragedy (*bürgerliches Trauerspiel*) and plays dealing with women who, because of inhumane laws and the intense social and religious stigma of illegitimacy, are driven to infanticide (*Kindesmörderinnen*). Landmark examples of the former are Lessing's *Emilia Galotti,* Schiller's *Kabale und Liebe* (*Love and Intrigue*), and Friedrich Hebbel's *Maria Magdalena*. These middle-class tragedies usually feature a seducer figure who, like Flamm, is from a superior social class and is motivated by sexual egotism. A further constant is the strongly patriarchal father of the victim, the embodiment of an obtuse and stubborn self-righteousness, who places greater emphasis on religious precepts and family honor than on simple humanity. One of the best examples is Hebbel's Master Anton, whose "morality" drives his daughter to suicide and (because she is pregnant) simultaneous infanticide. While Rose's father is a weaker and more confused example of the type, he is nonetheless a direct descendent of the Hebbel character. Notable precursors to *Rose Bernd* that stress more strongly the infanticide theme are Heinrich Leopold Wagner's Storm and Stress drama *Die Kindesmörderin* (The Infanticide) and Goethe's *Urfaust* and *Faust I*.

Like *Michael Kramer, Rose Bernd* is, among other things, a psychological tragedy of failed communication. Just as Arnold Kramer was incapable of confiding in his father, Rose, even in the decisive scene in which Mrs. Flamm makes every effort to help her, chooses denial over candor and, later in court, finds it easier to commit perjury than to confess the truth. Because each of the characters is conditioned to see reality from a different perspective, each is isolated from the others, and language assumes the role of gesture, largely impotent as a tool of direct communication but significant in revealing the psychology of the speaker. For example, the fact that Mrs. Flamm's speech is more strongly tinged with the local dialect than that of her husband gives it a sense of warmth and naturalness that contrasts sharply with his posturings and his habitual recourse to hunting imagery in expressing himself. Similarly, Keil's hesitant, inhibited language implies an honesty and sincerity of intention completely lacking in the devious, cynical, and threateningly allusive speech of Streckmann. This virtuosity in the use of linguistic nuance as characterization is especially evident in the figure of Rose. From the candor of her speech in the opening scene to the stammerings that reflect her growing torment and estrangement from reality as the play progress, we can trace the fever chart of the tragedy as it unfolds.[6]

As one critic has noted, "the actual details of the plot [of *Rose Bernd*] are exceedingly complex, because much remains unspoken, and misunderstood by the various characters."[7] For the same reason, what a particular reader or audience makes of the drama depends in part on the perspective from which it is approached. The consensus of recent criticism is that it is *not* primarily a social drama—the class differences here are neither the main motivating force of the tragedy nor are they so great as to preclude compromise. Instead, as in *Henschel*, Hauptmann focuses attention on a "natural" individual, one whose emotions and reactions are undiluted by an excess of civilization and who, for this reason, can serve more easily as a quintessential everyman. This archetypal aspect of the drama is enhanced by recourse to a few elemental symbols including, most prominently, those of hunter and hunted, nature and technology, and the progression of the seasons. The earliest note by Hauptmann relating to the drama refers to a "maid being hunted by master and inspector,"[8] and the opening scene firmly establishes Flamm as one of the hunters. In order to disguise his meeting with Rose, he has pretended to be out hunting, and now, his conquest accomplished, he cheerfully bursts forth with an erotically tinged hunting song. (Freudians take note: during the sex act his gun is concealed in a hollow cherry tree!) A much more brutal hunter is Streckmann—as implied by his name (*zur Strecke bringen* means "to hunt down, to bag").[9] That Rose sees herself as a hunted prey is expressed most directly when she complains bitterly to her father and Keil: " . . . they stuck to me like burrs . . . I couldn't cross the street! . . . all the men were after me! . . . I hid myself . . . I was afraid! I had such a fear of men! . . . it made no difference, it got worse and worse! Afterwards I stepped from snare to snare so that I no longer came to my senses" (2:256).

This theme of the unequal battle of the sexes is further intensified by the opposition between a destructive, powerful male technology (gun, steam engine) identified with Flamm and Streckmann, and nature (fecund landscape, pregnancy), Rose's natural domain. (Again the name Rose is revealing; an earlier version of the play includes her surname, Immoos [in the moss]). Judging from the play's early, tentative title, *Saat und Ernte* (Sowing and Harvest), it appears plausible that Hauptmann also intended to associate Rose's fate with the vegetation cycle of spring, summer, and fall, during which the action progresses. Whether or not we wish to go so far as Sprengel, who sees in Rose a "Silesian Demeter,"[10] Hauptmann's propensity for stressing the timeless universality of his themes (often within a modern, realistic context) seems by now firmly established.

In this drama as in earlier ones, the ambiguous ending has led to critical disagreement as to the extent of its alleged metaphysical tendency. Schrimpf and Sprengel see in it a variation of the theme of "learning through suffering" (5:177) or the "clairvoyance of pain" (6:813) expressed more explicitly in *Henschel* and *Kramer*.[11] Guthke sees a nihilistic tendency. "What is lacking," according to him, "is the abrupt transformation of earthly suffering into the mystical experience of proximity of God,"[12] more characteristic for Hauptmann. Osborne, finally, in what is definitely a minority opinion, warns against over-stressing the metaphysical aspects of the play, such as nihilism and fate, in general, arguing that "there is . . . little *positive* evidence . . . to support such interpretations."[13] Perhaps Alfred Kerr characterized the action and mood of *Rose Bernd* most memorably and succinctly when he wrote shortly after its appearance, "A song is its beginning; its conclusion a scream."[14]

## The Rats

"Perhaps *Die Ratten* (*The Rats*) simply represents Gerhart Hauptmann's most important contribution to modern world theater."[15] Although it would be difficult to dispute this estimation of Hauptmann's "Berlin Tragicomedy" (which premiered in 1911) by the distinguished German scholar Hans Mayer, it is not an opinion arrived at overnight. For many years Hauptmann's artistic intentions for the drama were misunderstood by both popular and academic critics. The initial response was to see in it little more than a reversion to a superseded form of naturalistic exposé while complaining about alleged psychological improbabilities, an excess of heterogeneous detail, and a clash of content and form. In retrospect and in the context of subsequent twentieth-century literary developments, it is now clear that the play was not behind but ahead of its time. Expressionism, the work of authors like Frank Wedekind and Kafka, the epic theater and alienation effects of Brecht, a modern propensity (as in Friedrich Dürrenmatt's work) for revealing tragedy through the grotesque, the collage technique of combining nondramatic forms such as the ballad or detective story with traditional dramatic ones, a saturation in Freud, and an image of "Sodom Berlin" as it became more widespread *after* 1911— all this and more had to find its place in the public consciousness before a deeper appreciation could prevail.

*The Rats,* Hauptmann's most successful tragicomedy and one of the most highly regarded tragicomedies in all of German literature, can be more easily approached through its characters than through its convoluted plot. To begin with, one might make the claim that the setting for the entire drama—different floors of a tenement building converted from a former cavalry barracks—is itself a significant protagonist. It teems with life: human beings of the most varied economic, moral, and social condition; rats and vermin (literal and figurative), and even ectoplasm—the ghost of a soldier named Sorgenfrei (carefree) who hanged himself in the attic when the building still served a military purpose. Based on the floors occupied by its various tenants from top to bottom, the claim has been made that the building recapitulates the prevailing social structure or even the Freudian schema of superego, ego, and id.[16]

Commenting shortly after it was written, Hauptmann himself claimed that "the idea of the drama consisted of the contrast between two worlds and had these two worlds as its starting point" (11:809). This remark suggests the advisability of separating the rather extensive dramatis personae into two main constellations. The first is made up of the near-proletarian, proletarian, or lumpenproletarian characters surrounding Mrs. John, including her husband, who is a foreman bricklayer [*Maurerpolierer*]; her younger, criminally inclined brother Bruno Mechelke; the drug addict and prostitute Sidonie Knobbe and her daughter Selma; the Polish servant girl Pauline Piperkarcka; and the house manager Quaquaro. The second constellation of characters is from the bourgeois world of the former director Harro Hassenreuter, who is temporarily reduced to eking out a living by renting theatrical costumes and props from the storage room in the attic. These characters include his daughter Walburga; Erich Spitta, a theology student and would-be actor in love with her; the pastor Spitta, the young man's father; and Alice Rütterbusch, an ingenue actress erotically involved with the considerably older Hassenreuter, her former director.

The John strand of the action derives from a basic human theme: thwarted motherhood. Like Mrs. Wolff (*The Beaver Coat*) and Mrs. Flamm (*Rose Bernd*), Mrs. John has lost an infant child, but, for social and economic reasons, it is harder for her to accept the loss. Because her husband cannot find employment in Berlin, he is forced to live and work in distant cities for months at a time. The separation, with its constant temptations of the flesh for her spouse, exacerbates Mrs. John's feelings of inadequacy as a wife. A strong-willed, enterprising woman, she exploits her husband's absence to deceive him. Knowing how much a son would mean to him, and hoping to strengthen her marriage, she persuades Pauline Piperkarcka, who is unmarried, pregnant, and desperate, to sell her her child. The birth takes place secretly amid the theatrical paraphernalia of Hassenreuter's attic, and for a short time the plan seems to succeed. Ecstatic over his unexpected "fatherhood," John even makes plans to move his little family out of Berlin and closer to his work so that he can spend more time at home. The euphoria is short-lived. The initial despair of illegitimacy behind her, Pauline decides that she wants her child back and, worse still, has reported his birth to the authorities. From this point on Mrs. John is driven to ever more desperate measures to maintain the fiction she has created and to keep the "son" to whom she has become so passionately attached that she keeps confusing him with her dead child. Predictably, given the extralegal nature of the "adoption," her frantic efforts only lead her into ever greater guilt. For a short time she confuses the biological mother and the authorities by foisting off on them as Pauline's the dying child of the prostitute Sidonie Knobbe; but when she asks her uncannily feral brother Bruno to threaten Pauline, he does his work all too well, killing her instead. Her deception exposed (Selma Knobbe has blurted out the remaining details), Mrs. John is utterly humiliated and reviled even by her husband. When the authorities arrive to take away "her" child to an orphanage, she dashes out into the street and dies under the wheels of a horse-drawn omnibus.

Counterpointing the John tragedy is the lighter, more humorous Hassenreuter strand of the action. Harro Hassenreuter, the ex-actor and director who prides himself on his perspicacity, is actually blind to what is happening under his nose: in the John household, in his own family, in the policies of his government, and in his profession. An actor who has played so many roles that any real-life authenticity he may once have had has all but evaporated, he speaks in school-Latin quotations and declaims Goethe and Schiller while wholeheartedly and uncritically subscribing to the militaristic excesses of the Bismarck regime. (He has even named his oldest son Otto.) He has no compunction about currying favors from the powerful and, by the end of the play, manages to regain his old position as director of the Strasbourg theater. Along the way he casually betrays both his wife (with Alice Rütterbusch) and his professed principles, the latter not only by tolerating the student Erich Spitta, whose artistic ideals are diametrically opposed to his own, but also by accepting the recalcitrant young man as his future son-in-law. (Walburga has exploited her knowledge of the Rütterbusch affair as a bit of persuasive blackmail.) The naive but likeable Spitta provides Hauptmann with a rostrum for expressing some opinions of his own. A hilarious acting lesson in the third act ridicules the antiquated Goethean *Regeln für Schauspieler* (*Rules for Actors*), to which Hassenreuter still vehemently subscribes, while the hypocrisy of contemporary Christianity is demonstrated by revelations the young man makes regarding his family life. We learn that his father, the pastor, has caused the suicide of a daughter because his rigid religious principles prevented him from forgiving her for her seduction by a nobleman. Unlike the John plot, this one has a happy if somewhat ironic ending. Spitta and Walburga are engaged to be married while Hassenreuter will return to his former position in Strassbourg, where, he has made clear, he intends to rehire Alice Rütterbusch.

The genesis of *The Rats*, based on both personal experience and actual events reported in newspapers, was long and complex. The Hassenreuter character derives by Hauptmann's own admission from a real person: Alexander Hessler, an impoverished former theater director from Strasbourg who supported his family by renting costumes and props and providing drama instruction in Berlin. While living in nearby Erkner, Hauptmann (like young Spitta) took acting lessons from him during the years 1884-86. During this same period he was also greatly impressed by the phantasmagoria of the gigantic metropolis whose red glow in the distance filled the night sky. On a number of occasions he voiced his intention of depicting the negative side of Berlin, as when he noted in his diary, "Perhaps one day I can hold a mirror up to this city. It must see itself as I see it . . . filled with demons, an inferno."[17] Several motifs found in *The Rats* (for example, a servant girl's insistence on the return of her illegitimate child; death under an omnibus) had been used earlier in a prose sketch, "Der Buchstabe tötet" (1887) (The Letter [of the law] Kills) and in a dramatic fragment, "Neue Tragikomödie" (1906) (New Tragicomedy), but the complex machinations of Mrs. John, including the attempt to substitute a kidnapped child to fool the authorities, are remarkably similar to a recently discovered story reported in a Berlin newspaper in 1907—the main differences being that here the court was apparently so moved by the pathetic plight of the distraught culprit that it sentenced her to prison for only a week.[18] Finally, in May of 1910, while Hauptmann was writing the play, his newborn son (Gerhart Erasmus) died; soon thereafter the motif of the early death of Mrs. John's son was introduced into the play, along with a number of remarks and recollections of dreams supplied by Margarete.[19]

Hauptmann's admission that writing the drama was "very difficult" has been convincingly substantiated by Skinner, who has isolated nine different drafts of the work.[20] Of particular interest here are the relatively late introduction of the underworld character Bruno Mechelke and the author's long vacillation between madness and suicide as a fitting end to Mrs. John's suffering.

Hauptmann's intention in using the unlikely microcosm of a Berlin tenement as a setting for *The Rats* seems to have included at least the following: criticism of the sociopolitical status quo in Germany during the Wilhelminian era, critique of an antiquated theater tradition cherished and maintained by the bourgeois class of that era, and a demonstration of what a genuine tragedy should look like.

The "lies of society" that Hauptmann exposes are especially manifest in the better-off characters: a theater director who has no real commitment to the theater who conceives of drama only as empty pathos; a Christian clergyman practiced in all the appropriate platitudes about morality but unable to forgive his own daughter her sexual victimization by a member of the upper classes. Among such characters marriage vows are taken lightly and there is a discrepancy between the piously proclaimed ideal of feminine virtue and actual behavior. It is in regard to such social aspects of the drama that the rat symbolism comes most openly into play. For at least one segment of Hauptmann's audience, John, a worker representing the social democratic perspective, was describing the alleged dilapidated condition of a sociopolitical structure as well as a physical building when he remarked, "Listen how it's cracking, how the plaster comes trickling down behind the wallpaper! Everything here is decayed, everything rotten wood! Everything undermined by vermin, eaten by rats and mice! . . . Everything is wobbling! At any minute everything can break through to the cellar" (2:824). For Hassenreuter, the political reactionary, on the other hand, the symbol of destructive rats is more appropriate for liberals like young Spitta (his future son-in-law!). "You are a symptom," he rants at him, "you are a rat! But these rats are beginning . . . rat plague!—to undermine our splendid, newly united German empire. They cheat us of the rewards of our effort! and, in the garden of German art—rat plague!—they eat away the roots of the tree of idealism: they want to by all means pull the crown into the muck.—Into the dust, into the dust, into the dust with you!'' (2:779-80). Certainly the most rat-like character of the play is Bruno Mechelke. With his black, penetrating eyes, ''low receding forehead, small round skull, brutal face with a torn and scarred left nostril,'' (2:737) he even looks like a rat, and we first encounter him setting traps. Pauline Piperkaracka is completely unnerved by him—for good reason, it turns out. In Bruno the rat symbolism transcends sociopolitical considerations, suggesting instead treacherous forces inherent in human nature, forces lurking in the dark and ready to burst forth into the civilized world at the slightest provocation.

Anticipating such works as Brecht's *The Brass Purchase* (*Der Messingkauf*) or Pirandello's *Six Characters in Search of an Author,* in which drama becomes a forum for the discussion of drama, Hauptmann uses *The Rats* to examine the nature of tragedy. The subject is broached most directly in the arguments between Hassenreuter and Spitta, but in light of the fate which overtakes Pauline Piperkarcka, Mrs. John, and even Sidonie Knobbe, these arguments seem abstract and literary. The views of Hassenreuter, and to a somewhat lesser extent Spitta, represent superseded stages in Hauptmann's own artistic development. During his art school days (in his writing as well as his sculpture) he was still in thrall to the same nationalistic and epigonic ideals espoused by Hassenreuter. By the time he wrote *Before Sunrise* he had experienced—and was well on the way to overcoming—the somewhat dogmatic, socially oriented brand of Naturalism embraced with such naive vigor by Erich Spitta. Gradually (and here the influence of Nietzsche is rather obvious) his views had begun to deepen and coalesce into his concept of the *Urdrama* (''primeval drama''). A trip to Greece in 1907 marks a final stage in this development. In his travel diary *Griechischer Frühling* (1908) (*Greek Spring*) he rejects the Goethean idea of Classical antiquity as the embodiment of ''noble simplicity, quiet grandeur'' in favor of an archetypal, cultic, and Dionysian view. ''It cannot be denied,'' he now concludes, ''that tragedy means: enmity, persecution, hatred, and love as a rage to live! Tragedy means: fear, anguish, danger, pain, torture, martyrdom . . . malice, crime, baseness . . . murder, bloodlust, incest, butchery. . . . To see a true tragedy would be to catch sight of Medusa's face while almost being turned into stone; it would mean to anticipate horror in a way that life secretly always holds it in readiness, even for Fortune's favorite'' (7:80).

The John plot gives us such a glimpse of ''Medusa's face'' in society's cruelty to Pauline Piperkarcka, which drives her to the verge of suicide and infanticide; in Mrs. Knobbe's child, who dies of neglect during an argument over who owns him; in Bruno's trance-like murder of Pauline under a lilac bush; and in Mrs. John herself, whose motherly attachment to an infant leads to incipient madness and then death.

One of the most remarkable features of *The Rats* is the way in which the author orchestrates comic and tragic elements of the drama for maximum effect. Hauptmann is never satisfied simply to alternate these elements, but in a process Guthke has described as "synthetic tragicomedy"[21] he uses comedy to enhance his tragic effects and vice versa. In a manner presaged by Molière he allows virtues such as Mrs. John's motherly instincts or pastor Spitta's sense of moral probity to become exaggerated to the point of humorous grotesqueness and at times (as in such earlier works as *The Beaver Coat*) reverts to an unabashed humor of cruelty. One of the best examples of the latter in *The Rats* occurs early in the first act when the Polish maid Piperkarcka describes her appallingly tragic situation to Mrs. John in an excited but humorously inadequate broken German. On an even darker note, the fact that Hauptmann chose a Polish woman as the butt of his humor—and that in his work Polish surnames are invariably reserved for weak, ridiculous, or negative characters[22]—may also suggest complicity in the pervasive anti-Polish sentiments of Hauptmann's German contemporaries.

## NOTES

1. See Hans Daiber, *Gerhart Hauptmann. Oder der letzte Klassiker* (Vienna, Munich, Zurich: Molden, 1971), p. 105.

2. See Eberhard Hilscher, *Gerhart Hauptmann. Leben und Werk* (Frankfurt/M.: Athenäum, 1988), p. 247.

3. Quoted by Bernhard Zeller, ed., *Gerhart Hauptmann. Leben und Werk: Eine Gedächtnisausstellung des Deutschen Literaturarchivs* (Stuttgart: Turmhaus-Druckerei, 1962), p. 115.

4. Karl S. Guthke, *Gerhart Hauptmann: Weltbild im Werk* (Munich: Francke, 1980), p. 107.

5. See Daiber, 134.

6. See Hans Joachim Schrimpf, "Hauptmann: 'Rose Bernd,' " in Benno von Wiese, ed., *Das deutsche Drama*, 2 vols. (Düsseldorf: Bagel, 1968) 2:178.

7. John Osborne, *The Naturalist Drama in Germany* (Manchester: Manchester University Press; Totowa N.J.: Rowan & Littlefield, 1971), p. 153.

8. Quoted by Peter Sprengel, *Gerhart Hauptmann, Epoche–Werk–Wirkung* (Munich: Beck, 1984), p. 137.

9. Sprengel, 137.

10. Sprengel, 138.

11. Schrimpf, 184; and Sprengel, 134.

12. Guthke, 113.

13. Osborne, 148.

14. See Zeller, 143.

15. Hans Mayer, *Hauptmann* (Velber: Friedrich, 1973), p. 68.

16. See Hugh F. Garten, *Gerhart Hauptmann* (New Haven: Yale University Press, 1954), p. 23; and Sprengel, *Epoche*, 145.

17. Quoted by Sprengel, 142.

18. See Sprengel, 141–42.

19. See Sprengel, 142.

20. See Gerhart Hauptmann, *Die Ratten: Berliner Tragikomödie mit Materialien*, ed. Anna Stroka (Stuttgart: Klett, 1982), p. 126; and Charles Bronson Skinner, "The Texts of Hauptmann's *Ratten*," *Modern Philology* 77 (1979): 163–71.

21. Karl S. Guthke, *Geschichte und Poetik der deutschen Tragikömödie* (Göttingen: Vandenhoeck & Ruprecht, 1961), p. 22.

22. See Warren R. Maurer, "Gerhart Hauptmann's Character Names," *German Quarterly* 52 (1979): 459.

# CHAPTER SEVEN

# Quintessential Hauptmann?

## *And Pippa Dances!*

*Und Pippa tanzt! Ein Glashüttenmärchen* (*And Pippa Dances! A Glass-works Fairy Tale*) was written in October and November of 1905 in Berlin, where it was also first performed on January 1, 1906. Like *The Sunken Bell* it combines realistic and romantic elements, and like that "German Fairy Tale Drama" it too aroused considerable puzzlement upon its appearance. When asked point-blank about the meaning of his new play, the author, allegedly somewhat in his cups, is quoted as having replied, "If I knew that, I wouldn't have needed to write down the whole nonsense (*Quatsch*)."[1] Later, in a less caustic mood, he described the work as a "*mysterium* in a small setting" and as a quest drama, "a symbolization of inner searching [in which] the external plot is only a pretext. But not only in this fairy tale, but also in my realistic dramas the story line—or the episodes—hardly play a role. My truth seekers are distinguished by the fact that I only show their search but never the truth. And how could I, since I haven't yet found it myself!"[2] More, perhaps, than any other drama (and certainly more deservedly so than *The Sunken Bell*) *Pippa* assumes a central place in Hauptmann's artistic development. As Guthke has pointed out, "here not only do numerous lines of the previous oeuvre converge in a focal point, but they also radiate outward as far as the [author's] last works."[3]

The first act of *And Pippa Dances!* opens in a naturalistic mode and closes with just a hint of more mysterious, transcendental forces at work behind the facade of mundane reality. The setting is a not very reputable tavern in the Riesengebirge mountains where workers from the declining local glass industry congregate. The season is snowy mid-winter, and, although not explicitly mentioned, the time appears to be contemporaneous with that during which the play was written, shortly after the turn of the century. Because of its reflective tendency Hauptmann was faced with the difficult task of avoiding stasis by keeping his audience constantly alert and involved. Although he manages to do this throughout the drama, the first act especially represents a masterful example of stagecraft incorporating setting, striking verbal description, noisy quarreling, music, dance, and physical violence. Progressing from back to front, the stage is simultaneously filled by several groups: forest workers who are only occasionally drawn into the main action; a group of rough gamblers whose presence is felt more strongly; and the director of the local glassworks, something of a blowhard who draws a great deal of attention to himself and becomes noisily involved with most of the characters milling about the stage. Gradually the dominant characters are introduced and a minimal plot begins to crystallize out of the general confusion. The Director (set apart from the others by his generic appellation) is a virtual caricature of the capitalist businessman. He is as insensitive to the plight of unemployed workers as he is to nature (he has ridden his magnificent mare half to death through deep snow drifts in order to enjoy a trout dinner in the tavern); his saving grace as a member of the human race is an irresistible attraction to the ethereal charm of a beautiful adolescent girl named Pippa who has insinuated herself into his very dreams. The unlikely offspring of the most prominent of the gamblers, Tagliazoni, an audacious, disreputable Italian craftsman who has brought the fine art of Venetian glass manufacture to the northern clime of the Riesengebirge, she introduces a delicate touch of vulnerable femininity into the raucous male surroundings. Professing boredom but obviously acting out of a more complex motivation, the Director offers Tagliazoni a hundred lire to see Pippa dance. At this time the action is briefly interrupted by the appearance of Michel Hellriegel, an eccentric, child-like German apprentice who is wandering about in search of the ultimate secret of fine glassmaking; but then the dance begins, although it is initiated by an old man named Huhn rather than by the Director. Huhn is described as "a gigantic man with long red hair, red bushy brows and red beard, covered from head to foot with rags" (2:267) whose uncanny nature is perhaps best summed up by the Director's remark: "If one looks at the old man and thinks of Paris, one doesn't believe in Paris" (2:268). His filthy, rough exterior notwithstanding, Huhn too creates beautiful glass objects and is obsessed by dreams of Pippa. Slowly, clumsily, and to the primitive music of an ocarina played by a little man with a goiter, Huhn circles and grasps for the gracefully elusive Pippa, who seems simultaneously to entice and fear him. Just as the dance reaches its frenzied climax there is a violent commotion among the gamblers. Tagliazoni has used his daughter's diversion to cheat at cards. Although he draws a knife to defend himself and flees out into the cold night, a blood-curdling scream signals his murder by the pursuing German gamblers. Cowering in fear, Pippa falls into a faint and is carried off in Huhn's hairy arms.

Act 2 is set in Huhn's primitive, decrepit hut. Having revived her with a sip of brandy, Huhn is solicitous of Pippa, providing her with blankets and goat's milk while a blizzard rages outside. A knock on the window entices Huhn out of the hut, with a club, to investigate, while the exhausted girl relapses into sleep. As soon as Huhn leaves Hellriegel appears, plays a few notes on the ocarina, and watches as Pippa slowly rises and begins to dance in her sleep. After she awakens she begs Hellriegel to take her away with him—something he is only too pleased to do. Like the first, this act also ends with a scream, but one of joy and celebration rather than terror. Drawn out and powerful, it consists of the single mysterious word "Jumalai," which Hellriegel translates as "joy for everyone" (2:291).

The third act introduces and features Wann, the last of the main characters. Described in the dramatis personae as "a mythical personality" (2:263), he nevertheless seems a very human, robust, and intelligent old man of ninety who lives alone, except for a mute servant, in a comfortable home high on a mountain top. He is visited by the Director, who cannot get his mind off Pippa; by Huhn, who is also pursuing her and has slipped unnoticed into Wann's home and hidden behind the stove; and by Hellriegel and Pippa herself, who arrive just in time to avoid freezing to death. Using a small model of a Venetian gondola and the sound Pippa produces by rubbing her moistened finger on the lip of a crystal wine glass, Wann fulfills Hellriegel's romantic yearning for a trip to Venice by hypnotically transporting him there. Upon returning from his "trip," Hellriegel is reminded that Huhn is still pursuing Pippa, and, before retiring for the night, he obtains Wann's promise to protect her. After she has been shown to her room, Huhn suddenly confronts Wann, and Wann struggles with him to keep him away from the girl. Again the act closes with "a frightful scream" (2:310), this time from Huhn, who, seemingly in the throes of death, has collapsed in Wann's arms.

As Rasch has pointed out, *And Pippa Dances!* would seem logically to be a three-act drama, with the stations of Hellriegel's wanderings represented by the tavern, by Huhn's hut, and by Wann's mountain retreat and the victory of Wann's wisdom over Huhn's instinct.[4] Apparently dissatisfied with the implications of such an unambiguous ending, Hauptmann reprieved Huhn and gave him a major role in a fourth act, somewhat to the confusion of his audiences. In spite of the death rattle in his throat at the end of act 3, Huhn is still alive when the curtain rises once more, and Wann sends Hellriegel out for a bucket of snow to place on his heart to revive him further. When the young man returns from his errand, however, he is changed. He claims to have seen an assemblage of horrible demons and soon loses his sight—apparently through snow blindness. Huhn gradually regains his strength, and when Pippa begins a bacchantic dance to the music of Hellriegel's ocarina, he is strong enough to beat out the rhythm with his fists. Catching sight of

Wann, however, he suddenly crushes one of Wann's beautiful Venetian glasses in his fist. As the pieces fall to the floor, Pippa collapses and dies. The audience hears Huhn repeat his earlier triumphant cry of "Jumalai!!" (2:318), and then he too expires. Hellriegel no longer sees any of this. Encouraging his fantasy, Wann pretends to marry him to Pippa, presses his staff into his hand, and sends the happy, giggling youth out into the winter sunlight. The music of the ocarina slowly fades in the distance as Wann painfully contemplates the tiny gondola from Pippa's homeland.

Like *The Sunken Bell* Hauptmann's *Pippa* is firmly rooted in the folklore and cultural landscape of the Silesian Riesengebirge mountains. A trip with Carl to the vacation town of Schreiberhau in that region in 1890 had acquainted him with the fascinating art of glass manufacture and left an "impression . . . that was very deep and lasting" (7:539). It was here, in 1842, that the famous glass artisan Franz Pohl had founded the Josephinenhütte glass works and where he later discovered a secret of Venetian glass making: the method for manufacturing fine mesh glass. The glass industry and its connection to Venice also had a long history in this part of Germany. As early as 1430 the Venetian nobleman Antonio de' Medici had visited the area while searching for gold and precious stones and, on returning home, mentioned in his memoirs a glassworks he had seen there.[5] Such a shared preoccupation with glass undoubtedly accounts for much of the interest in Venice reflected in the folklore of the Riesengebirge area, folklore that Hauptmann had studied intensively since 1897 and that supplied him with such motifs as that of the magical ability to fly that was attributed to Venetians.[6] In a more general sense too, as Hauptmann himself recalled later,[7] there had been a long–standing preoccupation with Venice (often as a symbolic antipode to a physically and spiritually cold north), which flourished especially around the turn of the century and which found artistic expression in the works of such authors as Rainer Maria Rilke, Hugo von Hofmannsthal, Friedrich Nietzsche, and Thomas Mann. It also seems plausible, as Sprengel has suggested, that Hauptmann expanded the evocative complex of emotions often associated with Venice (the real Italian city that he knew intimately at first hand) by amalgamating it with Vineta, the legendary city beneath the sea that has served as a familiar topos for generations of German authors.[8] He had already exploited the fabled city as a symbolic realm of art and death in the fragmentary drama "Der Mutter Fluch" Curse of the Mother, on which he worked during his trip to the United States in 1894, and returned to it in early drafts of *Gabriel Schilling's Flight* produced in 1905–06, at the time he was writing *Pippa*.

The most direct precursor to *Pippa* is, however, Hauptmann's "Der Venezianer" (The Venetian). An unfinished novel, this work contains striking parallels to *Pippa*. In it there is a character named Wann who is depicted as representing an ideal of wisdom and humanity acquired over many years and apparently personifying a wish projection of the author himself. This early variant of the Wann figure (he was reincarnated by Hauptmann in a number of later works) was the son of a wild, hirsute, athletic man resembling Huhn and a beautiful Venetian mother who had, like Pippa, caught the eye of a glassworks director. Before she was carried off by the Huhn-like character, she had been the wife of an Italian glass furnace builder named Tagliazoni, who, like his namesake in *Pippa*, was killed in a tavern fight.

The final form of the Pippa character, as is so often the case in Hauptmann's dramas, owes a great deal to an intimate personal experience. In 1905, the year after his long-awaited marriage to Margarethe Marschalk, he met a sixteen-year-old actress, Ida Orloff, who had caused something of a sensation with her stage portrayal of Hannele. Born Ida Margarethe Weissbeck in St. Petersburg, this daughter of German parents had adopted a Russian stage name to benefit from the vogue that Russian theater was then enjoying. The combination of her wide-eyed, blond, childish beauty with an aura of sexual depravity (she claimed to have been deflowered at the age of thirteen and seemed to enjoy flaunting her promiscuity) was too much for the forty-three-year old author to resist, and he remained completely under her spell for about a year. Although his young wife was able to cope with the "other woman" problem much better than Marie had earlier (she allowed her rival sufficient leeway to scuttle the affair with her impossible, childish demands), the experience made such a deep and lasting impression on Hauptmann as to provide inspiration for some thirty of his female characters ranging from Pippa to the title figure of *Mignon*, written when he was eighty-one years old.[9]

These *femme enfant* figures invariably have the letter *i* in their names (e.g., Gersuind, Ingigerd, Melitta, Hamida, Irina, Siri, and so on), and they are usually blond, delicate, and dangerously seductive. In his letters to Ida, which he sometimes signed "Your Wann," Hauptmann described her as a moth flirting with flames, as a bewitching Siren, as a mermaid, or as a cruel spider. "How," he laments, "can I extricate myself from the spiderweb of this love that threatens to strangle me?"[10] Since Hauptmann wrote *Pippa* while he was under her spell, it is not surprising that he chose Ida Orloff to play the title role for its premiere or that it was to remain her most memorable part. Although her career as a significant actress soon went into decline (she antagonized the powerful director of the Burgtheater in Vienna and suffered the consequences), she continued to be identified with Hauptmann in the public mind. In 1913 she starred in the film adaptation of the novel *Atlantis*, in which, as Ingigerd Hahlström, she performed a sensational "spider-dance"; and in 1941 Hauptmann witnessed her last performance (in a run of fifty) as Mrs. Fielitz of *The Conflagration*, staged in a small, insignificant theater. She died in Berlin at the age of fifty-seven, during the final weeks of the Second World War. Believing that her ability to speak Russian would spare her the fate of many German women who fell into the hands of Soviet soldiers, she neglected to go into hiding—a mistake, as it turned out. A victim of rape and abuse, she killed herself with an overdose of sleeping pills on April 9, 1945. No obituaries or newspaper announcements reported her death.[11]

Considering the form, language, and characters of *Pippa*, one is tempted to agree with Garten's assessment that the drama represents "probably [Hauptmann's] most perfect integration of the realistic and the symbolic."[12] On a superficial, sometimes almost banal level, the author takes pains to make even the more magical actions of his characters conform to common, ordinary reality. Thus Hellriegel's previously mentioned trip to Venice is explained by hypnosis, and when Wann seemingly conjures up the sudden appearance of Pippa with a clap of his hands in the third act—and in so doing astounds and perplexes the Director—he is able to do so only because, instead of the magic mirror attributed to certain Venetians, he possesses a telescope and has been observing her arrival from afar. Similarly, from a formal perspective, while monologues are hardly realistic and were strenuously rejected by the Naturalists, Hauptmann makes them plausible in the mouth of Hellriegel, a youth with a very tenuous hold on reality who would be likely indeed to converse with himself.

Just as in his naturalistic dramas, the author takes pains here to individualize each of his characters through their speech patterns. This is especially obvious in the first act, in which the glassblowers and woodcutters speak Silesian dialect; the tavern owner speaks a somewhat negligent High German; Tagliazoni peppers his makeshift, broken German with bits of his native Italian; the Director expresses himself in flippant trivialities and Berlin inflections; Huhn rumbles in difficult to comprehend Silesian; Hellriegel, ever cheerful, naive, and articulate, lards his speech with the vocabulary of German Romanticism; and Pippa hardly speaks at all, expressing herself much more adequately through gesture and dance. By the time Wann appears, in the third act, there is a gradual, almost imperceptible introduction of poetic, rhythmic language; and, under hypnosis, Hellriegel bursts forth in a rhapsodic verse description of flight over aureate mountain tops and descent to a magnificent underwater portico with a golden gate upon which he knocks three times before being abruptly snatched back to life and crass reality by Wann.

Greatly enhancing the lyrical quality of the drama are the musical effects that support especially the high points of the action, including the dancing of Pippa and Huhn. Dominant here is the primitive sound of the ocarina that accompanies Hellriegel and Pippa like a leitmotif throughout the play; but other, more complex musical interludes are also invoked as required, such as the unlikely sounds produced by Wann's wine glass. Here the stage direction prescribes, "From the glass, whose edge Pippa rubs, issues a gentle sound which becomes stronger and stronger until the tones link up in harmonies which, swelling, grow to a short but powerful musical storm that suddenly ebbs and dies away" (2:306).

Like its consort music, dance begins where spoken language ends. Infinitely more allusive than the denotative power of words, it too facilitates the expression of emotions and states of being that elude logical comprehension. Although dance is perhaps not as frequently and prominently on display in Hauptmann's work as music, *Pippa* reveals his appreciation of the potential of this art form. In later years he went out of his way to meet such admired dancers as Ruth St. Denis and Isadora Duncan, and it even seems possible that the choice of Pippa's surname—Tagliazoni—may conceal a tribute to Maria Taglioni, the celebrated Italian dancer whose name, at the turn of the century, was still synonymous with the dance.[13] Pippa's dance is, of course, replete with erotic overtones, and in this also Hauptmann had a familiar example: Marie's dance with the drum major in Büchners *Woyzeck*. In addition, Nietzsche's contribution to the appreciation of the significance of dance can hardly be underestimated for a dramatist at work around the turn of the century. As Sprengel has pointed out, in his *Birth of Tragedy* Nietzsche goes so far as to "derive . . . the tragic art form from the danced dithyramb as the objectification of Dionysian intoxication."[14]

Responding to the criticism of an alleged "neglect of dramatic form" (11:1148) in *Pippa*, in 1937 Hauptmann collected his thoughts concerning the drama in a short essay first published in 1963. In it he cautions that "interpretations and explanations cannot solve the mystery of a genuine dramatic creation, and they are not intended to do so. One can no more reduce it to rational formulae than a musical symphony" (11:1151–52). This cautionary note notwithstanding, Hauptmann nevertheless supplies clues with which the mystery can at least be approached. Starting with the love of an older man for a beautiful young girl, he describes the inception of the work not in terms of a sovereign, voluntary creation but as a desperate act of catharsis from an all-consuming passion. By splitting "himself and his passion" into four figures (Hellriegel, the Director, Huhn, and Wann) and by elevating "hard reality to a divine game. . . . the man struggling with passion attempts to become its master" (11:1150). With these remarks Hauptmann again suggests the ascendancy of character over plot action and justifies a closer look at the four male characters and their competition for the "eternal feminine" embodied in Pippa.

Although Pippa is the most elusive of the protagonists, her central position as the title figure is fully justified. The quintessence of femininity, she provokes a variety of reactions from her suitors according to their type: the animal-like persistence of Huhn; the rather crude advances of the Director; the Romantic longing of Hellriegel; and the subtle, resigned, spiritualized love of the wise old Wann. This is not to suggest, of course, that Pippa cannot also reflect more limited, contemporary ideals of womanhood or embody symbolic values. As the imagery associated with her suggests, she docs both. Described in terms of slender reeds, clinging vines, a mermaid-like affinity for water, and childish beauty, she, like her model Ida Orloff, closely approximates the Art Nouveau (*Jugendstil*) ideal of the *femme fragile*. The connection to this fashionable art style is further enhanced if we recall its affinity for fine glass objects and Pippa's own strong identification with the manufacture, beauty, and fragility of glass (her Venetian origin and the beautiful, slender wine glasses that provide the musical accompaniment for Hellriegel's journey and signal her death when one is crushed in Huhn's hand).[15]

Other imagery associated with Pippa suggests that Hauptmann had more profound intentions for her than to have her serve as a contemporary ideal of female beauty. Throughout the play she is described variously in terms of light, sparks, birds, and butterflies—all traditional metaphors for the soul—and Wann, perhaps, comes closest to unveiling her mystery. Upon her arrival in his mountain-top aerie, he describes her to the Director as "a little spark" that has found its way "out of the paradises of light" into the "black Hades fires" (2:299) of the everyday, contemporary world. Having severed its ties with the numinous reality preserved in Pippa, this modern world has become an impoverished, cold place saturated in cosmic loneliness. (Wann sums it up in the Kierkegaardian remark that "boredom is where God is not" [2:296].) Born in Venice at "the heart of the world" (2:304) and identified repeatedly with the warmth radiated from the glass furnace, Pippa is both a reminder of a lost paradise and a faint promise that it might still be regained.

Of the suitors crowding around Pippa in the hope of sharing the remnants of cosmic warmth that still cling to her, the Director is the least successful and the least deserving of success. Although even he shares certain traits with his creator (as his publisher Samuel Fischer discovered, Hauptmann could be a hard-nosed, pragmatic businessman; and his sybaritic tendencies were also well known), his main function seems to be to demonstrate the triviality of the cold world of modern commerce and technology. In this he serves as a contrast to Wann, Huhn, and Hellriegel, each of whom in his own way retains more intimate ties to "the heart of the world."

In spite of the fact that he too represents a "type," Hellriegel is a more complex character. As is so often true in Hauptmann's work, the name itself suggests clues as to how he is to be perceived. To begin with, the surname, divided into its component parts *hell* (bright, luminous, light) and *Riegel* (bar, bolt, latch) may contain both personal and symbolic allusions. As has been pointed out elsewhere, many of Hauptmann's fictional names for characters with strong autobiographical overtones relate to light, warmth, and the sun.[16] As a youth the author was nicknamed Lichtel (an affectionate diminutive of *Licht* [light]) "on account of the quiet, deep glow in his face," and his ex libris bears the motto "Ex corde lux."[17] More literally, the name Hellriegel suggests various forms of blindness. As long as he has his physical sight he sees reality enchanted; when he loses it he acquires a state of visionary blindness. The "bolt" (*Riegel*) locks out the bright external world, allowing him to become immersed in an inner life in which Pippa, and all she represents, becomes alive and present to him as never before. The name Michel, although it may also allude to the Biblical archangel St. Michael, who conquered the devil, is more readily identified with that quintessential German *der deutsche Michel* (the equivalent of the British John Bull or the American John Doe). As such he is a natural Romanticist, a wanderer, a dreamer, and an artist descendent of Novalis and Eichendorff. His seemingly impossible ambition is to learn to "form water into spheres," but, as Wann reminds him, he already does so "with his eyes" (2:321)—a further affirmation of Hauptmann's conviction that "suffering is the basis of artistic vision."[18]

When Wann is introduced in act 3, he is described as a "man [who] appears to be ninety or more years old, but . . . as if age were magnified energy, beauty, and youth" (2:293). That Hauptmann identified strongly with this character is suggested not only by the fact that he kept returning to him in subsequent works but by his signing some of his letters to Ida Orloff "Your Wann."[19] As. C. W. F. Behl, his loyal friend and faithful Boswell, remarked, he saw in this vigorous old man "a wish projection of his own future perfection."[20] An ideal figure in which age has finally distilled the experience of a lifetime into a cool, contemplative wisdom, he nevertheless remains susceptible to the mysteries he perceives behind the veil of palpable reality and is himself something of a mystery. Although he laughingly rejects the Director's attempt to identify him with the local *Walen* legends (*Walen* being Venetian gold-seekers with alleged magical abilities) his enigmatic name (*Wann* = when) and its apparent source suggests that Hauptmann himself had made the same connection. In a book Hauptmann used in his research for *Pippa* it is written that "A citizen of Wunsiedel, finally, Siegmund Wann, is said to have had a wife who was able to separate gold from zinc and made her husband the richest man in town."[21]

The sooty giant Huhn is as antipodal to the highly cultivated Wann as the dreamer Hellriegel is to the prosaic Director. If Wann can be compared to Shakespeare's Prospero (*The Tempest*), Huhn is Hauptmann's half-wild Caliban. Bearing the name of an animal (albeit a somewhat incongruous one [*Huhn* = chicken]), he talks to his goat and a pet jackdaw and is himself described as a bird of prey and (humorously) as a gorilla. In addition to this strong identification with the animal realm, he has something of a forest sprite about him. He threatens Pippa with the *Nachtjäger* (night hunter) of local folklore, and when he greets the rising sun with his cry of "Jumalai!" he looks to Hellriegel like "a frightful forest god" (2:291).

That Hauptmann had difficulty deciding what final impression his audience should have of *Pippa* is implied by the fact that he experimented with several endings: in one of them Hellriegel goes off to become a clown; in another he and Pippa are found frozen to death in a deserted glassworks.[22] If questions about "meaning" are raised at the conclusion of a discussion of a drama whose strength may well be its elusiveness, it may be more productive to examine more carefully the relationship between Wann and Huhn than that between Pippa and Hellriegel. Although it would be quite plausible to see in them respectively the personification of the Freudian superego and id, it is more likely that Hauptmann saw in their titanic wrestling match a battle between Apollonian and Dionysian forces; Nietzsche was very much in vogue at the time. As has again recently been pointed out, the mythology of antiquity distinguishes two variants of Dionysus, one white and the other black. In this interpretation Huhn, the representative of the wintery Riesengebirge, is seen as a black, Silesian Dionysus who in the delirium of his death throes suffers the same fate as his classical predecessor—dismemberment.[23] The facts that he loses the wrestling match with Wann at the end of the third act and that Wann survives him at the end of the fourth cannot be construed as an Apollonian victory of light, reason, and civilization over Dionysian darkness, instinct, and chaos. It is Huhn who, in the end, succeeds in capturing Pippa (as was foreshadowed in their first act dance), and, with his victorious cry of "Jumalai!!!" (2:318), taking her with him into the larger reality of death.

## NOTES

1. See Karl S. Guthke, "Gerhart Hauptmann und der Nihilismus," *German Quarterly* 36 (1963): 434.

2. Quoted by Hans Daiber, *Gerhart Hauptmann. Oder der letzte Klassiker* (Vienna, Munich, Zurich: Molden, 1971), p. 141.

3. Karl S. Guthke, *Gerhart Hauptmann: Weltbild im Werk* (Munich: Francke, 1980) p. 116.

4. Wolfdietrich Rasch, "Hauptmann 'Und Pippa tanzt!'" in *Das deutsche Drama*, Benno von Wiese, ed., 2 vols. (Düsseldorf: Bagel, 1968) 2:204.

5. See Daiber, 62.

6. See Rasch, 189.

7. Carl F. W. Behl, *Zwiesprache mit Gerhart Hauptmann: Tagebuchblätter* (Munich: Desch, 1949), p. 225.

8. See Peter Sprengel, *Gerhart Hauptmann. Epoche–Werk–Wirkung* (Munich: Beck, 1984), p. 182. For a detailed examination of this and numerous related legends in Germany see Warren R. Maurer, "German Sunken City Legends," *Fabula* 17 (1976): 189–214.

9. On Ida Orloff and her influence on Hauptmann see esp. Frederick W. J. Heuser, *Gerhart Hauptmann: Zu seinem Leben und Schaffen* (Tübingen: Niemeyer, 1961), pp. 100–54, and Wolfgang Leppmann, *Gerhart Hauptmanns Leben, Werk und Zeit* (Bern, Munich, Vienna: Scherz, 1986), pp. 237–57.

10. Quoted by H. D. Tschörtner, *Ungeheures erhofft. Gerhart Hauptmann—Werk und Wirkung* (Berlin: Der Morgen, 1986), p. 97.

11. See Heuser, 111.

12. Hugh F. Garten, *Gerhart Hauptmann* (New Haven: Yale University Press, 1954), p. 34.

13. See Warren R. Maurer, "Gerhart Hauptmann's Character Names," *German Quarterly* 52 (1979): 460.

14. Quoted by Peter Sprengel, *Die Wirklichkeit der Mythen: Untersuchungen zum Werk Gerhart Hauptmann* (Berlin: E. Schmidt, 1982), p. 246.

15. See Sprengel, *Epoche*, 184.

16. See Maurer, "Names," 465.

17. See Maurer, "Names," 471 n. 33.

18. See Sprengel, *Epoche*, 184.

19. Heuser, 123.

20. Carl F. W. Behl, "Die Metamorphosen des alten Wann," *Gerhart Hauptmann Jahrbuch* (1948): 97.

21. See Maurer, "Names," 468.

22. See Sprengel, *Epoche*, 182.

23. See Sprengel, *Epoche*, 180.

# CHAPTER EIGHT

# A Poor Man Such as Hamlet

## An Excursus

For more than a decade—from about 1924 to 1936—Hauptmann devoted himself extensively to the study, elucidation, and creative adaptation of Shakespeare's *Hamlet*. With the exception of completing projects already begun, he largely neglected other work during this period. And although the works that resulted from this preoccupation cannot be numbered among his most illustrious achievements, they cannot be completely ignored without slighting an important aspect of his creativity. Aside from personal experience, Shakespeare ranks with Büchner, Goethe, and classical antiquity as one of the major influences on Hauptmann's work.[1] This influence began in 1870 when, as a child, he received the gift of a primitive toy stage with a yellow-haired cardboard figure of Hamlet. It manifested itself in his eagerness to attend Shakespearean performances at every opportunity; later inspired him to take acting lessons in the hope that he would someday be able to play Hamlet on the stage; and, in 1905, took him on a virtual pilgrimage to Stratford-upon-Avon. Shakespeare's influence has been detected in numerous characters from Loth (*Before Sunrise*) to Orestes and Electra from Hauptmann's last major dramatic work, the *Atriden-Tetralogie* (1940–44) (*Atridae-Tetralogy*); and in such disparate dramas as *Germanic Tribes and Romans, Schluck und Jau* (1899) (compare *The Taming of the Shrew*), *Indipohdi* (1920), strongly reminiscent of *The Tempest*, and *Die Tochter der Kathedrale* (1939) *(The Daughter of the Cathedral)*.[2]

To appreciate this preoccupation with Shakespeare it is necessary to understand that it had both a personal and a national component. Germans were obsessed with him, especially since the appearance of the Schlegel-Tieck translation of his works between 1797 and 1840; and Hauptmann, writing in 1915 on behalf of the German Shakespeare Society (in jeopardy because of the animosities of the First World War), expressed a typically proprietary attitude: "There is no nation, not even the English, which has, like the German, earned a right to Shakespeare. Shakespeare's figures have become a part of our world; his soul has become one with ours. And, though he was born and buried in England, Germany is the country in which he truly lives" (6:292–30). On a more personal, artistic level, he sees in Shakespeare an exemplar of his own concept of the *Urdrama:* "Shakespeare's creations reveal the *Urdrama* which is saturated with life and death, love and hatred, blood and tears, honey and gall, in which madness and sense constitute a mad-sense *(Wahnsinn)*, before which a higher sense flees into resignation; a *Wahnsinn* with whose most varied forms mankind undermines, dismembers, and slaughters itself" (7:927).

The fruits of Hauptmann's labors on behalf of Shakespeare during the decade in question are most evident in three works: *Shakespeares tragische Geschichte von Hamlet Prinzen von Dänemark in deutscher Nachdichtung und neu eingerichtet* (1928) (*Shakespeare's Tragic History of Hamlet, Prince of Denmark, in German Adaptation and Newly Arranged*); the more independent drama *Hamlet in Wittenberg* (1935); and the strongly autobiographical novel *Im Wirbel der Berufung* (1936) *(In the Maelstrom of Vocation)*.

Of these works the first found the least and the least positive public and critical response. Proceeding from the premise that Shakespeare's drama, as it has come down to us, is at best a magnificent torso but one that hardly represents the ultimate intentions of its author, Hauptmann set out to reconstruct it in accord with his own poetic intuition. Formally he leans heavily on Schlegel-Tieck—more than half of his text is identical with their translation—and the changes in plot are also conservative. In essence he follows the tack set by Goethe in *Wilhelm Meister's Apprenticeship* by making Hamlet rather than Laertes the leader of the rebellion in the third act (in Shakespeare the play threatens to become Laertes's drama at this point); emphasizes the historical and political background of the action more than Shakespeare had done; and shifts the stress from Hamlet's Werther-like passivity (a dominant German interpretation since Goethe's Storm and Stress novel) to a more active, decisive, and manly role. The fact that the prince hesitates at all can be largely ascribed to the humanistic atmosphere of Wittenberg. Here he feels most strongly the depravity of his own family milieu and is desperately intent upon cleansing himself of it.

The significance of the Wittenberg episode is explored in even greater detail in *Hamlet in Wittenberg*. Bringing to bear an impressive historical expertise, Hauptmann depicts all social strata of this teeming university town and uses its varied milieu to demonstrate the growing complexity of his hero, whom Wahr has succinctly described as follows:

He admires the authors of classical humanism and the disputations of the University classroom. He is an idealist and visionary who youth-like would right the wrongs and incongruities of life, a lonely thinker who cares neither for rank nor for station; a passionate lover, a cheerful companion ready for fight or frolic, faithful to his friends and his principles, genuine, with the many-sidedness of genius. He suffers fitful moods of brooding melancholy and introspection, and then with impetuous daring he rushes forth into adventures to display rare courage and magnanimous generosity. He rescues others from distress and suffering at the cost of personal comfort and safety. He possesses a strong sense of justice and equality.[3]

As this description suggests, the character of Hauptmann's Hamlet is depicted more directly and explicitly than that of the Shakespearean original. That this makes him an inherently more interesting hero—or that it substantially enhances the understanding of Shakespeare's plot—can hardly be claimed. Instead, *Hamlet in Wittenberg* remains a largely original play, inspired by Shakespeare, of which the most interesting aspect is the lively evocation of an historical era and a place.

Of the three works centering on *Hamlet,* the novel *Im Wirbel der Berufung* (In the Maelstrom of Vocation) (1936) preoccupied Hauptmann longest—from August 1924 to the summer of 1935. Highly autobiographical in both an intellectual and a personal sense, it depicts the general situation of its author around 1886–88, when he took acting lessons and spent a summer away from his family in Putbus on the island of Rügen. On a personal level it depicts the author (thinly disguised as Erasmus Gotter) and his domestic problems with three women: Kitty (wife Marie), Irina Bell (Ida Orloff), and Princess Ditta (modeled after Elizabeth von Schaumburg-Lippe, to whom his son Benvenuto was married for a short time in 1928). By his own admission Hauptmann considered the autobiographical elements largely in terms of a framework for an extended discussion of the problems of Shakespeare's *Hamlet.* As in earlier works, the influence of Goethe's *Wilhelm Meister's Apprenticeship* is obvious here. Dr. Gotter, "a poet by God's Grace" (5:1090), finds himself in the aristocratic duchy of Granitz (Putbus) during the summer of 1885 and is given an opportunity to stage his own reconstructed version of *Hamlet,* basically Hauptmann's version of 1927. A series of circumstances, including love for the three women, illness, and indecision regarding his calling, plunges the author into an emotional "maelstrom" leading to nervous collapse. Like Wilhelm Meister before him he plans to retreat to the serenity of a country estate to regain his equilibrium.

In addition to some revealing discussions on his theories about acting, staging, and directing, Hauptmann stresses what he considers central importance of Hamlet's father's ghost in the play. Here (in the spiritual vicinity of the *Urdrama*) we are dealing with a death cult (*Totenkult*) or, more accurately, a cult of the hero (*Heroenkult*). As the classical philologist Dr. Trautvetter explains, "The soul of a great man, especially if he has died through murder or assassination, must be appeased, otherwise his wrath, and the power to assert it, will be devastating. After death the hero has rank and authority similar to that of the chthonic, that is subterreanean, gods" (5:1224). *Hamlet,* according to Hauptmann, is such a *Heroenkult* drama, an atavistic, archetypal funeral play demanding blood sacrifice, the product of Shakespeare's unconscious. This explains, among other things, Hamlet's black clothing, black being both the preferred color of sacrificial victims and of the garb of priests whose duty it is to perform sacrifices to the gods.

Not too surprisingly, *Im Wirbel der Berufung* was not very popular. The autobiographical and essayistic elements of the novel clash; the hero is painfully identical with his creator; and the number of traumatic experiences that befall Gotter within the space of four weeks stretches credibility.

Although Hauptmann had been involved with Shakespeare too long and too intensely ever to be completely free of his influence, his active preoccupation began to wane after 1936. In 1943 he was to confess, "Previously I always thought only of Shakespeare, as if there were nothing besides him. Now I have come completely away from that. Too much and too exclusive [a preoccupation with] Shakespeare can be an inhibition. . . . "[4]

## NOTES

1. See Felix A. Voigt and Walter A. Reichart, *Hauptmann und Shakespeare: Ein Beitrag zur Geschichte des Fortlebens Shakespeares in Deutschland* (Breslau: Maruschke & Berendt, 1938), pp. 1–2.

2. Voigt and Reichart, 19–41.

3. Fred B. Wahr, "The Hauptmann 'Hamlet,'" *Philological Quarterly* 16 (1937): 134.

4. Carl F. W. Behl, *Zwiesprache mit Gerhart Hauptmann: Tagebuchblätter* (Munich: Desch, 1949), p. 185.

# CHAPTER NINE

# Darkness Descending

*Magnus Garbe*

The tragedy *Magnus Garbe,* written in 1914 and 1915 but not published until 1942, is one of Hauptmann's darkest. Set in the sixteenth century in an unnamed city, it depicts the precipitous fall of two exemplary human beings: the strong and prosperous mayor, Magnus Garbe, and his beautiful, virtuous wife Felicia. Unprepared by the happy circumstances of their lives to recognize and deal with evil—satanically personified in a papal inquisition—they are inexorably destroyed by it.

The external elements of the plot are as sparse and drastic as a medieval woodcut. Shocked and indignant over the ragings of the "pious" executioners who exploit the denunciations of innocent victims (obtained through torture from equally innocent denunciators), Garbe nevertheless underestimates the threat to his own family. While he relaxes in one of his vineyards, his wife is accused of witchcraft; removed to a dungeon, where she gives birth to a son; and horribly abused by a team of torturers who would have felt at home working in Auschwitz—they too perform their unspeakable cruelties from a combination of motives including sadism, unquestioning obedience, and pride in their grisly craftsmanship. Upon learning of his wife's fate at the end of the second act, Magnus suffers a stroke and falls to the ground. Three weeks later, in the third and final act, he appears broken and half-paralyzed at the prison tower to take leave of his wife; she is to be executed in the morning. After the two finally recognize each other—Felicia, like Goethe's Gretchen, has found some refuge from her sufferings in madness—they fall together upon the straw of the dungeon floor and reconsecrate their marriage. When the executioner comes to fetch Felicia to be burned at the stake, he is exasperated to find two stiffly intertwined corpses which will have to be delivered up to the flames together. The newborn son is rescued by friends and taken to a neighboring country.

As Hauptmann liked to emphasize in later years, the mood of this drama was nourished by gloomy personal experiences: the start of the First World War, a period of severe illness for his wife, and a political witch-hunt directed against him for the pacifist tendencies expressed in his *Festspiel in deutschen Reimen* (1913) (*Commemoration Masque*)—a spectacular project commissioned by the city fathers of Breslau in commemoration of the centenary of the German uprising against the Napoleonic yoke, which fell considerably short of its sponsors' patriotic expectations and was soon banned. It is this personal component that helps to elevate *Magnus Garbe* above the level of a merely historical play or an attack on the Church. Setting, time, and characters are more symbolic than real, and the themes are archetypal and parabolic: absolute evil, fate, envy, anxiety, human sacrifice, and regeneration. And while the hero himself undergoes a reverse conversion, to the conviction that "there is no God, only the devil," (2:1072) the escape of the son with the telling name Magnus Felix and the *Liebestod* that deprives the hangman of his triumph provide a hint of catharsis and a flickering ray of light in the dark dungeon of the world.

Underlining the sense of inevitability and timelessness that permeates this tragedy are elements of its form. Meaningful repetitions of words and phrases are frequent; animal images (for example, a mad dog roaming the city) recur again and again, and character names transcend the simple function of appellation (by the end of the play, for instance, the names Magnus [great] and Felicia [happy] have become cruel mockeries). The most striking of such symbolic devices, however, is that of the "golden ball" that appears as a kind of leitmotif throughout the drama. Traditionally identified with perfection and happiness—but here the identifying sign-ornament of the Garbe house—it comes to rest, as a minor character observes, "in the filth of the street" (2:1060).

## Before Sunset

The premiere of *Vor Sonnenuntergang* (*Before Sunset*) on February 16, 1932, in the Deutsches Theater in Berlin marks a significant turning point in Hauptmann's literary and personal fortunes. Staged by Max Reinhardt with the renowned actors Werner Kraus and Helene Thimig in the main roles (as Matthias Clausen and Inken Peters), this production was to be the author's last widely acclaimed premiere and the last significant theater premiere of the rapidly expiring Weimar Republic.[1]

Beginning as early as 1912, the year he was awarded the Nobel Prize for literature, Hauptmann's literary persona underwent a gradual metamorphosis from that of vibrant, popular dramatist to that of a writer who increasingly indulged irrational and mystical tendencies with a much more limited appeal and whose occasional public successes (such as *Der Ketzer von Soana* [*The Heretic of Soana*] of 1918) were likely to be in nondramatic genres. Remarkably (at least from the perspective of societies not accustomed to paying much attention to serious authors of fiction), as his active literary contribution waned, his popularity as a personality grew. As early as 1906 a newspaper poll had identified him as second only to Kaiser Wilhelm in popular recognition in Germany.[2] By now frequently compared with Goethe's, his work soon became part of the public school curriculum, and he gradually assumed something of the role of a spiritual figurehead for his nation. Though he had begun his career on a note of rebellion (largely artistic in *Before Sunrise*, more political in *The Weavers*), he had also subscribed to the notion that an artist worthy of the name is ipso facto apolitical. By the outbreak of the First World War, however, he is alleged to have declared his willingness to forego literature entirely in order to devote himself to politics; but then, in a paroxysm of nationalist fervor, he wrote a number of propagandistic poems such as one commemorating his third son's induction into the army, entitled "Komm, wir wollen sterben gehn" ("Come, Let Us Go to Die"). By 1921 he had become so strongly identified with the political life of the Weimar Republic that he felt obliged publically to deny widespread rumors that he was a presidential candidate. Nevertheless Thomas Mann (and probably others) continued to see in him an unofficial "King of the Republic." On the occasion of his sixtieth birthday—celebrated throughout Germany in 1922—Reichspräsident Friedrich Ebert declared, "By honoring Gerhart Hauptmann the German nation honors itself."[3]

The pinnacle of Hauptmann's renown came ten years later, in 1932, shortly before the Nazi takeover. The year-long celebration of his seventieth birthday, which by a kind quirk of fate coincided with the centennial of the death of Goethe (with whom he identified ever more strongly as he grew older) brought a harvest of acclaim including the Goethe Prize of Frankfurt; a theater named after him in Breslau;.a celebration and speech by Thomas Mann honoring him in Munich; and similar celebrations in Prague, Vienna, Dresden, Hamburg, and Leipzig.

In America he had achieved a modicum of recognition. The Nobel Prize had, of course, helped in this regard, and the history of translations of his works in this country chronicles a growing awareness of his importance. Excerpts from William Archer's translation of *Hannele* had appeared as early as 1894 in *Werner's Readings and Recitations*, and individual scenes were also published in *A Library of the World's Best Literature* in 1896 and in the *Ridpath Library of Universal Literature* in 1898. By 1900 complete translations of *Lonely Lives*, *The Sunken Bell*, and *The Weavers* were also available. But the most ambitious and successful project was the translation and publication of *The Dramatic Work of Gerhart Hauptmann*. This nine–volume edition, which appeared in New York between 1913 and 1929, represents the effort of a number of translators under the editorship of Ludwig Lewisohn. It contains thirty dramatic works, including all of Hauptmann's best-known plays from *Before Sunrise* to *Veland* (1925).[4]

Just as in Germany, the high point of Hauptmann's acclaim as a public figure in America came in 1932, when he made his second and final visit to this country. Principal organizer, impresario, press agent, interpreter, general factotum, and eventual historian of the visit was Columbia University professor and long-time Hauptmann friend and admirer Frederick W. J. Heuser.[5] Never before, according to Heuser, had a German national been so celebrated in America, and never had the press preoccupied itself to such an extent for three whole weeks with a "mere" author. From his triumphal motorcade arrival in New York's City Hall, where (in stark contrast to his previous humiliating experience with that building thirty-eight years earlier because of the *Hannele* debacle) he was warmly received by the popular mayor James A. ("Jimmy") Walker on February 26, to his tumultuous farewell on March 16, the daily stream of honors bestowed upon him was avidly reported by the *New York Times* and other leading newspapers. And while the ostensible occasion for the trip was his centennial Goethe address, Hauptmann also enjoyed the benefits of a highly privileged tourist. The main celebration occurred at Columbia University on February 29, where he was awarded an honorary doctorate and graciously responded to the praise of his hosts with the remark that "if I were not a German I should like to be an American."[6] The following day, before a sell-out crowd, he delivered his Goethe address, which was also broadcast by radio to the entire United States, Canada, and Germany. Repetitions of the speech took him to Harvard, Johns Hopkins, and George Washington universities. Other highlights included visits to Harlem and to a house once occupied by Edgar Allen Poe; a three-day stay in Cambridge, Massachusetts, at Craigie House, in which Longfellow had lived; a meeting with President Hoover in the White House and a reception in his honor by the political elite of Washington, as well as introductions to such notables as Theodore Dreiser, Sinclair Lewis, Helen Keller, Lillian Gish, and Eugene O'Neill—whose *Mourning Becomes Electra* he had an opportunity to see and admire. Finally, at a Lotos Club dinner in his honor, Ethel Barrymore, the doyenne of American actresses, provided what was perhaps the most moving testimonial. Having rushed to New York by train from an engagement in Ohio just to meet the author, she stammered this tribute:

It is a very difficult place to speak after Dr. Hauptmann. I am not a speaker, but I wish just to tell you that it is the greatest moment of my life tonight to be sitting at the table with Dr. Hauptmann. It makes me feel as if I were sitting with Beethoven, with Goethe, and Hauptmann.

I feel that so much, I have nothing else that I can say. It is true . . . that my favorite role is Rose Bernd of Hauptmann of all that I have ever played—and I have played many, many roles. Thank you! I can't say any more.[7]

As Hauptmann harvested the fruits of a long, productive lifetime, so, too, does Matthias Clausen, the hero of *Before Sunset*. Privy councillor, industrialist, owner of a publishing house, and cultured man of letters, he appears to possess a devoted family, friends, admirers, distinguished standing in the world, and everything a man of his station could wish for. As the play opens, amidst the joyful revelry of his seventieth birthday and the sounds of a jazz band, it even appears that the depression he suffered over the death of his beloved spouse three years earlier has finally been overcome. Largely responsible for the improved outlook is Inken Peters, the niece of a gardener on one of his estates who works as a seamstress and conducts a small kindergarten. In spite of an age difference of half a century and radical disparities in social background, the two have fallen in love, and the old man is making plans to marry Inken and to live out the remainder of his days with her in a house in Switzerland. The Clausen children and their spouses do everything in their power to prevent the marriage, ostensibly because they worry about the seemliness of a match between such an odd couple but, as soon becomes clear, much more from mercenary motives. A symbolic climax of their animosity occurs at a breakfast gathering when a place setting for Inken, whom Clausen had intended to introduce formally to his family, is removed before her arrival. When threats, blackmail, and bribery fail to produce the desired results, the plotters, aided and abetted by the Protestant pastor Immoos and the legal counsel Hanefeldt, succeed in having Clausen declared incompetent. Devastated by the meanness of those closest to him (only his youngest son, Egmont, has shown occasional compassion and understanding), in the last act Clausen finds himself—desperate, confused, and in ill health—in the modest home of Inken's uncle, the gardener. Still trying to flee to Switzerland but with his enemies in close pursuit, he kills himself by taking poison. To the concern voiced by Pastor Immoos that the family should be spared the sight of the dead man, Professor Geiger, an old friend from Cambridge who has come to support Clausen in his hour of need, replies with the final words of the play: "But why, Pastor? It has what it wants" (3:377).

123

*Before Sunset* represents Hauptmann's elegiac farewell to an era still characterized by high cultural aspirations but already afflicted by premonitions of the darkness that was soon to descend over civilized Europe. Adolf Hitler came to power in January of 1933, and by July of that year the author presciently concluded, "My epoch begins in 1870 and ends with the burning of the Reichstag."[8] Too well known to be completely excluded from the cultural life of his nation, Hauptmann nevertheless found himself crowded more and more into offstage obscurity. There is cruel irony in the fact that a 1937 film version of *Before Sunset* (*The Ruler* [*Der Herrscher*]) starring Emil Jannings was placed in the service of the Nazi propaganda mill.

Hauptmann's work is at least three plays in one: a love drama, a drama of social criticism, and yet another embodiment of the *Urdrama*. As a love drama it reflects the author's predilection for May-December romances deriving from his own personal proclivities, but also perhaps from the example of a grandfather who was over sixty when he remarried and fathered four more children and that of Goethe's famous love affair at the age of seventy-three with a woman more than fifty years his junior. As a drama of social criticism, *Before Sunset* is easily seen as a pendant to the early Naturalist family dramas. Like *Before Sunrise* it depicts the decline of a family, albeit with a somewhat stronger psychological emphasis. Whereas the earlier drama placed the blame for the decline on alcohol, heredity, and a nouveau riche environment, *Before Sunset* depicts an era of such brutal, cynical materialism that it even turns children and parents against each other. The most drastic exemplar of this soulless new age, and Clausen's most insidious antagonist, is his son-in-law Erich Klamroth, a Darwinian capitalist of whom it can truly be said that he knows the price of everything and the value of nothing. The familiar elements of the *Urdrama* come into play near its end. Inken describes the pursuers of her lover as a "dehumanized horde," a pack of "staghounds," (3:372) and Clausen develops a "thirst for destruction" that causes "the blood to freeze in one's veins" (3:373). By the time he swallows the poison, illumination is at hand; he does so in a state of exaltation, while listening to "a fugue, a motet or an oratorio" (3:373) audible only to himself.

While *Before Sunset* may also owe something to Shakespeare (its original title was *Der neue Lear* [The New Lear], and the theme of the ungrateful children is very prominent), the humane spirit with which Clausen is identified owes much more to Goethe, especially in the latter's old age. Thus the drama represents not only a significant contribution to the observance of the "Goethe Year" (1932), but it also marks a growing tendency on Hauptmann's part to adapt existing works by his illustrious "father" (he considered himself, only half-jokingly, as Goethe's "son") for his own, very different ends. Among the more obvious examples are the drama *Iphigenie in Aulis* (1944); the narratives *Das Märchen* (The Fairytale)[9] of 1941; and *Mignon,* completed in 1944. *Before Sunset* has numerous reminders of Goethe. Perhaps somewhat too hubristically Clausen has given his children Goethean names (Wolfgang, Egmont, Bettina, and Ottilie) they can hardly hope to live up to, at least to their father's expectations. Goethean quotations (and parodies of Goethean quotations) occur throughout the work, and, in a risky flirtation with kitsch, Hauptmann even has Inken reenact the all too familiar scene from *Werther* in which the charming Lotte slices bread for the children crowding around her. Clausen himself embodies much of Goethe's "pure humanity," but at a time when such old-fashioned virtues are ridiculed as weakness by the likes of his son-in-law and are, at any rate, no longer a bulwark against the rapaciousness of modern commercial and political reality.

In addition to paying homage to Goethe, *Before Sunset* also memorializes several of the author's personal friends. The character of Geiger is based on Hermann G. Fiedler (*Fiedler/Geiger* = fiddler/violinist), a professor of German literature at Oxford who was instrumental in the award of Hauptmann's first honorary doctorate. Clausen himself is a composite figure embodying characteristics of Walter Rathenau, the idealist, industrialist, and politician who, as Foreign Minister of the Weimar Republic, was assassinated in 1922; and in particular of Max Pinkus, a manufacturer, art patron, book collector, and early Hauptmann bibliographer whose problems with his own children, resulting from the widower's love for a much younger woman, are very similar to Clausen's. Paradigmatic for what such culturally sophisticated and high-minded individuals could expect from the immediate future in Germany is the humiliating experience of Pinkus. By 1934 he found himself persona non grata in his native land for the unpardonable crime of Jewishness.[10]

## NOTES

1. See Wolfgang Leppmann, *Gerhart Hauptmanns Leben, Werk und Zeit* (Bern, Munich, Vienna: Scherz, 1986), p. 353.

2. See Peter Sprengel, *Gerhart Hauptmann, Epoche–Werk–Wirkung* (Munich: Beck, 1984), p. 226.

3. Quoted by Sprengel, 226. For a detailed account of Hauptmann's political stance see Karl S. Guthke, "The King of the Weimar Republic: Gerhart Hauptmann's Role in Political Life, 1919–1933," in *Probleme der Moderne: Studien zur deutschen Literatur von Nietzsche bis Brecht, Festschrift für Walter Sokel* (Tübingen: Niemeyer, 1983), pp. 369–87.

4. For detailed bibliographical information about these and more than a hundred additional translations of Hauptmann's works into English see Sigfrid Hoefert, *Internationale Bibliographie* 1:369–87.

5. For a day-by-day account of Hauptmann's 1932 trip to America see Frederick W. J. Heuser, *Gerhart Hauptmann: Zu seinem Leben und Schaffen* (Tübingen: Niemeyer, 1961), pp. 67–91.

6. Quoted by Heuser, 78.

7. Quoted by Walter A. Reichart, "Gerhart Hauptmann's Dramas on the American Stage," *Maske und Kothern* 8 (1962): 225.

8. Quoted by Carl F. W. Behl, *Zwiesprache mit Gerhart Hauptmann: Tagebuchblätter* (Munich: Desch, 1949), p. 25.

9. For an interpretation of this work that compares and contrasts Goethe's and Hauptmann's treatments see Robin A. Clouser, "The Pilgrim of Consciousness: Hauptmann's Syncretistic Fairy Tale," in *Hauptmann-Forschung: Neue Beiträge; Hauptmann Research: New Directions,* eds. Peter Sprengel and Philip Mellen (Frankfurt/M., Bern, New York: Peter Lang, 1986), pp. 303–22.

10. For a description of Pinkus's circumstances, his role as a model for Matthias Clausen, and his friendship with Hauptmann, see Walter A. Reichart, "In Memoriam Max Pinkus," in Hans Joachim Schrimpf, ed., *Gerhart Hauptmann* (Darmstadt: Wissenschaftliche Buchgesellschaft, 1976), p. 33.

# CHAPTER TEN

# Symphony in Prose

## Flagman Thiel

In Hauptmann's development as a dramatist, a distinct progression in the mastery of his craft is discernible from 1889 (*Before Sunrise*) to about 1911 (*The Rats*). In contrast to this pattern, *Bahnwärter Thiel* (1888) (*Flagman Thiel*) is a highly acclaimed masterpiece of prose fiction created at the beginning of his literary career and never quite equaled afterwards.[1] Written in Erkner during the early morning hours around the period of the birth of his second son and published in the Munich Naturalist periodical *Die Gesellschaft* (Society), this remarkable German novella marked Hauptmann's debut as an author of great potential. Although considerably milder than that occasioned by such dramas as *Before Sunrise, The Weavers,* or *Hannele,* this work also provoked its share of controversy. While some early readers welcomed in it primarily a Zolaesque Naturalism applied to the portrayal of distinctly German characters and circumstances, conservatives and Marxists alike decried its seemingly bleak and pessimistic depiction of the human condition.[2] Unconvincing Marxist interpretations to the contrary, the causes of the Thiel family tragedy derive more directly from universal human circumstances than from socioeconomic problems.[3] And while the novella has been widely read in German schools since around the end of the First World War as a classic example of Naturalism, it has also long been recognized by critics and scholars that such a rigid classification is much too narrow. *Flagman Thiel* features an early (but as we know from *Rose Bernd, The Rats,* and *Magnus Garbe,* recurrent) thematic complex of marriage, birth, and death, presented in a literary form skillfully amalgamated from naturalistic, symbolic, and mystical elements. In many respects it is paradigmatic for much of Hauptmann's future oeuvre; and, as a work with an established place in German literary history, it represents a transitional landmark reflecting past, contemporary, and future periods such as Poetic Realism, Naturalism, and Neoromanticism.

Because the story's salient characteristics are more powerfully atmospheric, lyrical, and musical than narrative (it has been convincingly described as a "symphonic poem"),[4] the plot of *Flagman Thiel* can be summarized in a few words. It examines the life, conflicts, and eventual destruction of a simple, almost child-like railroad—crossing guard and his family, whose situation is similar in many respects to the situation in *Drayman Henschel*. Like Henschel, Thiel is a widower who, ostensibly to provide a mother for Tobias, the son he has had with his deceased wife Minna, marries and becomes the guilt-ridden victim of a brutally sensual woman, Lene, who dominates him through the overwhelming power of her sexuality while simultaneously neglecting the child she had been expected to nurture. The climactic event is an accident in which the boy is struck and killed by a racing express train. Although neglectful of his safety, Lene can hardly be accused of consciously causing Tobias's death. Thiel, however, in an explosion of long-repressed and unarticulated rage, slaughters her and the child she has in the meantime borne him. The destructive paroxysm having run its course, Thiel lapses into a state of benign, lethargic insanity and is last seen in a charity hospital ward for the insane, guarding in his hands Tobias's little brown cap "with jealous care and tenderness" (6:67).

In spite of considerable effort expended on finding a real—life counterpart to the plot of *Flagman Thiel* (of the kind available for *The Rats,* for example), such searches have remained unproductive. When asked about a model for Thiel, Hauptmann was able to recall later only that he had spoken a great deal with a crossing guard in his little railroad shack located near the village of Fangschleuse.[5] The "humus" from which this particular narrative grew must, therefore, be sought elsewhere: in more general personal experiences of its author, in literary sources, and in the zeitgeist.

From the perspectives of personal experience two periods in Hauptmann's life seem especially promising here: the years immediately after 1877 and those following his move to Erkner with Marie in 1885. When Robert Hauptmann lost his hotel to creditors in 1877 and was reduced to the socially inferior status of running a mere railroad restaurant in Sorgau, the move was humiliating for the sensitive adolescent Gerhart, but it also steeped him in the railroad atmosphere that so thoroughly permeates *Flagman Thiel*. Difficult as it may be for someone in an age of hydrogen bombs and rockets to the moon to imagine, the steam engine was for young Hauptmann the embodiment of an awe-inspiring, quasi-diabolical technology. The noise and speed of "these iron colossi of locomotives" and their "inescapable, powerful rhythm" (7:724) stood in strong contrast to the idyllic natural surroundings of his boyhood. That he was both fascinated and repelled by these monstrous intrusions into the landscape is clear from two early poems, "Der Nachtzug" (The Night Train) and "Der Wärter" (The Crossing Guard). The former plainly anticipates the admixture of romanticism, mysticism, and technology of

*Thiel,* while the latter is more strongly oriented towards social criticism; it depicts the sufferings of a poor, deathly ill railway employee with a wife and child desperately in need of his support who collapses and dies beside the tracks.

While the Sorgau experience acquainted Hauptmann with the technology of the railroad (and with a variety of people employed in its demanding service), a second important aspect of the novella, the atmosphere and natural beauty of its setting, derives largely from the author's life in Erkner. "I had never been so close to nature as then," he was to recall later. "Through the mystery of birth [of a son] it was as though the earth too had opened itself up to me. The forests, lakes, meadows, and fields exhaled the same mystery. There was contained within it a somehow disconsolate magnificence, a grandeur through which one was placed before the gate (closed, to be sure) of ultimate comprehension" (7:1033).

In a search for literary models for *Thiel* it soon becomes obvious that, more than for any other of Hauptmann's works, Büchner is of central importance. Hauptmann confessed that "Georg Büchner's works, about which I had given a lecture before the *Durch* society [in 1887], had made an enormous impression on me. The incomparable monument that he had left behind after only twenty-three years of life, the novella *Lenz,* the *Woyzeck* fragment, had for me the significance of great discoveries" (7:1061). The importance of this Büchner "cult" (7:1061) has long been recognized and thoroughly explored in relation to *Thiel.*[6] Attention has been focused on similarities between the two authors' weltanschauung, formal attributes of their prose, and characters. Both Büchner and Hauptmann are strongly fatalistic, and because the lives of their characters are determined by forces over which they have little or no control, their creators refuse to subject them to moral censure, preferring instead to reply to their failings and transgressions with compassion. Both authors are skillful at depicting stages of mental deterioration resulting in madness (see *Lenz*), and both employ a combination of realism and symbolism to achieve their desired results. Comparing Büchner's Franz Woyzeck with Hauptmann's Franz Thiel, Silz has pointed out that "both are simple, not to say simple-minded, faithful, 'kinderlieb,' inarticulate, concealing profound spiritual depths beneath a usually tranquil surface; easy-going, slow to suspicion and wrath, but finally capable of murderous violence against the women who have failed them."[7] Although neither of these antiheroes can escape completely the consequences of their low social status, it is their irrepressible and universal human qualities that shine forth in the end. Both are victims of a "progress" that has, outwardly at least, reduced them to a mechanical existence. For Woyzeck the dehumanizing force is embodied in the sadistic experiments of the medical doctor who sees in him only a human guinea pig; for Thiel it is a pedantic punctuality engendered by the demands of his railroad employment. Whereas Woyzeck has order imposed upon him by his superiors (and finds it difficult to subjugate his nature to their demands), Thiel seems to have adopted order as a defense mechanism. It is expressed not only in the mechanical precision with which he exercises his occupational obligations, in his regular church attendance, in the pedantic treatment of his few personal possessions, and in the monotonous rhythm of his daily existence, but, especially, in his effort to compartmentalize the central conflict of his life: his enthrallment by two women of totally opposite natures. Unable to resist the animalistic, physical blandishments of Lene (and feeling guilt for succumbing to them), he has established a shrine to his ethereal, spiritual, dead wife Minna in his lonely railroad shack, where he communes with her nightly. By keeping the physical and spiritual halves of his life scrupulously separated in this way, by imposing on them the same mechanical order he observes in his daily activities, he hopes to control them. However, as we know from Hauptmann's concept of the *Urdrama,* life is too chaotic to be managed so easily. A momentary lapse of caution, during which Thiel reveals that he has received a small strip of land near the tracks for his own use, becomes a fateful turning point when it leads to a merging of the two realms. Having once heard about it, Lene cannot be restrained from the urge to plant potatoes in the little plot—a necessity, she claims, for the poor family. As usual her forcefulness prevails, and tragedy is the result. Diverted by her work, she neglects to keep an eye on Tobias; he is killed, and Thiel's repressed emotions explode in fury.

Hauptmann has been aptly described as a "seismograph of his time."[8] Literarily this description seems especially apt for his early successes and can be illustrated by a closer look at the female characters depicted in *Flagman Thiel.* While Thiel is reasonably well-rounded and individualized, both Minna and Lene come close to representing melodramatic types who would have been at home in much of the popular literature of the day and who embody naturalistic stereotypes of women in general. At a time when women were struggling to achieve an enhancement of their status in society (equality with men remained a wistful dream), male writers and intellectuals found it both expedient and consoling to reduce them to two contradictory types: the idealized, pure—not to say immaculate—mother, and the sexually destructive whore, usually from the lower classes. Minna and Lene reflect these stereotypes. Minna (whose name associates readily with the medieval concept of

*Minne*, a sublimated, spiritualized form of eros) is described as "a slender, sickly looking woman . . . who hadn't suited well Thiel's Herculean stature" (6:37) but who had been bound to him by "a more spiritualized love" (6:39). Outwardly Lene appears the more suitable spouse for Thiel. In strong contrast to her predecessor, "the former cowherd appeared as though made for the flagman. She was barely half a head shorter than he and surpassed him in fullness of limb. Also her face was carved quite as crudely as his, only that, in contrast to that of the flagman, it lacked soul" (6:38).

Although scornful of Strindberg's simplistic depictions of the battle of the sexes, Hauptmann, apparently unknowingly, shares a good deal of the Swede's misogyny. Not only is he partial to what he sees as an obsessive Strindbergian theme—the man trapped between and destroyed by two women[9] (compare *Henschel* and *Schilling*)—but he too seems to revel in the depiction of vulnerable males threatened by an all-powerful female sexuality. Surprised by Thiel as she is beating Tobias, Lene escapes her husband's wrath by paralyzing his ability to react: "Her full, half-naked breasts swelled from excitement and threatened to burst her bodice, and her gathered skirts made her broad hips appear even broader. An invincible, inescapable power, which Thiel felt unable to control, emanated from the woman" (6:47). Only the death of his son and the depths of suffering caused by it break the spell, and Thiel acts with devastating physical violence to escape and get revenge for the bondage he has been powerless to resist.

Perhaps because Lene's domination of Thiel is so blatant, Minna's role in his destruction tends to be overlooked. His love for his first wife is just as compulsive, irrational, and abnormal as his sensual enslavement by Lene. From a psychological perspective, Thiel (and some would claim his creator) fears both women. The good, spiritualized woman is banned to the realm of the dead; the evil, sensual one is beaten and butchered.[10] As Jofen has pointed out, the theme of *mariage à trois* tends to assume a special variation in Hauptmann's work, with the third person, a dead mother, continuing to dominate the unfortunate father from the grave.[11] (Compare not only *Thiel* and *Henschel* but also such later dramas as *Winterballade* [1917] [*Winter Ballad*] and *Veland* [1925]). Personally familiar to Hauptmann since the death of his cousin Georg and the death cult practiced on his behalf by his aunt in Lederose, such infatuation with the dead can exert a powerful influence on the daily lives of the living. By continuing to cede to Minna a controlling force over his inner life, Thiel, of course, exacerbates his anguish over Tobias.

It has been frequently noted that what separates Hauptmann's Thiel character from those of his Poetic Realist predecessors is a modern mood of isolation, an existential loneliness and sense of ultimate futility, and that his characteristic taciturnity and inarticulateness mirror a feeling of "external and inner abandonment."[12] This sense of abandonment is of a kind expressed by the famous "fairy tale" related by the character of the grandmother in Büchner's *Woyzeck*[13] and is manifested most poignantly in little Tobias, a sickly, abused child deprived of the warmth and emotional security of a loving, caring mother. As Klaus D. Post has convincingly shown, such a quintessential motherless state assumed for Hauptmann the force of a potent, recurring metaphor through which to express the inhumane coldness of modern existence.[14] Again it derives from a congruence of personal and zeitgeist elements. Although Hauptmann was strongly attached to his own mother, during his earliest formative years, as has been noted, her duties in helping run the hotel often deprived him of her coveted attention and left him to fend for himself or, worse still, in the dubious care of a brutal nursemaid. Even years later he vividly recalled a cosmic dream, reminiscent of the Büchner scene mentioned above, that epitomized his feelings of abandonment from that time: "There were dimensions of the most monstrous kind which were made graphic to me. I saw nothing less than the earth rolling along in space. I myself, however, was stuck to it, hopelessly, like a dizzying, minimal speck of life, doomed to death, in danger at every moment of plunging off into endless expanses" (7:489).

Leaving aside the autobiographical dimension, the Tobias character must have been of particular interest to Hauptmann's contemporaries. In no previous epoch had so much attention been focused on the study (social, political, pedagogical, or scientific) of childhood as during the Naturalist era. Given the appalling conditions in which children were often forced to work and live (see *The Weavers*), such attention was long overdue. The economic conditions which made it necessary for mothers to spend long hours each day away from home frequently resulted in their virtual abandonment of their offspring. A typical contemporary exposé provides a context within which readers of Hauptmann's novella could appreciate the emotional state of "motherless" children like Tobias. It reads in part, "A most horrible fact: Infants in their cradle, without care, day after day, without nursing, without motherly attention. Not a breath of love can warm them, no tender hand caress them, no mouth kiss them. No one to rock them to sleep, no one to sing songs to them, to laugh with them, to bathe them, to arrange their pillow, to enliven and refresh their little souls with games and dallying. The flat is empty and locked. No human being breathes in it, except the small, helpless mite of a child. The mother slaves in a factory. . . . "[15] Although Tobias's situation is somewhat different, the sense of motherless isolation it engenders is equally pervasive. His biological mother died when he was born, bequeathing him only her own delicate constitution and none of the benefits of genuine motherhood, and Lene actively abuses him both physically and psychologically—the latter in the time-honored manner of wicked stepmothers by letting him know how worthless he is.

More important than plot or characterization for an estimation of Hauptmann's narrative talent at this early stage of his career are some of the more formal aspects of his story. Although he was careful to label it a "study" (6:36)—thereby implying a more modest, tentative, and experimental approach—*Flagman Thiel* shares many of the attributes of the *Novelle* genre that flourished in Germany and Switzerland especially during the late nineteenth century. Silz includes among these its brevity; at least a relative limitation as to time and place; few adult characters; no real evaluation of character but, instead, the revelation of a hitherto submerged aspect of character under the stress of crisis; a striking central event (the death of Tobias); a turning point (Thiel's first vision of his dead wife); a straightforward plot easily summarized in a few sentences; a sharply profiled "silhouette"; and even, perhaps, Paul Heyse's notorious "falcon"—a physical object which plays a memorable role in the story (Tobias's little brown cap).[16]

Yet, in spite of such familiar traits, contemporaries must have been struck by Hauptmann's radical adaptation of the *Novelle* genre to a changed, modern zeitgeist. *Flagman Thiel* ends in chaos and disorder instead of the harmony more typical of Poetic Realism, and the shock of a brutal multiple murder (at a time when such crimes were still extremely rare) was not something readers of Gottfried Keller or Theodor Storm would have been prepared for. Indeed, it was such naturalistic elements that served most clearly to distance the work from more conventional literature of the day. These elements include the depiction of a passive central character from a lower-class background in a specific milieu; attention to details of heredity (Tobias has his father's red hair and his mother's frailty); an undisguised emphasis on sexuality; the rather clinical description of progressive mental derangement; a minutely detailed narrative style that, at times, comes close to Arno Holz's *Sekundenstil;* a preoccupation with technology; the use of actual place names; and the depiction of ugly, crass reality (Lene's abuse of Tobias, Thiel's aborted strangulation of Lene's infant, and the final discovery of the mutilated bodies).

Nonetheless, such an impressive catalogue of naturalist traits notwithstanding, to simply consign Hauptmann's novella to the Naturalist movement is much too restrictive. Particularly in the character of Franz Thiel, for example, there is still a strong residue of Romantic ideology (for example, the belief that simple, down-to-earth, uneducated human beings have easier access to numinous levels of existence than their more sophisticated brethren). At the opposite extreme, there is considerable anticipation of future literary developments such as fin de siècle symbolism. The complex, virtuoso manipulation and control of every aspect of composition (symbols, leitmotifs, nature descriptions, and the like) is of such a higher order that it bears favorable comparison with Thomas Mann's *Death in Venice* (1912). (Like such rare masterpieces it must be absorbed whole through multiple readings, yields different secrets to individual readers of varied background, and will always retain elements of an ineffable, residual obscurity.)

Some sense of Hauptmann's "irrational realism"[17] can be conveyed by a closer inspection of a few symbols that provide for much of the compositional unity of the work. Superficially (and with the caveat that neatly separating them is contrary to the author's obvious intention) they can be categorized, for our purpose, as relating to technology and nature. Of the former, the railroad and its tracks, steam locomotive, telegraph wires, crossing-guard shack, and other accouterments figure most prominently.

Because of its omnipresence and the vitalistic terms in which it is depicted, it would not be too farfetched to consider the railroad as an important character in the story. It is a governing force of Thiel's external life as well as the locus of his inner existence. During ten years of servitude in its behalf, the reader learns in the first paragraph, he has suffered only two lapses of duty— both occasioned by the dangerous railroad itself: one as the result of a lump of coal that had fallen from the tender of a passing locomotive and "had struck him and flung him with a smashed leg into the ditch beside the track; the other time on account of a wine bottle which had flown out of an express train racing by, and had struck him in the middle of his chest" (6:37). At the end of the story, after the murders and the retreat into insanity, Thiel is found sitting between the rails at the precise spot where Tobias was killed. Briefly, for the first and only time, he is able to prevail over the train by forcing it to stop, but he is soon overpowered, bound hand and foot, and dispatched to the Charité hospital in Berlin. Throughout the novella the railroad is depicted in anthropomorphic terms as an all-powerful, demonic beast of destruction before which mere human beings are as helpless as before a natural cataclysm. "Panting" (6:63) or "stretching its sinews" (6:60), by night with "two red, round lights penetrating the darkness like the goggle-eyes of a gigantic monster" (6:53), it appears in daylight out of infinity, a dark point on the horizon, suddenly expanding into an enormous, black presence before disappearing into unearthly stillness as mysteriously as it arrived—paralleling Thiel's own fate in its inscrutable origin, sudden destructive force, and equally sudden lapse into deathly calm. It is almost as though this piece of cold technology were capable of mocking its human victims. After Tobias has been reduced to a lifeless object, "thrown to and fro between the wheels like a rubber ball," (6:58) a herd of deer watched over by a stag is seen standing on the tracks but gracefully escapes the oncoming locomotive.

Whereas the locomotive assumes vital, malicious overtones, Lene tends to be described in terms of a soulless machine. Depersonalized at one point with the inappropriate neuter definite article as "*das Mensch*" (6:38) (instead of *der Mensch* = human being), she beats Tobias "as though pieces of clothing were being dusted out" (6:46) and tills her little plot of land "with the speed and endurance of a machine" (6:56). Gradually and subtly Hauptmann establishes a parallel between Lene and the train so that when the catastrophe occurs they both seem culpable victimizers.

It is not only the train, however, but also the tracks which deserve attention. It may be stretching things to ascribe phallic significance to them as Jean Jofen does (she refers to the contention of Stekel, a disciple of Freud, that tracks—referred to at one point as resembling "firey snakes"—signify "path to woman"),[18] but it does seem clear that Hauptmann too has weighted them with symbolic value. Spatially, and as an irresistible "track of fate," they seem to run right through the middle of the narrative; and, running parallel to each other, like Thiel's attempt to keep the two halves of his life parallel but separate, they nevertheless converge in a "dark point" (6:49).

Thiel's mystical inclinations flourish especially in the railroad shack, which at night becomes a chapel for Minna. "A faded photograph of the dead woman before him on the table, open song book and Bible, he read and sang alternately throughout the long night, only interrupted at intervals by trains raging by, and, in so doing, fell into an ecstasy which intensified into visions in which he saw the departed bodily before him" (6:40). Reflections of his sexual bondage to Lene and of his guilt over his failure to protect Tobias from her abuse, these visions help push Thiel to the edge of insanity and make the subsequent catastrophe, if not inevitable, at least highly plausible.

Hauptmann's skill at saturating mundane, technological locales and artifacts with atmospheric significance is also shown by his recurring reference to the telegraph wires strung along the railroad embankment. The wind passing over them contributes to the subtle acoustical effects that complement so well the striking visual images of the narrative. Walking along the track with his son shortly before the accident, Thiel shares with him the pleasure of the mysterious music they produce.

> Holding little Tobias by the hand he often stopped to listen to the wonderful sounds that streamed forth out of the wood [of the telegraph poles] like sonorous chorales from the interior of a church. The pole at the south end of his section had an especially full and beautiful harmony. There was a turmoil of tones in its interior which continued to resound, without interruption as though from a single breath, and Tobias ran around the weathered wood in order, as he believed, to discover the originator of the lovely sound through an opening. The flagman fell into a solemn mood, as though in church. Additionally, with time, he identified a voice which reminded him of his dead wife. He imagined it was a chorus of blessed spirits, into which she also mingled her voice, and this notion awakened a longing in him, a longing close to tears. (6:56–57)

This passage, which freely mixes technology, nature, religion, and psychology in a kind of magic realism, by no means exhausts the telegraph wire symbolism. While it successfully illustrates his dead wife's spiritual hold on Thiel, at a crucial point in the story the author is also able to expand the same imagery to include the threatening sexuality of Lene. Her strong identification with machines and technology, mentioned earlier, is further enhanced by association with the recurrent image of an iron net, based on both the iron rails of the railroad and the wires of the telegraph. "The black, parallel tracks . . . resemble . . . an enormous *iron mesh net* . . . and . . . . On the wires, which crept from pole to pole like the *web of a giant spider,* flocks of twittering birds were stuck in dense rows. A woodpecker flew away laughing over Thiel's head . . . " (emphasis added [6:49]). Two pages earlier Lene's feeling of dominance over Thiel had been suggested in similar terms. "Easily, like a fine *spider web,* and yet as tightly as a *web of iron,* it wrapped itself around him, binding, overpowering, and enervating him (emphasis added [6:47]). As original as such imagery may seem to us today, it too derives from that stock arsenal of symbols frequently invoked by contemporary authors and graphic artists at the turn of the century to epitomize lethal femininity—woman as black widow intent upon enticing, paralyzing, and devouring her mate.[19] Unlike the laughing bird, but very much like so many of Hauptmann's heroes and heroines still waiting in the wings, Thiel is unable to escape his own fateful "web of iron" without paying a heavy price—in this case his loss of sanity.

Among the most unnaturalistic aspects of *Flagman Thiel* are its nature descriptions and use of animal and color imagery. Although close to the author's own experiences—long walks in the forest solitude (*Waldeinsamkeit* [6:47]) of the pine woods near Erkner—nature is used to enhance the sense of a transparent reality behind which fateful, mysterious forces are constantly lurking. For Hauptmann "religious feeling has its deepest roots in nature,"[20] and in his novella nature descriptions are finely attuned to the requirements of plot, character, and atmosphere. As Martini has shown, the author, by his generous use of verbs of motion in describing nature, insures that it is rarely static.[21] In addition, he makes nature an integral part of his fictional cosmos by merging images appropriate to disparate aspects of Thiel's environment: tree trunks glow "like iron" (6:49); rain drops suffused by the red of a locomotive headlight are changed into "drops of blood" (6:53); the noise of a train is described in terms of a charging "cavalry squadron" (6:49); steel railroad tracks "suck up the pale moonlight" (6:52); and the moon itself becomes a "pale golden bowl" (6:52) or a "signal lamp" (6:65). Not surprisingly, Hauptmann also orchestrates nature freely to reflect Thiel's changing emotions and moods (fear, loneliness, calm, inner turmoil) or as a dramatic setting for enhancing the power of his visions. After Tobias's accident nature even seems to share his grief: "A gentle breath of evening air moved softly, steadily over the forest, and pink-flamed curls of clouds hovered over the western heavens" (6:62), and the moon shining on them "paints the faces of the men [carrying Tobias's body] in corpse-like tones" (6:65).

Animals also play a significant role in the artistic economy of *Flagman Thiel*, although those mentioned (including birds, squirrels, deer, and a poodle) do not belong to the "fang and claw" species so frequently identified with Naturalism. Instead, and appropriate for a hero who communes with the dead, they tend to be associated with a variety of superstitions, sometimes local ones. From time immemorial birds have been seen as messengers between the worlds of the living and the dead, and the crows and woodpecker mentioned in the story are considered to have special demonic attributes. (In Hauptmann's Silesia crows are messengers of death. According to local folklore their call is "Grab! Grab!" [grave]).[22] The squirrel Tobias encounters with his father just before the accident is likewise thought to possess oracular powers. Tobias's question on seeing it ("Father, is that . . . God?") has caused considerable puzzlement among interpreters; but, given the mystical tenor of Hauptmann's story, it is doubtful that much would be gained by a definitive, explicit explanation. (For what it is worth—or to add yet another element of ironic ambiguity—the superstitious of Silesia were accused of readiness to believe that the devil is a squirrel.)[23]

Color symbolism (often in synesthetic combination with sounds) adds another strong element of originality to *Flagman Thiel*. And while it would require a separate essay to do justice to this topic, it seems safe to say that no German writer before Hauptmann had so thoroughly saturated such a short prose work with such a profusion of meaningful colors, and that even the later Expressionists failed to surpass him in this regard. Not only do certain colors such as the polarity of black and white (the colors of the demonic locomotive and the pallor of death), red (sunsets, blood, vitality of life), and brown (Tobias's cap, a deer killed on the tracks, the squirrel mentioned above) suggest a metalanguage of symbolic gesture, but, as Krämer has pointed out, even the sequence in which colors are introduced appears to recapitulate the cycle of events depicted in the novella.[24]

"Everything that belongs only to the present dies along with the present."[25] This remark by Mikhail Bakhtin, Russia's greatest twentieth-century literary theorist and critic, would certainly have appealed to Hauptmann, who rejected fanatical, time-bound dogmatism in literature and politics alike. What he aspired to in his best work was permanence, and this could best be achieved by concentrating his talent on the depiction of eternally human qualities that can never lose their topicality and are a staple of great world literature (for example, the Bible; classical literature of Greece and Rome, and Grimms' *Fairy Tales*). As noted before, in recent years attempts have been made to link even Hauptmann's early work to models of such mythic stature. And, while the role of coincidence cannot be entirely discounted—erotic entanglements, child neglect, and murder are not unique in the annals of world literature—Clouser has shown a considerable number of detailed and interesting correspondences between Hauptmann's novella and the Hellenic myth of Hercules. These include but are by no means limited to physical traits (Thiel's "Herculean physique" [6:37]), "an emotional religiosity, self-slaughtered families, and an ambivalent reaction to women."[26]

## NOTES

1. See also, however, the short narrative *Carnival* (*Fasching*, 1887), 6:13–34, discussed in Warren R. Maurer, *Gerhart Hauptmann* (Boston: Twayne, 1982), pp. 13–15.

2. Cf. Klaus D. Post, *Gerhart Hauptmann. Bahnwärter Thiel: Text, Materialien, Kommentar* (Munich, Vienna: Hanser, 1979), pp. 47–50.

3. See, for example, Irene Heerdegen, "Gerhart Hauptmanns Novelle 'Bahnwärter Thiel,'" *Weimarer Beiträge* 3 (1958): esp. 353 and 359–60.

4. See Larry Wells, "Words of Music: Gerhart Hauptmann's Composition *Bahnwärter Thiel*, in *Wege der Worte: Festschrift für Wolfgang Fleischhauer* (Cologne, Vienna: Böhlau, 1978), p. 385.

5. See Eberhard Hilscher, *Gerhart Hauptmann. Leben und Werk* (Frankfurt/M.: Athenäum, 1988), p. 90.

6. For a summary discussion and secondary literature relating to this topic see Post, 100–108.

7. See Walter Silz, *Realism and Reality: Studies in the German Novelle of Poetic Realism* (Chapel Hill: University of North Carolina Press, 1954), p. 146.

8. See Ralph Fiedler, *Die späten Dramen Gerhart Hauptmanns: Versuch einer Deutung* (Munich: Bergstadt, 1954), p. 135.

9. Cf. Peter Sprengel, *Die Wirklichkeit der Mythen: Untersuchungen zum Werk Gerhart Hauptmanns* (Berlin: E. Schmidt, 1982), p. 182.

10. See Herbert Krämer, *Gerhart Hauptmann: Bahnwärter Thiel* (Munich: R. Oldenbourg, 1980), 18.

11. Jean Jofen, *Das letzte Geheimnis: Eine psychologische Studie über die Brüder Gerhart und Carl Hauptmann* (Bern: Francke, 1972), p. 51.

12. See Fritz Martini, *Das Wagnis der Sprache: Interpretationen deutscher Prosa von Nietzsche bis Benn* (Stuttgart: Klett, 1954), p. 63. Cf. also Post, 55.

13. See Georg Büchner, *Sämtliche Werke und Briefe,* ed. Werner R. Lehmann (Munich: Hanser, 1978) 1:427.

14. See Post, 55–64.

15. Quoted by Post, 138.

16. Cf. Silz, 137.

17. Martini, 60.

18. Jofen, 206.

19. For an especially drastic example of this attitude expressed in a work of art, see Alfred Kubin's 1902 drawing "The Spider" (*Die Spinne*) in Wieland Schmied, *Alfred Kubin* (New York: Ferdinand A. Praeger, 1969), plate 38.

20. Quoted by Martini, 60.

21. See Martini, 79.

22. See Krämer, 23.

23. See Krämer, 37 n. 75.

24. See Krämer, 33–35.

25. Quoted by Gary Saul Morson, "Bakhtin and the Present Moment," *The American Scholar* 60 (1991): 220.

26. Robin A. Clouser, "The Spiritual Malaise of a Modern Hercules, Hauptmann's *Bahnwärter Thiel*," *The Germanic Review* 50 (1980): 105.

# CHAPTER ELEVEN

# Phallus and Cross

### The Apostle

Saturated from childhood in the rich mystical tradition of his Silesian homeland, Hauptmann never succumbed to the logical positivism of so many of his contemporaries. And, although his later works in particular reveal an intense preoccupation with a wide variety of religious experience,[1] he remains much better known for two works devoted to examining the viability of the Christian tradition in the modern world: his most accomplished novel *Der Narr in Christo Emanuel Quint* (1910) (*The Fool in Christ Emanuel Quint*), and his single most popular prose narrative, *Der Ketzer von Soana* (1918) (*The Heretic of Soana*). The author's preoccupation with the New Testament and Christ was both early and lasting. (When he was buried in 1946 on the island of Hiddensee, it was with the same worn copy of the New Testament in his hands that had led him to the verge of religious mania as an agricultural trainee in Lohnig and Lederose.) He had begun more detached, serious, and scholarly studies as early as the winter of 1885–86 with the outline of a projected (but never completed) drama on the life of Jesus, which already contained various motifs significant for later works. Subsequently he devoted much time and energy to a biographical study of the historical Christ and, in a similar vein, wrote a fragmentary "Evangelium Judae" intended to supplement and correct the four Gospels.[2] Not until March 1890, in a letter to Otto Brahm,[3] did he announce that he was finally abandoning his Jesus studies—a resolution only loosely adhered to, as a mere three months later he had completed *Der Apostel* (1890) (*The Apostle*), a psychological sketch that in some respects can be considered a precursor of *Quint*. Both works rely on abundant Biblical quotation and allusion to achieve their intended effect; both feature contemporary heroes who believe (or appear to believe) that they are the resurrected Christ and who in dream visions experience mystical union with Him; and both find themselves in the vicinity of the Saint Gotthard Pass at crucial stages of their lives. There are, to be sure, also some significant differences between the two protagonists. As Paul Fechter has pointed out, the Apostle is considerably further removed from Quint's Dostoyevskian humility; is, as an ex-military officer, a member of a more elevated social class than the lowly carpenter's son; and is much more open to the suspicion of fraudulent, narcissistic role playing.[4] Such differences (and the twenty years that separate the two works) notwithstanding, both narratives derive from a broadly similar autobiographical, sociopolitical, and religious background. The personal elements include Hauptmann's thoroughgoing immersion in the Bible and his exposure as a teenager to the religious frenzy of itinerant fire-and-brimstone preachers in rural Silesia while in the employ of his uncle and aunt Schubert, as well as the lasting impression made on him by Professor Forel's investigations into mental illness—especially hysteria—that he observed in Zurich in 1888.

The most immediate and direct inspiration for *The Apostle* also seems to have come out of the Zurich visit, albeit from two very different sources: his acquaintance with an eccentric religious zealot named Johannes Guttzeit and an intensified interest in Georg Büchner that flourished among Hauptmann's friends in the city where their idol had died young and lay buried. As Büchner had done in his tour de force psychological novella *Lenz*, Hauptmann exposes his hero's mental aberrations from within, as it were, "out of the consciousness of the paranoid himself."[5]

Although the approach and technique of Büchner and Hauptmann are similar, there is an element of ambiguity in *The Apostle* that is not nearly as prominent in *Lenz*. The reason for this can be traced in part to the respective real-life models of the two works. Büchner's psychological portrait was based on the troubled life of J. M. R. Lenz, the brilliant Storm and Stress dramatist popular among the Naturalists.[6] Like Büchner, Lenz proved to be far ahead of his time with his highly original dramas and ideas for the theater but, also like Büchner, was cut off in his prime—albeit in his case by increasingly frequent bouts with mental illness. Whatever else can be said about him, there is an aura of authenticity and sincerity about Lenz largely lacking in Johannes Guttzeit, an insignificant local personality who would hardly be remembered at all were it not for his portrayal by Hauptmann. To be sure, Hauptmann found in him a convenient model through which to give expression to a type of religious fervor prevalent at the time. He had witnessed Guttzeit's outdoor sermon on the evils of unbridled luxury on Whitsunday of 1888, near Lake Zurich, and even recalled it later as "a truly holy scene, which cannot be equalled by any Oberammergau."[7] Likewise the physical description of the Apostle, including his distinctive garb, derives from the "nature apostle," and the external similarity to the Hauptmann character was obvious enough for Guttzeit to take umbrage at the author's allegedly distorted "portrait" of himself. In a reply that concentrates in a nutshell his usual creative approach, Hauptmann answered his accuser, "Certain events in Zurich were, for me, at best stimuli. . . . I also never in my life feel so-to-speak photographic cravings. One of many possibilities is developed creatively on my own initiative."[8]

Guttzeit's complaints notwithstanding, Hauptmann was able to create an interesting, memorable character in his Apostle, one who manages not only to convey something of the prevailing fin de siécle religious spirit in Europe but who, at the same time, holds the reader's interest as a distinctive personality. And, although he has been dismissed in psychological terms as little more than "a vain and shallow neurotic whose Imitation of Christ is an incidental by-product of narcissism and exhibitionism, ultimately compounded with the unmistakable signs of an Oedipus complex,"[9] such a reduction to psychological jargon does both him and his creator a disservice. Regardless of how his views were arrived at—and they are frequently views with which Hauptmann himself could and did sympathize—they are expressed with a passion and sincerity that belie (or at least bring into question) the accusation of mere religious fraud. Like the author he has a reverence for nature and life in all its forms and an ingrained suspicion of the supposed advances of technology and human civilization. Having just arrived from Italy by train, he is described as hating "these railroads with their eternal jolting, stamping, and din, with their fleeting images; he hated them and along with them most of the so-called achievements of their so-called cultures" (6:71). Even the relatively bucolic city of Zurich offends his natural sensibilities. "[The city] appeared to him like a gray, disgusting crust, like a scab injected into this paradise which would continue to eat away at it: piles of stone beside piles of stone, sparse greenery between them. He realized that man is the most dangerous vermin of all. Indeed, that was beyond doubting: cities were no better than boils, excrescences of culture. Their sight caused him disgust and pain" (6:73). In a visionary, trance-like state he sees the fate of mankind in terms which anticipate Hauptmann's own conception of the *Urdrama:* "The smell of blood lay over the world. Flowing blood was the sign of the struggle. He heard this struggle rage, constantly, asleep and awake. They were brothers and brothers, sisters and sisters, who slew each other. He loved them all, he saw their raging and wrung his hands in pain and despair" (6:75). Such passages suggest the inadequacy of a purely psychological approach to the character of the Apostle and may even imply a productive component within his "madness."

From this perspective it is perhaps not too farfetched to follow Sprengel's lead and posit a distinct Dostoyevskian influence on *The Apostle.*[10] Literarily, during Hauptmann's stay in Zurich, Dostoyevski soon became his "greatest experience,'' (7:1058) and Hauptmann did everything he could to proselyte among his friends for the Russian novelist. He was, of course, familiar with the visionary figure of Alyosha from *The Brothers Karamazov,* and the first German translation of *The Idiot,* certainly the quintessential treatment of the synthesis of psychopathology with the Jesus redivivus theme, had appeared while *The Apostle* was still in progress. Given Hauptmann's intense interest in Dostoyevski, Pentecostal religion, and abnormal psychology during this period of his life, it is unlikely that these works would have passed him by without leaving some traces on his own creativity.

## The Fool in Christ Emanuel Quint

*Der Narr in Christo Emanuel Quint* (*The Fool in Christ Emanuel Quint*), published two decades after *The Apostle,* reveals more clearly than any other work the full extent of Hauptmann's intimacy with the New Testament and his ability to transmute into art the personal and cultural experiences of his epoch. Paul Schlenther claimed on the novel's appearance that "artistically, Gerhart Hauptmann never stood higher than here," and as late as 1954 Heuser still considered it "one of the greatest novels of the twentieth century."[11] Unfortunately, perhaps because it describes an epoch and a subject too far removed from the interests of the general reading public, *Quint* is hardly read today, even in Germany. Any attempt to rehabilitate the work, however modest, should begin therefore by stressing the general humanity of Hauptmann's hero, whose career, as Sinden has described it, "leads us. . . . through an extraordinarily rich and convincing picture of men, their doings, and their world, a picture as vivid and intense as those that Hauptmann achieved in his best plays."[12]

Most of the numerous studies devoted to the novel stress either a psychological or a religious interpretation, depending on their author's personal predilections and their understanding of the ambiguous word "fool" in the title. Should the word be interpreted in a strictly psychological sense, referring to an individual with diminished mental capacities, or in a more traditional Christian sense of a person wise in ways that transcend mere logical thinking? As might be expected from an author who makes no pretense to ultimate truth, Hauptmann, as in *The Apostle,* does little to prejudice the reader toward either position or any intermediate one, preferring that he examine the evidence as presented and draw his own conclusion.

As related by a chronicler who makes no claim to omniscience, the plot of the roughly four-hundred-page novel unfolds through an unobtrusive frame and depicts—now vaguely, now in great and vivid detail—what would seem to be the last year and a half of the twenty-eight-year-old hero's life. An illegitimate child who has grown up in Silesia under the abuse of an alcoholic stepfather, Quint has found consolation and refuge in the Bible and in the life of Christ. A first turning point occurs when, almost inadvertently, he finds himself preaching repentance in the marketplace of a nearby village. Although largely ridiculed by the crowd, he has impressed a few like-minded zealots; and gradually, helped along by an ambiguous and suspect faith healing, a variety of individuals gather around him, some sincerely eager to partake of God's realm on earth, about which he constantly preaches, and others hoping to witness the performance of sensational miracles. To his credit he tries hard to resist the temptations to which his celebrity exposes him and would prefer a hermit's life of contemplation and prayer. At the same time, however, his love of mankind and all living creatures cannot be suppressed; he is drawn into an active life of Christian servitude and the realization of his calling as an *imitatio Christi*.

This path brings him into contact with numerous strata of society which Hauptmann depicts in his usual uncompromising fashion: for example, the sadistic police who arrest him for vagrancy and, for a time, confine him in an insane asylum; a bigoted Protestant pastor whose loyalty to the Crown has long since stifled any remnants of Christian charity he may once have possessed; and a rich noblewoman from Gurau ("das Gurauer Fräulein") who believes in him, employs him as a gardener, and introduces him to her own varied society. Gradually his popularity reaches dangerous proportions. His enemies ridicule him and conflicts among his followers, the so-called Valley Brethren (*Talbrüder*), persuade him that it is time to leave Gurau.

The next stage of the novel takes us to the Valley Mill (*Talmühle*), where Quint's followers are found engaging in nocturnal religious orgies and are generally on the verge of losing control. Although his appearance among them has an initially sobering effect, the situation is complicated by the arrival of Ruth Heidebrand, the daughter of the gardener with whom Quint worked at the Gurau castle. Without his awareness the teenager has conceived a passion for him—compounded of pubertal eros and religious hysteria—and, although he quickly returns her to her parents, his role in the affair has been construed as that of an abductor, and the noblewoman of Gurau withdraws her support from him. Quint's subsequent rejection of his followers' dissolute behavior drives most of them away, and he is left with a small group of seven faithful. Continuing his wanderings, he searches for and finds his natural father, a Catholic priest, and, proclaiming his identity with Christ in the man's church, smashes the holy images and the implements on the altar.

Moving on to Breslau Quint sets himself up in a disreputable tavern, where he receives and advises people of various social levels. Although he initially gains new followers, most of them too soon desert him when their hopes for achieving God's Realm appear dashed. When Ruth Heidebrand falls victim to a sex murderer, Quint does nothing to allay the suspicion directed against him, but his innocence is nevertheless established. This ultimate (albeit tainted) martyrdom rejected, the identification with Christ sustains him a while longer as he wanders through Germany but, in the vicinity of the St. Gotthard Pass, the spring thaw exposes a frozen corpse—presumably his. A scrap of paper found on the body contains only the enigmatic question: "The secret of the Realm?" (5:414).

By his own admission Hauptmann "never wrote a line which he did not experience in that way, or live through in a similar manner, or which was not in some connection autobiography,"[13] and his *Quint* is certainly no exception in this respect. A number of autobiographical elements that found expression in the novel have already been discussed above in regard to *The Apostle* and can be subsumed under such catchwords as Lohnig/Lederose, Zurich, Forel, Jesus studies, and Dostoyevski. Not surprisingly, a four-hundred-page novel yields many more examples—so many, in fact, that they can only be sampled here. Among the characters, Kurt Simon, an eighteen-year-old farm estate secretary, is such a precise portrait of the young author himself during his year in Lohnig that it would not have been out of place in *The Adventure of my Youth*. (Even the poems Simon writes were later reproduced in Hauptmann's autobiography.) In Dominik, a sensitive, gifted, and troubled young man whose suicide is a relief to his father because now he no longer has to support his son, Hauptmann provided a monument to a real friend by that name who had introduced him to the poetry of Novalis and Hölderlin in 1877. The brothers Hassenpflug, whose condescending attitude toward Quint tends to reduce him to an object of scientific curiosity, were by the author's own admission modeled after Heinrich and Julius Hart, "those strong adherents of pathos (*starke Pathetiker*), honest haters, dashing dispatchers of fashionable writers,"[14] who were among the very earliest initiators of the Naturalist movement in Germany. Similarly, Peter Hullenkamp, "with bedfeathers in his dishevelled hair," (5:364) and Annette von Rhyn, "who ran along beside him everywhere like Antigone beside the blind Oedipus," (5:365) are thinly disguised portraits of the bohemian poets Peter Hille and Elsa Lasker-Schüler. Personal experience also adds an element of authenticity to the locales described. For example, anyone familiar with Hauptmann's descriptions of his own dissolute life as an art student will recognize the tavern in Breslau where Quint is found by the troubled sufferers as the disreputable dive and prostitute hangout in which the author squandered his own time and money; it even includes a faithful description of his frequent drinking companion the painter Professor James Marshall.

*Quint* is, of course, also much more than a roman à clef. As a seismograph of his age Hauptmann provides a sensitive description and critique of religious and sociopolitical attitudes prevalent in Germany at the turn of the century. (At the end of every century, and our own twentieth appears not to be an exception, the fever heat of millennialistic fervor tends to increase while the ignorant, superstitious, and disenfranchised fall victim to charlatans with simplistic answers to life's difficult questions.) Distinguishing features of the German zeitgeist during the period in question include a socialistic interpretation of the Christian gospel, a psychopathological explanation of the historical phenomenon of Jesus, and a tendency among artists to identify with the sufferings of Christ.[15] Various attempts were made to bring the Christian tradition into closer alignment with the gospel according to Marx: by stressing a more practical application of Christian precepts to social problems; by infusing an element of humane, Christian morality into scientific socialism; or by some other approach that would combine the best features of Christianity and socialism. In typically impudent tones bordering on blasphemy, Arno Holz speaks for a number of his Naturalist cohorts in the lines "For me that rabbi Jesus Christ / Is nothing—but the first socialist!"[16] Works of art in which Jesus appears among modern workers, or social reformist heroes assume the appearance and/or characteristics of Christ, are almost commonplace (for example, the proletarian paintings of Fritz von Uhde or novels by Hans Land or Max Kretzer). "Is there a subject matter," the future Bundespräsident Theodor Heuss asks rhetorically in his 1911 review of *Quint*, "which was more intimately connected with the problems which preoccupied German youth of that time [around 1890] than this one: Jesus of Nazareth wanders through the Germany of the present, the Germany of factories, of class struggles, of the orthodox state church. In numerous literary efforts one struggled with this antithesis. . . . "[17]

For the narrator of *Quint*, to be sure, this antithesis is more apparent than real. Describing the mood of his countrymen from the perspective of twenty intervening years, he concludes: "Over many of the tables of the populace engaged in discussing politics there hovered at that time, intermingled with beer and cigar fumes like a colorful, narcotic cloud, Utopia. What was called this by one person was called something else by others, but, essentially, it all grew out of the same . . . longing of the soul for salvation, purity, liberation, happiness and, generally speaking, perfection. Some called it social state; others freedom or paradise, and still others the millennium or heavenly realm'' (5:362). What all had in common, to a greater or lesser degree, was the desire to change the social, political, and religious status quo. Through the depiction of Quint's interaction with those who cross his path, Hauptmann reiterates many of the views familiar from his earlier works, such as the heartlessness of monopolistic capitalism, the arbitrariness of the criminal justice system, the hypocrisy of the orthodox clergy, and the foolish arrogance of the military. Somewhat typically, however, as a comparison of earlier drafts with the published novel shows, he chose to tone the political attack down considerably before exposing the work to public scrutiny.[18]

In addition to the tendency to intermingle socialism and Christianity, *Quint* also reflects a contemporary preoccupation with psychopathological biographies of Jesus and scientifically oriented studies devoted to such phenomena as genius and "divine madness." This trend had its inception in widely influential works like David Friedrich Strauß's *Das Leben Jesu* (*The Life of Jesus* [1835–36]) and Ernest Renan's *La vie de Jésus* (1863), on the one hand, which aimed to demystify Christ and reduce him to ordinary, human dimensions; and on the other hand the argument popularized by Cesare Lombroso in *Genio et follia* (1864) that genius is a function of psychological abnormality. Such views are reflected in the work of Dostoyevski and Nietzsche, and psychiatric studies devoted to the alleged mental problems of Jesus became so numerous that Albert Schweizer devoted his medical dissertation for the University of Strasbourg to refuting them.[19] All of these ideas were, of course, common currency to Hauptmann, as were the concepts of the relativity of mental health and the possibility, identified most strongly with Freud, that neurosis could be a spur to creativity. "Doesn't everyone," he later recalled thinking in Zurich, "have his *idée fixe*? The Protestant clergy as well as the Catholic? The philosopher, the physician, the scientist? And isn't the difference here between health and disease only one of degree?" (7:1063–64). Furthermore, and especially when fostered by a charismatic figure, individual mental aberrations can be transmitted to others. As the narrator of *Quint* puts it, "one knows that madness can seize entire nations; how much more then such small congregations [as Quint's]. It is a psychic fever which constantly increases through contagion" (5:204). Indeed, one of the special fascinations of Hauptmann's novel is the depiction of such collective madness and its description of how little is sometimes required to trigger it. The excessive consumption of alcohol, for example, combined with the epileptic fit of the young woman Therese Katzmarek, coming as they do at a critical juncture of events, are sufficient to spark a "universal paroxysm" (5:298) among Quint's susceptible followers.

Central as it is to the novel, it is the question of Quint's own sanity which has provoked the most intense speculation. And while a psychological interpretation of the work has on occasion been rejected outright,[20] a much more typical reaction is the one expressed by Geyer when he writes: "Reading Hauptmann's novel . . . is a special pleasure, particularly for the psychopathologist, because here the image of a primary mental disturbance is delineated with psychological mastery and striking fidelity."[21] The delusion of being identical with Christ is a relatively common one, and if we accept the conclusions of psychiatrists who have examined Quint's case history, it appears that Hauptmann has provided a model example of a transition from neurosis to paranoia. This transition, which has been described in considerable detail elsewhere[22] and which can be summarized in a few words only at the risk of oversimplification, proceeds through several stages. As an isolated, illegitimate, and abused child, Quint developed a deficient self-image. Bereft of human love and affection, he sought solace, even as a young boy, in a selfless, idealized love for Jesus that gradually became an obsession. Later, when his disciples insisted on seeing in him the Messiah (a view dangerously compatible with his own secret desires), he committed a major sin of omission by not rejecting their image of him vigorously enough. (According to Hauptmann, the historical Jesus had made the same mistake.)[23] Eventually, under the pressure of circumstances, a change occurred in his view of himself. From the mystical idea that Christ was alive within him (as in others) he took the fateful and irreversible step into psychosis—reflected in the conviction that he had become Christ. The mechanism cited that explains this development is the familiar one of escape from unbearable psychic pain. As Christ he could be everything that Quint was not. No longer despised and outcast, he could approve of himself now as a powerful, omnipotent savior and dismiss the evident antipathy of others as "a clear result of the hostile attitude of a humanity bent on rejecting Christ."[24] The very success with which he insinuated himself into the person of Christ, of course, also worked against him; and when, during his trip south through Germany at the end of the novel, he knocked on doors and calmly announced himself as the Savior, he was understandably met by fear and revulsion.

In addition to the amalgamation of socialism with Christianity, or the psychiatric approach to Jesus, *Quint* seems also to reflect a third common preoccupation of its day: the identification of the artist with the sufferings of Christ. Upon hearing of the death of Tolstoy in 1910 (the year *Quint* appeared in book form), Hauptmann wrote, "And again all this had to happen as it is written. Again the true Christ, the true anointed, is the stumbling block and the sacred nuisance. Many considered Tolstoy a fool. One also considered Jesus the Savior one. He was a human being. He was our brother" (6:915). A less exalted example, but one that shows how widespread this type of identification was among artists, can be found in Hermann Conradi, an early participant in the Naturalist movement. Not only did he consider himself something of a literary Messiah whose calling it was to spread a revolutionary gospel that would drive the philistines from the temple of art, but he also assumed Christlike airs and mannerisms amid his student friends in Leipzig. When he died suddenly, at the age of twenty-seven, *Die Gesellschaft* published a deathbed photo in May 1890 in which the corpse itself is highly stylized to resemble the Savior.[25] That Hauptmann made a similar connection between Christ and the artist of genius, and that he consciously employed it in his own work, seems adequately demonstrated by his *Michael Kramer.* For the elder Kramer, we recall, "art is religion" (1:1135), and he compares the torment of his gifted son at the hands of local boors with the sufferings of "the son of God" (1:1172). For Michael Kramer "the artist is always the true Hermit," (1:1134) and Hauptmann himself, not without a touch of dubious role-playing, took pleasure in proclaiming himself a "monk of poetry."[26] Symptomatic of this affectation is the Franciscan cowl he acquired in an Italian monastery in 1912, wore at times while vacationing on the island of Hiddensee, and was buried in-—by his own request—in 1946. The remark "every true genius has something of Jesus Christ [about him],"[27] noted down by Hauptmann in 1898, seems to have been one he could live with the rest of his life.

The intent of these last remarks regarding the artist as Christ figure is not, of course, to categorize *Quint* as an artist novel per se, or even primarily as an artist novel. Given Hauptmann's propensity for working from personal experience, however, it seems likely that some of his own feelings and attributes as an artist should have rubbed off on his fictional character. What must strike most readers as anomalous is the extraordinary sensitivity of this uneducated carpenter's son from the backwaters of Silesia: "his deep, penetrating eye for the sufferings and pains of the earth"; the "cautious, knowing hand" (5:30) with which he touches things; his susceptibility to the glories of nature;

and the finely nuanced theological arguments with which he refutes his critics. By making his character a part of himself in this way, Hauptmann, albeit perhaps with the sacrifice of some degree of realism, elevates and enriches Quint as a vital, multidimensional fictional character.

While it appears true, then, as Fechter claims, that Hauptmann identified with Quint and for pages at a time even used him as his mouthpiece,[28] he is obviously not identical with him. By the author's own account, much the same can be said about the narrator of the novel. Writing twenty years after the events he is describing, he naturally does so with a certain degree of historical detachment. As Weimar describes him, "Hauptmann's chronicler has gathered the facts about Quint and even followed his tracks. He is initially convinced that he is dealing with a fool or a half-fool; as he penetrates the fool's thoughts and dreams, he speaks of the 'sickly disposition' . . . of his nature. His attitude is ironic and skeptical but not unsympathetic. He makes every effort to be fair and he even tries to suspend judgment in favor of understanding and forgiving."[29] Although he is undoubtedly predisposed toward a rationalistic interpretation of the phenomena with which his investigation confronts him, Quint's story is so striking and authentic that even he, an exemplar of modern civilized man, is troubled by a touch of residual doubt at the end. "But how could one know,—" he asks, "although we pray: 'lead us not into temptation!'—whether it was not after all the true Savior, who, in the disguise of the poor fool, wanted to investigate to what extent His seed, sown by God, the seed of the Realm, had, in the meantime, ripened?" (5:413).

Whether because acoustical effects loom larger in spoken dialogue or because efforts to reproduce dialect are more distracting to readers, Hauptmann tends to avoid the type of linguistic verisimilitude found in his naturalistic dramas when writing prose narratives. As one would expect, the narrator of *Quint* presents his story in a cultivated and sophisticated German, but other characters, including those from much lower strata of society for whom dialect would be the normal form of expression, likewise avoid it. As Stirk has pointed out, "when [Hauptmann] is dealing with religion his style is often very similar to the Lutheran Bible: it is almost as if he were quoting directly from it."[30] *Quint* seems, like *Florian Geyer*, a linguistic tour de force. The earlier work, however, had required Hauptmann to reconstruct the German of the late Middle Ages piecemeal from a variety of sources; for *Quint* he had absorbed the content, style, and language of the New Testament so thoroughly that he could allow his characters—Quint in particular—to ramble on effortlessly for pages at a time in Biblical idiom. The overall tone established in this way provides the best possible ambiance for Quint's story and also serves as a counterbalance to the more abstract speech of the narrator.

The care lavished on the details of *Quint* is also evident in the work's larger structure. To begin with what is perhaps the most obvious structural feature, the novel is divided into two roughly equal parts. As Ziolkowski has aptly summarized, "in the first part Quint is imitating Christ and in the second part Jesus; in the first part he thinks of himself as the apostle of Christ's ethical teaching, while in the second part he sees himself as a new redeemer; in the first part he still distinguishes between reality and imagination, and in the second the two coalesce into a paranoic hallucination."[31] In the first part there are discernible parallels to the New Testament, but, as the end approaches, they become more numerous—as it also dawns on the reader that Quint is beginning to stage them himself or attempting to exploit such opportunities as present themselves, such as trying to use the murder of Ruth Heidebrand to achieve martyrdom. Within this bipartite division Weimar detects a series of subdivisions based on the principle of the mystical number seven. "The seventh chapter describes the experience of the *unio mystica;* seven chapters later (numbers fourteen and fifteen, the mid-point of the novel) the climactic experience of serenity and bliss in the seclusion of the country estate. Then again after seven chapters comes a critical turning point (chapters twenty-one and twenty-three), the arrival in Breslau and the impact of corrupt urban civilization; and finally climaxing the last group of seven chapters, the death of Quint."[32] Additionally, as he also tended to do in his dramas (see for example *The Sunken Bell* and *Rose Bernd*), Hauptmann uses the passing seasons as appropriate metaphors to reflect the spiritual "passages" through which his hero progresses, from spring's "vernal longing, [to] summer fulfillment, autumnal waning, and hibernal congelation."[33]

## The Heretic of Soana

In a review from 1919 the popular author Emil Ludwig described *Der Ketzer von Soana* (*The Heretic of Soana*) as "the story of an ascetic who becomes a pagan anchorite, the awakening of a saintly man to love, the transformation of a priest into a mountain shepherd. It is, although it takes place in our time and in the mountains of Lugana, a mutation from the Christian to the Greek, during which the Panic is dissolved with consummate art into that modern multiplicity which one customarily calls Naturalism. In this little work the author calls the maiden 'the fruit of the tree of life,' not [of] the tree of knowledge."[34] While (like Hesse's *Demian* or Rilke's *Coronet*) this short novel had a special attraction for the young, serious older critics also fell under its spell. Thus, for example, Hugh F. Garten still discovered in it as recently as 1954 "a prose of classic perfection" and called it "undoubtedly [Hauptmann's] finest prose work and, for that matter, one of the masterpieces of German narrative writing."[35] Perhaps inevitably, critical opinion has cooled somewhat in the meantime. Relatively speaking, the infatuation of a priest with a young woman has lost some of its piquancy, and at times the prose tends too much toward the purple end of the spectrum for present–day tastes. In a conversation with Thomas Mann (who, incidentally, also expressed his distaste for the author's "humoristic" treatment of Christianity in *The Heretic*), Hauptmann is alleged to have described his intentions for the new work as providing a Dionysian complement for his Christian *Quint*.[36] To be sure, the dualism implied here is not so stark as a superficial reading of both works might at first suggest. Quint's *imitatio Christi* and Biblical speech notwithstanding, his penchant for nudity; his sensual receptivity to the beauties of nature; his unabashed sun worship; his tendency to evoke rhapsodic, bacchantic behavior among his followers; his orgiastic dream of a woman "dancing, quite naked . . . before him, an Eve with voluptuous breasts" (5:56)—all these things and more suggest a not–so–veiled congruence between the "Christian" Quint and Francesco, the "heretic" of Soana. Perhaps, as Hilscher surmises, Francesco is indeed intended to represent "an ennobled, intensified Quint."[37] Quint's death presumably occurred on his way to Italy—in the German consciousness "the land where the lemons bloom," the land of passion and sensuality—and Francesco's adventures occur in northern Italy within a few miles of the St. Gotthard Pass. Both men are sincere, God-seeking outsiders who come more and more into conflict with the tenets of orthodox religion; both find revelation in dreams; and both are identified with the age-old occupation of shepherds: Quint as the symbolic "good shepherd," as which he is repeatedly apostrophized, and Francesco in literally becoming a shepherd after his excommunication.

Like all of Hauptmann's best work, *The Heretic* represents a seamless fusion of intensely personal, literary, and zeitgeist elements. While it has resulted in a downgrading of the significance of the author's trip to Greece in 1907 for an understanding of *The Heretic*, the availability of his literary estate in recent years has provided a number of interesting correspondences between real–life experience and fictional narrative. During the years 1897–1901, Hauptmann spent at least part of each spring in the northern Italian town of Rovio (the Soana of his story) on the slope of Monte Generoso. Here, amid the magnificent mountain terrain, he first learned of an incestuous family—brother, sister, and their children—that provided a model for the ill-famed Scarabota family that plays such a central role in the "conversion" of Francesco from Christian asceticism to a religion that not only incorporates but glorifies sensuality. Diary descriptions of the landscape surrounding the family's primitive dwelling later found their way, word for word, into the story, and during the 1900 visit Hauptmann witnessed the very goat birth—representative of "the deep mystery of birth in general" (6:88)—that serves to introduce the heroine. In addition, the cultic conception of sexuality espoused in the work had preoccupied Hauptmann at least as early as 1905. At that time he had actually dreamed the phallic monks' dream which was later incorporated in *The Heretic,* as were also various thoughts and ruminations on "the mystery of the black procreation" (6:92) and on the priapic experience of nature to which Francesco is so susceptible. That the author had a predilection for the theme of incest that may also have played a role in the genesis of the work remains an interesting but unprovable speculation.[38]

From the perspective of literary history *The Heretic* represents a curious blend of ancient and contemporary traditions. It not only shares a number of motifs with the late-classical, bucolic novel of Longos, *Daphnis and Chloe,* but quotes directly a significant aperçu from that work: "that Eros is older and also more powerful than Cronos" (6:91). The theme of the fallen priest, on the other hand, was popular among Naturalist writers, and various attempts have been made to link *The Heretic,* in this regard, to such works as Ludwig Anzengruber's drama *Der Pfarrer von Kirchfeld* (1870) (*The Parson of Kirchfeld*) and Zola's sensational novel of 1875, *La faute de l'abbé Mouret.* The latter especially reveals a number of striking parallels that seem all the more significant, from a cultural–historical perspective, if one accepts Hauptmann's denial that he had read the work. To be sure, Zola's emphasis had been on the contrast between natural human sexuality and the allegedly life-denying tendencies of Christianity, whereas Hauptmann's intent seems to have been the melding of sensuality into a superior, more humane form of that religion.[39] Here the all-pervasive legacy of Nietzsche appears, once again, to surface. Familiar as he certainly was with such Nietzschean concepts as the Dionysian/Apollonian dichotomy, Hauptmann had made it clear in diary entries from 1892–94 where his sympathies lay: "The Christian sickness. The pagan healthiness. But also the pagan natural religion, sun-worship. . . . Christianity trains (*dressiert*) human beings for heaven; i.e., for death and to death;" or: "Christianity has deprived the man from the country of poetry and made him dull. A pagan flower, he became a Christian blockhead."[40] As Oberembdt has shown, Hauptmann's attempt to synthesize the "delusional systems'' (*Wahnsysteme*) of paganism and Christianity, which he insisted were ''not pathological'' (because ''only the numbing, the petrification of such systems demonstrates the death of the spirit''),[41] goes back at least as far as *Hannele*.[42]

The formal challenge of *The Heretic* consists in the need to elevate a rather sordid, naturalistic plot involving what could easily be misconstrued as simple moral depravity (incest and the sexual bondage of a priest) to a level of mythic timelessness. An important first step (and one to which Hauptmann would resort again in later works) was the introduction of a frame device that tends to blur past and present. In the Tessin mountains the ''editor'' of the story hears the shepherd Ludovico, known locally as the heretic of Soana, relate an allegedly older legend about Francesco Vela—the central content of the narrative. (Although it is never stated explicitly, the suspicion is unavoidable that what is presented here is actually a thinly disguised narration of Ludovico's own experiences.) Further enhancing the sense of timelessness is the magnificent natural scenery in which the events are played out. A series of recurrent images—the monotonous background roar of the waterfall; the tireless, slow circling of the noble ospreys hovering in the sky above; and the massive blocks of white stone towering around Soana—evoke a sense of the eternal that tends to overpower merely temporal human concerns. The apotheosis of this experience, which provides the hero with access to deeper, archetypal levels of his psyche, occurs during a night of love he spends with Agata Scarabota on a secluded, paradisiacal island.

> In this paradise, into which [Francesco] now took the first enraptured steps, timelessness reigned. He no longer felt himself to be a human being of any time, or of any age at all. Just as timeless was the nocturnal world around him. And because the time of expulsion, the world of banishment and original sin, now lay behind him, before the guarded gate of paradise, he also no longer felt the slightest fear of it. No one out there could harm him. It wasn't in the power of his superiors, nor in the power of the Pope himself to hinder his enjoyment of the smallest fruit of paradise, nor to rob him in the slightest of the charitable gift of bliss which had now become his own. His superiors had become inferiors. They lived, forgotten, in a lost world of howling and gnashing of teeth. Francesco was no longer Francesco; as the first human being, just now awakened by divine breath, he was the lone Adam, the lone lord of the Garden of Eden. (6:158)

Yet in spite of his powerful nocturnal experience—tantamount to a religious illumination—there is a strong undertone of resignation in the fate of

Ludovico/Francesco. After a number of years in exile in South America, he has returned home to Soana, where he is found living the isolated life of a shepherd with a woman who, by the author's description, is a veritable Earth Mother (and presumably the matured Agata). Like *Quint, The Heretic* ends on a note of ambiguity. Just as we are left with a residue of doubt regarding Quint's fate and the authenticity of his religious experience, Hauptmann avoids explicitly identifying Ludovico with Francesco (although readers and critics routinely do so) and clouds the ultimate nature of his hero's conversion. Being only human the heretic cannot, under the circumstances, distinguish clearly between animal sexuality and the more exalted forms of love. Perhaps, therefore, Fechter is correct when he concludes that "Eros' Song of Songs has, in the final analysis, become a Song of Songs of sex—here secretly disguised as Eros."[43]

## The Island of the Great Mother

Hauptmann's continued fascination with the relationship between eros and religion is also reflected in a popular novel with the baroque title *Die Insel der Großen Mutter oder Das Wunder von Ile des Dames* (1924) (*The Island of the Great Mother or the Miracle of the Ile de Dames: A Story from the Utopian Archipelago.*) This work, begun in 1916, was considered quite daring in its day; it is suffused with a light irony we would be more likely to expect from Thomas Mann. Because of the book's general tone, it comes as no surprise that Hauptmann should have enjoyed writing it or that its pervasive sensuality owes something to personal experience. "I certainly would never have written it," he recalled in 1942, "if I had not, for years, seen the many beautiful, often completely naked, women's bodies on [the island of] Hiddensee and observed the carryings on there."[44] Indeed, when taken out of its artistic and ideational context, the plot could be dismissed as little more than the product of an overheated, adolescent male fantasy.

A considerable willingness to suspend disbelief is presumed from the very beginning. As the result of a shipwreck, more than a hundred women of mixed nationality and one twelve-year-old boy, Phaon,[45] find themselves stranded on a South Sea island paradise. Compounding the implausibility of there being no adult males among the rescued, the lifeboats contain an unlikely variety and abundance of supplies, including carpentry tools, seeds for growing grain, a coffee grinder, and even a violin—but nothing as ultimately practical as an emergency shortwave radio transmitter. What has not been salvaged in the boats is easily provided by the island. Clothing, of which the women wear little or none, is not a problem in the tropical climate, and there is bamboo for construction, coffee for the grinder, fine slate for writing purposes, flowers and wild fruit in abundance, and even tobacco for the smokers. After about a year (during which a simple form of participatory government has been set up; the fear of potential dangers on the island has proven groundless; and, with a minimum of effort, a cozy habitat has been established) a miracle of sorts occurs. Babette, a suggestible, somewhat hysterical young woman, gives birth to a son. Although no one is comfortable accepting her claim of a fatherless conception, with the possible exception of the mother herself, the women do so out of feminine pride, preferring to reject the rude mechanics of natural procreation in favor of a belief in divine intervention— in this case allegedly by a mysterious snake king. Through the precocious sexual activity of Phaon (Hauptmann nowhere in the novel overtly acknowledges his responsibility but removes all doubt with many a wink and smirk), the island is soon swarming with infants. Because many of these children are male, they eventually represent a threat to the previously intact matriarchy. Not willing to resort to the Amazonian solution of keeping males only for breeding purposes and then disposing of them, the mothers resettle them on a distant part of the island under the guidance of Phaon. With its supposed innate male talent for logic and technology (the youths' god is the "Thinking Hand"), the new masculine state soon surpasses that of the women in both practical and artistic accomplishments (for example, on the one hand, such trades as boat construction and the domestication of animals, and, on the other, the production and virtuoso employment of musical instruments). Led by Babette's now mature son Bianor and exacerbated by hotheads from both male and female camps, a rebellion develops. When the twelve "Sons of Heaven," chosen according to the established conventions of the matriarchy, refuse to avail the women of their procreational services, the tabus that have kept the sexes apart collapse and a feverish Dionysian orgy ensues, which presages the rise of a new patriarchy. The patriarch Phaon, however, sets sail for a Polynesian island with his chosen spouse, Diotima. Here, according to an epilogue published by Hauptmann in 1925 in *Die neue Rundschau,* he created the fictionalized world of the novel, which has in the meantime found its way to the reading public.[46]

From a thematic perspective *The Island* partakes of at least three familiar literary traditions: the *Robinsonade,* in imitation of Defoe's *Robinson Crusoe* (1719) and quite popular in German–speaking countries for many years; the "Ship of Fools" topos, in which a group of disparate individuals is forced to live together and their behavior is described; and the Utopian novel. Of the three the *Robinsonade* (except for the shipwreck and a certain amount of ingenuity displayed in adjusting to a different environment) is of little significance here. The "Ship of Fools" topos, of which Katherine Anne Porter's 1962 novel by that name and Thomas Mann's *The Magic Mountain* (1924) (*Der Zauberberg*) are good modern examples, comes much closer to Hauptmann's intentions, as has been demonstrated by a comparison of his and Mann's novels.[47] In addition to the pervasive ironic tone common to both *The Island* and *The Magic Mountain*, in both novels too an international group of individuals lives in an isolated "pedagogical province" and experiments (practically in Hauptmann, more theoretically in Mann) with varied forms of social structure. Both authors derive much of their symbolism from an eclectic mixture of mythology and literary allusion (to Goethe's *Faust*, for example); both works are replete with essayistic passages that display the erudition of their authors to good advantage; and even some of their characters, such as Phaon and Hans Castorp, share certain similarities. (It will be recalled, of course, that Mann's inarticulate but majestic Peeperkorn was actually modeled after Hauptmann.) Probably the most striking difference between the two novels is that *The Magic Mountain* issues into the slaughter of the First World War while *The Island*, after the air has been cleared by the orgy, ends more optimistically with Cronos apparently in control.

As the subtitle of the work suggests, it was the Utopian theme that attracted Hauptmann most strongly. For him the idea of Utopia was "by no means merely an idle game for fantasists" (7:206) but a serious preoccupation. "Everyone," he went on to claim, "whoever he may be, works at his Utopia every day" (7:206). The desire to create a happier, more meaningful existence is a universal attribute that, in Hauptmann's case and in that of many of his contemporaries, was abetted by a debilitating *Europamüdigkeit*—a "tiredness with Europe" ·like that described by Friedrich von Kammacher, the autobiographical hero of *Atlantis:* "Almost the entire world, at any rate, however, Europe, is for me a cold plate left standing on a railroad station buffet, which no longer tempts me" (5:421). The idea of retreat to an island as a refuge from the negative aspects of modern civilization is one that Hauptmann toyed with in his personal life; and the island, perhaps as an intermediary realm between the temporal and spiritual, plays a role in his work from the early "Helios" fragment of 1896 to *Gabriel Schilling, Veland* (1925), and the novella *The Sea Miracle* (1934) (*Das Meerwunder*).

While it would be futile to try to isolate all of the literary, religious, or historical reminiscences that found their way into *The Island*, a number of them have been so clearly established and are so significant that they must be mentioned here, at least in passing. Hauptmann himself stressed the importance of the cultural historian Johann Jakob Bachofen to his own thought and claimed in 1942 that "without him . . . I would never have written *The Island of the Great Mother.*"[48] From Bachofen (as also perhaps from Franz Grillparzer's drama *Libussa* [1848]) Hauptmann may have been encouraged in the notion of a utopia based on archetypal female virtues rather than on the typically more aggressive forms of male morality that have allegedly perverted modern Western civilization. Bachofen's matriarchy, furthermore, is also destroyed in a paroxysm of Dionysian celebration from which a patriarchy arises victorious, and the upper and lower spheres into which Hauptmann divides his island correspond to his predecessor's dichotomy of a Uranian and a tellurian—a heavenly and an earthbound—Aphrodite.[49] A good case has also been made for the significant influence of Dante on *The Island.* A central symbol of the novel, the sun, which traditionally represents God or divine revelation, is expanded here, as it was by Dante, into "a symbol of hope for a better, if inscrutable, future for mankind in the struggle to grasp the complexities of a dualistic existence."[50] More generally the novel reflects a myriad of ancient Greek, Hindu, Buddhistic, and Christian elements that the author attempts to synthesize into a kind of universal, humanistic religion.

Like other utopian thinkers before and after him, Hauptmann touches on such topics as government, economics, family life, sexual ethics, and the collection and dissemination of knowledge.[51] Rather atypically, however, he slights these areas in favor of speculation regarding the origin of myth, its importance, and the role it plays in human life. By stripping away the elements of civilization from his adventuresses (insofar as that is possible for individuals who, after all, are adult products of modern civilization), the author constructs a *roman expérimental* designed to demonstrate the necessity of myth for the enjoyment of a truly human existence. The direction that such an appropriate myth must follow is spelled out by the philosopher-priestess Laurence Hobbema in a sermon delivered in the "bamboo church of Notre Dame des Dames" (5:774). Like the Romantic poet Novalis in his essay "Die Christenheit oder Europa" (Christianity or Europe), she begins with a lament for the missed opportunity of Christianity to provide modern humanity with an adequate source of spiritual sustenance.

Europe enjoyed a great epoch. I mean the one during which the Romanesque and Gothic cathedrals rose up under the holy reign of the Church. It was great because its highest claim was the claim of religion. But it was also not great, and had of necessity to collapse into ruins, because it had crushed, debased, and made thoroughly despicable the human basis upon which it stood. One must not wish to found life on the contempt for life; human bliss on the contempt for that which is human; nor human society on contempt for woman, the begetter of humanity. (5:776–77)

Hobemma goes on to plead for a gynecocratic society in which caritas and a "fruitful motherly way of thinking" (5:777) will displace the peripheral concerns, empty materialism, and sense of cosmic loneliness engendered by contemporary male-dominated society. It is instinctively appreciated by the elite of the *Ile des Dames* that such a radical transformation can only be founded on a powerful new mythology and that the "truth" on which such a mythology is based is of secondary concern. (If Christ was conceived without benefit of an earthly father, the birth of Bianor and his siblings can be attributed to the Hindu god Mukalinda.) Reduced to prosaic definition, myths are lies, albeit sometimes productive lies upon which civilizations can build. It is particularly ironic, however, that the women of *The Island* succumb to the flaw for which they castigate the Christian church: the unnatural, perverted inhibition of the same basic human instinct, sexuality. Nor is it surprising therefore that from an extreme feminist perspective, the experiment ends in failure. The forced repression, the symptoms of which are as evident in the females as in the males, is revenged in a Dionysian orgy. That this orgy serves as "a kind of a spring storm" (5:798) that will prepare the way for a more fruitful era to follow is a possibility. That the balance between matriarchy and patriarchy has shifted once more to the latter is beyond dispute.[52]

## NOTES

1. For a detailed study of Hauptmann's interest in this area see Philip Mellen, *Gerhart Hauptmann: Religious Syncretism and Eastern Religions* (New York, Berne, Frankfurt/M.: Lang, 1984).

2. See Peter Sprengel, *Gerhart Hauptmann. Epoche-Werk-Wirkung* (Munich: Beck, 1984), p. 198.

3. Ibid.

4. See Paul Fechter, *Gerhart Hauptmann* (Dresden: Sibyllen-Verlag, 1922), p. 127.

5. Theodore Ziolkowski, *Fictional Transfigurations of Jesus* (Princeton: Princeton University Press, 1972), p. 109.

6. See Warren R. Maurer, *The Naturalist Image of German Literature* (Munich: Fink, 1972), esp. pp. 81–84 and 90–92.

7. Quoted by Peter Sprengel, *Die Wirklichkeit der Mythen: Untersuchungen zum Werk Gerhart Hauptmanns* (Berlin: E. Schmidt, 1982), p. 89.

8. Quoted by Carl F. W. Behl and Felix A. Voigt, *Chronik von Gerhart Hauptmanns Leben und Schaffen* (Munich: Bergstadtverlag, 1957), p. 33.

9. Karl S. Weimar, "Another Look at Gerhart Hauptmann's *Der Narr in Christo Emanuel Quint*," *Germanic Review* 34 (1959): 208.

10. See Sprengel, *Mythen*, 89–90.

11. See Bernhard Zeller, ed., *Gerhard Hauptmann. Leben und Werk: Eine Gedächtnisausstellung des Deutschen Literaturarchivs* (Stuttgart: Turmhaus-Druckerei, 1962), p. 170.

12. Margaret Sinden, "Hauptmann's *Emanuel Quint*," *Germanic Review* 29 (1954): 271.

13. Quoted by F. A. Voigt, *Gerhart Hauptmann der Schlesier* (Munich: Bergstadt, 1953), p. 67.

14. Albert Soergel, *Dichtung und Dichter der Zeit: Eine Schilderung der deutschen Literatur der letzten Jahrzehnte* (Leipzig: R. Voigtländer, 1911), p. 69.

15. See Sprengel, *Epoche*, 196–97.

16. Arno Holz, *Werke*, eds. Wilhelm Emrich and Anita Holz (Berlin: Luchterhand, 1964) 5:14.

17. Zeller, 171.

18. See Sprengel, *Epoche*, 203.

19. See Sprengel, *Epoche*, 197.

20. See Paul Krauß, " 'Der Narr in Christo Emanuel Quint' aus psychiatrischer Sicht," in Sprengel/Mellen, *Research*, 272.

21. Horst Geyer, *Dichter des Wahnsinns* (Göttingen: Musterschmidt, 1955), p. 215.

22. See Krauß, 249–74.

23. See Krauß, 261.

24. Krauß, 263.

25. See Gotthart Wunberg, "Utopie und fin de siècle. Zur deutschen Literaturkritik vor der Jahrhundertwende," *Deutsche Vierteljahresschrift* 43 (1969): 695.

26. Quoted by Sprengel, *Epoche*, 206.

27. Sprengel, *Epoche*, 206.

28. See Fechter, 124.

29. Weimar, 212.

30. S. D. Stirk, "Gerhart Hauptmann's Jesus Drama: An Unprinted Fragment," *Gerhart Hauptmann Jahrbuch* 1 (1936): 130.

31. Ziolkowski, 114.

32. Weimar, 220.

33. Weimar, 214.

34. See Zeller, 205.

35. Hugh F. Garten, *Gerhart Hauptmann* (New Haven: Yale University Press, 1954), p. 41.

36. See Zeller, 206.

37. Eberhard Hilscher, *Gerhart Hauptmann. Leben und Werk* (Frankfurt/M.: Athenäum, 1988), p. 281.

38. See Jean Jofen, *Das letzte Geheimnis: Eine psychologische Studie über die Brüder Gerhart und Carl Hauptmann* (Bern: Francke, 1972), esp. 33, 78; see also Sprengel, *Epoche*, 211–12.

39. Cf. Sprengel, *Epoche*, 212.

40. Quoted by Gert Oberembt in "Kunst aus dem Geist des Mythos. Bemerkungen zu 'Hanneles Himmelfahrt,' " in *Hauptmann-Forschung: Neue Beiträge; Hauptmann Research: New Directions,* eds. Peter Sprengel and Philip Mellen (Frankfurt/M., Bern, New York: Peter Lang, 1986), p. 48.

41. Ibid.

42. Oberembt, 45–49.

43. Fechter, 143.

44. Carl F. W. Behl, *Zwiesprache mit Gerhart Hauptmann: Tagebuchblätter* (Munich: Desch, 1949), p. 111.

45. The name is ironic and derives from the legend according to which, because of a potion given to Phaon by Aphrodite, all the women of Lesbos are passionately attracted to him. Phaon, however, remains cold and distant. See Sprengel, *Mythen*, 314 n. 139.

46. Reprinted in Hans-Egon Hass and Martin Machazke, eds., *Gerhart Hauptmann: Sämtliche Werke*, 11 vols., (Frankfurt/M.: Propyläen, 1966–74) 11:357–71.

47. See Hilscher, 379–80.

48. Behl, *Zwiesprache*, 84.

49. See Sprengel, *Mythen*, 315.

50. See Philip Mellen, "Gerhart Hauptmann and Dante," *Seminar* 16 (1980): 18.

51. See Philip Mellen, *Gerhart Hauptmann and Utopia* (Stuttgart: Akademischer Verlag Hans-Dieter Heinz, 1976), esp. pp. 52–60.

52. Much as Hauptmann seems to have enjoyed presenting a case for matriarchy in *The Island*, the novel can also be read as ridicule of an exaggerated feminism. In addition to Bachofen as an inspiration for the book, he admitted motivation from "another old idea . . . that, namely, one man and a thousand women could continue to populate the world; never, however, one woman and a thousand men." See Behl, *Zwiesprache*, p. 84.

# CHAPTER TWELVE

# Conclusion

It would be misleading and unfair to Hauptmann to end this discussion so abruptly with a work that is at best only an average product of his talent. Written more than two decades before his death (decades during which his remarkable productivity continued apace), *The Island of the Great Mother* is simply too lighthearted and optimistic to serve as a representative capstone to a study such as this, and at least a few corrective remarks and final reminders of the magnitude of the author's achievement would seem in order. It is typical for Hauptmann, whose works often appear as complementary pairs, that the drama *Veland* (1925), following directly after *The Island*, presents a much more negative view of the Dionysian impulse; and such works as *Till Eulenspiegel* (1928), *The Sea Miracle* (1934), and the *Atriden-Tetrologie*[1] depict a much bleaker image of mankind's isolation in a vast, insensate universe.

The years after 1933 often proved a particularly heavy burden for Hauptmann. He was unable or unwilling to separate himself resolutely from his homeland when it was taken over by the Nazis, and his indecisiveness cost him the loss of former friends and admirers without ever earning him more than a grudging tolerance on the part of the new political masters. Whether we ascribe this fateful lapse to an unfortunate congruence of weltanschauung with that professed by the Hitler regime (Leppmann goes so far as to note biographical parallels between Hauptmann and Hitler), accept an alleged confession of simple personal cowardice, or blame an excessive political flexibility that at the end of the Second World War found Hauptmann succumbing to the enticements of East German Communists who wished to exploit his reputation for their own dubious purposes, the fact remains that Hauptmann stayed in Germany and, outwardly at least, arranged his life so as to avoid excessive unpleasantness.[2] There were, to be sure, some mitigating circumstances. In contrast to such famous emigrés as Thomas Mann, Franz Werfel, and Bertolt Brecht, Hauptmann was not forced into exile by anti-Jewish legislation (also affecting spouses) or anti-Bolshevism. The fact that he was already seventy-one years old in 1933, his belief—right or wrong—that emigration would stifle his artistry, and his wish to be buried in native soil may be mentioned in his defense by the charitably inclined.[3] Had he joined the ranks of fellow German artists, scientists, and intellectuals in America, he would undoubtedly have been spared some of the hardship and bitterness of his last years. Perhaps the low point came on the night of February 14, 1945, when he witnessed from a distant hillside one of the most destructive conflagrations of the war. In a statement which soon became a staple of Communist propaganda he wrote, "I have personally experienced the demise of Dresden under the Sodom and Gomorrah hells of English and American airplanes. Splendid rivers flowed from Dresden throughout the world, and England and America drank thirstily from them. Have they forgotten this?"[4] Broken in body and spirit, he died of pneumonia on June 6, 1946—his last words were "Am I still in my house?"—and lies buried on his beloved island of Hiddensee.[5]

This is a necessarily incomplete survey of the life's work of an author whose fecundity and creativity spanned more than sixty years. If one succumbs to the temptation to abstract from it a few patterns and conclusions, it must be with the understanding that this can be done only at the price of a certain amount of oversimplification. Perhaps the least controversial conclusion consists of a final reminder of the extent to which Hauptmann's works are intimately autobiographical—"fragments of a great confession," to borrow Goethe's famous remark. Especially the characters in the early dramas (Robert and Wilhelm Scholz, Johannes Vockerat, Crampton, Mrs. Wolff, and bell founder Heinrich, among others) frequently owe a great deal to Hauptmann's family members, friends, acquaintances, and/or his personal experiences. Although some of his characters were at times close enough to their "originals" to elicit complaints (Mrs. Henze and her fictional counterpart Mrs. Wolff or Johannes Guttzeit and the Apostle figure, for example), Hauptmann always strove to embellish and elevate them into memorable types, transcending their real–life models. Similarly his works invariably benefited from the keen sense of landscape and atmosphere he acquired through travel and through the years he spent in various distinctive locales. Without his firsthand experience of life in Erkner, Lederose, Berlin, the Riesengebirge mountains, northern Italy, Breslau, and Hiddensee, *Flagman Thiel, Quint, The Rats, Pippa, The Heretic, Michael Kramer,* and *Schilling* would be much paler and more prosaic than they are. Not only did Hauptmann open himself to a wide variety of experiences (people, travel, landscapes, music, sculpture, literature, and religions), but from an early age he attempted to fix and preserve these experiences in poetry and journals for later use. As his literary estate in Berlin demonstrates, such activity amounted to a veritable collector's mania that provided him with a vast storehouse of names, incidents, newspaper stories, and other materials, often separated by decades, from which to draw as the need arose.

Like another famous autodidact, his contemporary Thomas Mann, Hauptmann was also such a voracious reader that he sometimes worried about striking a proper balance between informing himself and writing. Among the many literary figures who influenced his work, Ibsen, Zola, Goethe, Büchner, Shakespeare, Sophocles, Dante, Tolstoy, and Dostoyevski deserve special mention. As this discussion has shown (and his library confirms), Hauptmann also roamed freely through areas of history (for *The Weavers* and *Florian Geyer*), folklore, (*The Sunken Bell, Pippa*), and religious lore (*The Island*). As Mellen points out, "we find a clue to the private Gerhart Hauptmann in his ca. 1885–1945 study of religious texts. His quest for that which underlies and binds the myriad perspectives of supernatural existence into a cohesive whole . . . leads him, for instance, to intense studies of Buddhism, Taoism, Confusianism, Tibetan Lamaism, Islam, Christianity, and the writings of Jacob Boehme."[6] As a "seismograph of his age," he was also responsive to more contemporaneous currents of European thought, including ideas from Schopenhauer, Nietzsche, Marx, and Freud. Yet, while they always benefit from an intimate familiarity with the times and conditions out of which they grew, Hauptmann's greatest works invariably transcend, and will presumably continue to transcend, these times and conditions.

Although his reputation is based largely on his naturalistic dramas, Hauptmann never accepted the Naturalist label. Looking back from the perspective of seventy-five years, he remarked that "once they called me the 'naturalistic' writer, others found in me the 'classical' author. I myself, if you don't construe the term too narrowly and pedantically, profess myself a *Romantic*."[7] Concerned by what he considered "the danger and ambiguity of mere reason,"[8] he preferred to see his role as that of a medium through which the perennial dualisms of human existence (suffering and compassion, love and hatred, light and darkness, life and death) could find expression. Siding with instinct over reason, he preferred to end his works with a question rather than a definitive answer, emphasized the evocation of mood over plot construction, and preferred a communication via gesture (physical or verbal) rather than verbiage. Like many modern authors he had a few favorite themes, ideas, and images to which he remained faithful: the *Urdrama* as expressed in family tragedies from *Before Sunrise* to the *Atridae,* the belief that simple people (Thiel) and women (Rose Bernd and Pippa) are closer to the "heart of the world" than excessively rationalized men (Wehrhahn), and a conviction that the human predicament can best be captured in elemental imagery (the hunter and his prey). Not surprisingly, from this perspective, he felt himself both unwilling and ultimately incapable of subscribing to any rigid, abstract weltanschauung, with the result that little can be added to Heuser's summation:

> Few other writers have delved so deeply into the contradictions and irrationalities of human behavior, few have looked at the facts of life and of nature with the same honesty and candor. While he believed in a Supreme Being and felt a cosmic oneness with nature, he could not reconcile with the existence of evil and suffering the Christian Concept of God as a loving father. Life was to him a nonrational mystery which must be accepted. It can be portrayed; it cannot be explained . . . the reader is left with the depressing senselessness of human events, the brutality of life, and the dominating role played by error and chance.[9]

While hardly a household name today in Anglo-Saxon countries (where he has been largely relegated to the semi-obscurity of the academy) Gerhart Hauptmann has earned a significant niche in world literary history, especially through his influence on the international Naturalist movement and on a diversity of foreign authors. In Germany, where he single-handedly revived a moribund theater tradition of which the last great dramatist had been Friedrich Hebbel, he remains, after such giants as Goethe, Schiller, and Kleist, one of the most popular playwrights.

## NOTES

1. For discussions of *The Sea Miracle* and the *Atridae-Tetrology* see Warren R. Maurer, *Gerhart Hauptmann* (Boston: Twayne, 1982), pp. 121–23 and 123–30. The complete *Atridae-Tetrology* was first published in 1949.

2. See Wolfgang Leppmann, *Gerhart Hauptmanns Leben, Werk und Zeit* (Bern, Munich, Vienna: Scherz, 1986), pp. 8, 353, 359–60; Ferenc Kormendi, "A Walk with Gerhart Hauptmann," *The Reporter,* 2 November 1967, p. 50; and Peter Sprengel, *Gerhart Hauptmann. Epoche-Werk-Wirkung* (Munich: Beck, 1984), pp. 230–35.

3. See also Maurer, 3–4.

4. Gerhart Hauptmann, "Die Untat von Dresden," *Aufbau,* 6 (1950): 109.

5. See Eberhard Hilscher, *Gerhart Hauptmann. Leben und Werk* (Frankfurt/M.: Athenäum, 1988), p. 506.

6. Philip Mellen, *Gerhart Hauptmann: Religious Syncretism and Eastern Religions* (New York, Bern, Frankfurt/M.: Peter Lang, 1984), p. ix.

7. Quoted by Bernhard Zeller, ed., *Gerhard Hauptmann. Leben und Werk: Eine Gedächtnisausstellung des Deutschen Literaturarchivs* (Stuttgart: Turmhaus-Druckerei, 1962), p. 312.

8. Carl F. W. Behl, *Zwiesprache mit Gerhart Hauptmann: Tagebuchblätter* (Munich: Francke, 1980), p. 82.

9. Quoted by Hans Joachim Schrimpf, ed., *Gerhart Hauptmann* (Darmstadt: Wissenschaftliche Buchgesellschaft, 1976), p. 393.

# SELECT BIBLIOGRAPHY

## WORKS BY GERHART HAUPTMANN

*Das Gesammelte Werk. Ausgabe letzter Hand zum 80. Geburtstag des Dichters am 15. November 1942,* 17 vols. Berlin: S. Fischer, 1942. Because of the limited time available to assemble this edition (approx. one year) and because the work involved was largely accomplished by C. F. W. Behl and Felix A. Voigt, the designation "Ausgabe letzter Hand" is dubious at best.

*Gesammelte Werke.* 8 vols. Ed. Hans Mayer. Berlin: Aufbau 1962. Contains most of Hauptmann's best-known works (notable exception: *Die versunkene Glocke*).

*Sämtliche Werke. Centenar-Ausgabe zum 100. Geburtstag des Dichters, 15. November 1962.* 11 vols. Ed. Hans-Egon Hass and continued by Martin Machatzke. Frankfurt/M.: Propyläen, 1966–74. Although not a "definitive" or a historical-critical edition, this edition is likely to remain the most useful for some time to come. Indispensable for any serious scholarly work on Hauptmann.

*Die Kunst des Dramas: Über Schauspiel und Theater.* Ed. Martin Machatzke. Frankfurt/M.: Propyläen, 1963. Very useful compilation of Hauptmann's comments relating to this subject.

*Die großen Dramen.* Berlin: Propyläen, 1965. Useful one-volume anthology which ignores the early "family" tragedies.

*Die großen Beichten.* Berlin: Propyläen, 1966. Hauptmann's most overtly autobiographical works.

*Die großen Erzählungen.* Berlin: Propyläen, 1967.

*Die großen Romane.* Berlin: Propyläen, 1968. Includes *Quint, Die Insel der Großen Mutter,* and *Wanda.*

*Das dramatische Werk.* 4 vols. Berlin: Propyläen, 1974. Includes all of the completed dramas but not the fragments or variants.

*Italienische Reise 1897: Tagebuchaufzeichnungen.* Ed. Martin Machatzke. Berlin: Propyläen, 1976. Important documents for Hauptmann's aesthetic development after his turn from the more extreme forms of Naturalism.

### English Translations

*The Dramatic Work of Gerhart Hauptmann.* Trans. numerous translators. 9 vols. Ed. Ludwig Lewisohn. New York: B. W. Huebsch, 1913–29. Contains thirty dramatic works, including translations of all of Hauptmann's best-known plays from *Vor Sonnenaufgang* to *Veland.*

*Atlantis*. Trans. Adele and Thomas Seltzer. New York: B. W. Heubsch, 1912.

*The Island of the Great Mother*. Trans. Willa and Edwin Muir. New York: B. W. Huebsch and Viking Press, 1925.

*The Fool in Christ: Emanuel Quint*. Trans. Thomas Seltzer. New York: Viking Press, 1926.

*Flagman Thiel*. Trans. Adele S. Seltzer. In *Great German Short Novels and Stories*, ed. Victor Lange. New York: Modern Library, 1952. Pp. 332–62.

*The Heretic of Soana*. Trans. Bayard Q. Morgan. New York: Frederick Ungar, 1958.

*The Weavers, Rose Bernd, Drayman Henschel, The Beaver Coat, Hannele: Five Plays by Gerhart Hauptmann*. Trans. Theodore H. Lustig. New York: Bantam Books, 1961.

*Gerhart Hauptmann's "Before Daybreak": A Translation and An Introduction*. Trans. and intro. by Peter Bauland. University of North Carolina Press, 1978. Translation of *Vor Sonnenaufgang* for modern American audiences; useful introduction.

## WORKS ABOUT GERHART HAUPTMANN

### Bibliography

Hoefert, Sigfrid. *Internationale Bibliographie zum Werk Gerhart Hauptmanns*. 2 vols. Berlin: Erich Schmidt Verlag, 1986–89. The first volume (327 pp.) of this indispensable bibliography provides an exhaustive listing of the editions and translations of Hauptmann's oeuvre published throughout the world, as well as a generous sampling of the criticism elicited by each work during the first ten years following its publication. The second volume (589 pp.) catalogues the massive amount of secondary literature devoted to Hauptmann and his works in numerous languages during the years 1886 to 1987. (Subsequent publications relating to the author and his work are listed in the annual *MLA International Bibliography of Books and Articles on the Modern Languages and Literatures*. New York: Publications of the Modern Languages and Literatures).

### Books and Articles

Alexander, Neville E. *Studien zum Stilwandel im dramatischen Werk Gerhart Hauptmanns*. Stuttgart: Metzler, 1964. Demonstrates the unity of Hauptmann's oeuvre on the basis of a consistent (and largely pessimistic) determinism.

Bachman, Charles R. "Life into Art: Gerhart Hauptmann and Michael Kramer." *German Quarterly* 42 (1969): 381–92.

Behl, Carl F. W. *Zwiesprache mit Gerhart Hauptmann: Tagebuchblätter*. Munich: Desch, 1949. Indispensable source for Hauptmann's comments on his life, times, and works.

———, and Voigt, Felix A. *Chronik von Gerhart Hauptmanns Leben und Schaffen*. Munich: Bergstadtverlag, 1957. Detailed, extremely useful chronology.

Böckmann, Paul. "Der Naturalismus Gerhart Hauptmanns." In *Interpretationen,* ed. Jost Schillement, 2: 269–94. Frankfurt/M.: Fischer, 1966.

Brauneck, Manfred. *Literatur und Öffentlichkeit im ausgehenden 19. Jahrhundert: Studien zur Rezeption des naturalistischen Theaters in Deutschland.* Stuttgart: Metzler, 1974. Mainly devoted to the political circumstances surrounding and influencing the reception of *Die Weber.* Carefully researched.

Brescius, Hans von. *Gerhart Hauptmann: Zeitgeschehen und Bewußtsein in unbekannten Selbstzeugnissen: Eine politisch-biographische Studie.* Bonn: Bouvier, 1976. Almost a collection of Hauptmann quotations (many previously unpublished) which afford an insight into the author's political views, especially during the period of the Third Reich.

Clouser, Robin A. "The Spiritual Malaise of a Modern Hercules: Hauptmann's *Bahnwärter Thiel." Germanic Review* 55 (1980): 98–108.

Coupe, William A. "An Ambiguous Hero: In Defense of Alfred Loth." *German Life and Letters* 31 (1977–78): 13–22.

Cowen, Roy C. *Hauptmann Kommentar zum dramatischen Werk.* Munich: Winkler, 1980. Convenient summary of relevant facts and materials for all of Hauptmann's completed dramas.

Dussère, Carolyn T. *The Image of the Primitive Giant in the Work of Gerhart Hauptmann.* Stuttgart: Heinz, 1979.

Ellis, John M. *Narration in the German Novelle: Theory and Interpretation.* London: Cambridge University Press, 1974. A close analysis of the role of the narrator in *Bahnwärter Thiel,* pp. 167–87.

Emrich, Wilhelm. "Der Tragödientypus Gerhart Hauptmanns." In *Protest und Verheissung: Studien zur klassischen und modernen Dichtung.* Frankfurt/M., Bonn: Athenäum, 1960.

Furst, Lilian R., and Skrine, Peter N. *Naturalism.* London: Methuen, 1971. Good introduction to the European roots and spreading of the Naturalist movement.

Garten, Hugh F. *Gerhart Hauptmann.* New Haven: Yale University Press, 1954. Introduction to Hauptmann and his work partly superseded by later German scholarship.

Guthke, Karl S. "Authentischer oder authorisierter Text? Die Centenar-Ausgabe der Werke Gerhart Hauptmanns." *Göttingische Gelehrte Anzeigen.* 228 (1976): 115–48. In-depth appraisal of the strengths and weaknesses of the most authoritative edition of Hauptmann's work.

———, *Gerhart Hauptmann: Weltbild im Werk.* Göttingen: Vandenhoeck & Ruprecht, 1961. A landmark of postwar Hauptmann criticism. Available in a second, completely reworked and expanded edition: Munich: Francke Verlag, 1980.

———. "The King of the Weimar Republic: Gerhart Hauptmann's Role in Political Life, 1919–1933." In *Probleme der Moderne: Studien zur deutschen Literatur von Nietzsche bis Brecht, Festschrift für Walter Sokel.* Tübingen: Niemeyer, 1983, pp. 367–87. The most detailed study in English of Hauptmann's political views, his celebrated status during the Weimar Republic, and his ambivalent reaction to the Nazi takeover.

Hilscher, Walter A. *Gerhart Hauptmann. Leben und Werk*. Frankfurt/M.: Athenäum, 1988. Best and most comprehensive treatment of Hauptmann and his work by a Marxist scholar.

Hoefert, Sigfrid. *Gerhart Hauptmann*. Stuttgart: Metzler, 1982. Very useful biographical, literary, and bibliographical survey.

Knight, K. G., and F. Norman, eds. *Hauptmann Centenary Lectures*. London: University of London Press, 1964. An excellent collection of essays covering a wide range of topics.

Lea, Henry A. "The Specter of Romanticism: Hauptmann's Use of Quotations." *Germanic Review* 49 (1974): 267–83.

McInnes, Edward. "The Domestic Dramas of Gerhart Hauptmann: Tragedy or Sentimental Pathos?" *German Life and Letters* 20 (1966): 53–60.

McMillan, Dougald. "Influences of Gerhart Hauptmann in Joyce's *Ulysses*." *James Joyce Quarterly* 4 (1967): 107–19.

Marshall, Alan. *The German Naturalists and Gerhart Hauptmann*. Frankfurt/M.: Peter Lang, 1982. Especially useful as a study of Hauptmann's early reception by critics and his German public.

Martini, Fritz. *Das Wagnis der Sprache: Interpretationen deutscher Prosa von Nietzsche bis Benn*. Stuttgart: Klett, 1954. Sensitive interpretation of *Flagmen Thiel*, pp. 56–98.

Maurer, Warren R. *Gerhart Hauptmann*. Boston: Twayne, 1982.

———. "Gerhart Hauptmann in the United States." In *The Fortunes of German Writers in America: Studies in Literary Reception*, ed. Wolfgang Elfe, James Hardin, and Gunther Holst. Columbia: University of South Carolina Press, 1992. Pp. 99–120.

———. "Gerhart Hauptmann's Character Names." *German Quarterly* 52 (1972): 457–71.

———. "Hauptmann's 'Die versunkene Glocke' and Ibsen's 'Auf den Höhen.' " *Monatshefte* 25 (1960): 189–93.

———. *The Naturalist Image of German Literature: A Study of the German Naturalists' Appraisal of Their·Literary Heritage*. Munich: Fink, 1972.

May, Kurt. "Hauptmann: 'Die Weber.' " In *Das deutsche Drama vom Barock bis zur Gegenwart: Interpretationen*, ed. Benno von Wiese, 2: 158–66. Düsseldorf: Bagel, 1968.

Mellen, Philip. *Gerhart Hauptmann and Utopia*. Stuttgart: Heinz, 1976. Interesting study of Hauptmann's place within the context of historical utopian thought. Emphasis on *The Island of the Great Mother*.

———. *Gerhart Hauptmann: Religious Syncretism and Eastern Religions*. New York: Peter Lang, 1984. Based to a large extent on previously unpublished materials from the Hauptmann Archives of the Staatsbibliothek Preussischer Kulturbesitz in Berlin, this study reveals the extent of the author's enduring preoccupation with German mysticism and the religious philosophies of the Orient.

Michaelis, Rolf. *Der schwarze Zeus: Gerhart Hauptmanns zweiter Weg.* Berlin: Argon, 1962. Defends later dramas as stageworthy. Ignores much secondary literature but provides some good, close readings.

Muller, Siegfried H. "Gerhart Hauptmann's Relation to American Literature and His Concept of America." *Monatshefte* 44 (1952): 333–39.

Oberembt, Gert. *Gerhart Hauptmann. Der Biberpelz.* Paderborn, Munich, Vienna, Zurich: Schöningh, 1987. Thorough introduction to all aspects of Hauptmann's greatest comedy.

Osborne, John. *The Naturalist Drama in Germany.* Manchester: Manchester University Press; Totowa, N.J.: Rowan and Littlefield, 1971. Strong preference for Hauptmann's Naturalist dramas.

Post, Klaus D. *Gerhart Hauptmann. Bahnwärter Thiel: Text, Materialien, Kommentar.* Munich, Vienna: Hanser, 1979. Good summarizing introduction to *Flagman Thiel* with interesting commentary on the mother-child relationship.

Reichart, Walter A. "Grundbegriffe im dramatischen Schaffen Gerhart Hauptmanns." *PMLA,* 82 (1967): 142–54.

———. "The Totality of Hauptmann's Work." *Germanic Review* 21 (1946): 143–49. A good introduction to the wide range of Hauptmann's works.

Reichert, Herbert W. "Hauptmann's Frau Wolff and Brecht's Mutter Courage." *German Quarterly* 34 (1961): 439–48.

Rey, William H. "Der offene Schluß der Weber. Zur Aktualität Gerhart Hauptmanns in unserer Zeit." *German Quarterly* 55 (1982): 141–63. Defends Hauptmann against political attack from Bertold Brecht while providing a common-sense interpretation of the ending of *The Weavers.*

Scheuer, Helmut, ed. *Naturalismus: Bürgerliche Dichtung und soziales Engagement.* Stuttgart, Berlin, Cologne, Mainz: W. Kohlhammer, 1974. Nine essays on sociopolitical aspects in the work of Hauptmann and other German writers. Uneven quality.

Schlenther, Paul. *Gerhart Hauptmann: Leben und Werk.* Revised and expanded by Arthur Eloesser. Berlin: Fischer, 1922. A basic biographical study by one who knew the author well.

Schrimpf, Hans Joachim, ed. *Gerhart Hauptmann.* Darmstadt: Wissenschaftliche Buchgesellschaft, 1976. Excellent anthology of Hauptmann criticism from 1889 to 1971.

Shaw, Leroy R. *Witness of Deceit: Gerhart Hauptmann as Critic of Society.* Berkeley and Los Angeles: University of California Press, 1958.

Sinden, Margaret. *Gerhart Hauptmann: The Prose Plays.* Toronto: University Press, 1957.

————. "Hauptmann's Emanuel Quint." *Germanic Review* 29 (1954): 269–81.

Sprengel, Peter. *Gerhart Hauptmann. Epoche-Werk-Wirkung.* Munich: C. H. Beck, 1984. Useful summarizing introductions to major works by Hauptmann and a good chapter on his political outlook.

————. *Die Wirklichkeit der Mythen. Untersuchungen zum Werk Gerhart Hauptmanns aufgrund des handschriftlichen Nachlasses.* Berlin: E. Schmidt, 1982. Outstanding investigation of the (often hidden) relationship of Hauptmann's works to classical mythology.

————, and Philip Mellen, eds. *Hauptmann-Forschung: Neue Beiträge: Hauptmann Research: New Directions.* Frankfurt/M.: Berne; New York: Peter Lang, 1986. Anthology of recent essays in English and German on Hauptmann and his work.

Voigt, Felix A. *Gerhart Hauptmann und die Antike.* 2d revised edition. Berlin: Erich Schmidt, 1965.

————. and Walter A. Reichart, *Hauptmann und Shakespeare.* Breslau: Maruschke & Berendt, 1938. Traces the strong impact of Shakespeare on Hauptmann from his childhood through his "Shakespeare decade." A standard work by two of Hauptmann's most knowledgeable critics.

Washington, Ida H. "The Symbolism of Contrast in Gerhart Hauptmann's 'Fasching.' " *German Quarterly* 52 (1972): 248–51.

Weigand, Hermann J. "Gerhart Hauptmann's Range as a Dramatist." *Monatshefte* 44 (1952): 317–32.

Weimar, Karl S. "Another Look at Gerhart Hauptmann's *Der Narr in Christo Emanuel Quint. Germanic Review* 34 (1959): 209–22.

Zeller, Bernhard, ed. *Gerhart Hauptmann. Leben und Werk: Eine Gedächtnisausstellung zum 100. Geburtstag des Dichters im Schiller-Nationalmuseum Marbach a.N.* Marbach/N.: Schiller-Nationalmuseum, 1962. Much previously inaccessible material on Hauptmann and his work.

Ziolkowski, Theodore. *Fictional Transfigurations of Jesus.* Princeton: Princeton University Press, 1972. Erudite study which places *Quint* in the context of a popular theme of Western literature.

# INDEX